THE ANTIGONE COMPLEX

Cultural Memory
in
the
Present

Mieke Bal and Hent de Vries, Editors

THE ANTIGONE COMPLEX

Ethics and the Invention of Feminine Desire

Cecilia Sjöholm

STANFORD UNIVERSITY PRESS

STANFORD, CALIFORNIA

2004

Stanford University Press
Stanford, California

Printed in the United States of America on acid-free, archival-quality paper

Library of Congress Cataloging-in-Publication Data

Sjöholm, Cecilia.
    The Antigone complex : ethics and the invention of feminine desire /
Cecilia Sjöholm.
        p. cm.—(Cultural memory in the present)
    Includes bibliographical references and index.
    ISBN 0-8047-4892-6 (alk. paper)
    1. Feminist ethics.   2. Desire (Philosophy)   3. Femininity (Philosophy)
4. Antigone (Greek mythology)   I. Title.   II. Series.
BJ1395 .S57 2004
170'.82—dc22

                                                                2003026001

Original Printing 2004

Last figure below indicates year of this printing:
13   12   11   10   09   08   07   06   05   04

Contents

Acknowledgments

Many people have participated in the intellectual work leading to the completion of this book. I do not have space to list them all, but where names would be too abundant, I would at least like to point to the contexts and places that have served as an inspiration. First of all I would like to thank the institutions that have generously contributed research funding: FRN or the Swedish Research Council, the Swedish Institute, and the Knut and Alice Wallenberg Foundation. The Center for Theoretical Studies at Essex University, where I have spent a lot of time as a visiting fellow throughout my writing of this project, proved an extraordinarily fruitful place to pursue research of this kind. I am particularly grateful to Noreen Harburt for having lent me her office. The Philosophy Department at De-Paul University had the kindness to invite me as a visiting professor in 1998–99. The graduate course on Lacan that I gave there, and the response by the graduate students who attended, was crucial to the development of the project.

The response from audiences to whom I have had the chance to present this material has been of great importance: the University of Essex, University of Memphis, University of Michigan, Middlesex University, the New School of Social Research, Université de Louvaine, Katholieke Universiteit Nijmegen, University of Gothenburg, University of Stockholm, South Stockholm University College, and the Université de Toulouse. I would particularly like to thank those who invited me to present the material: Sara Beardsworth, Peg Birmingham, Fabienne Bruguère, Eva-Lena Dahl, Bernard Flynn, Philippe van Haute, Peter Osborne, Renata Salecl, Stella Sandford, and Slavoj Žižek. Moreover, I would like to thank the colleagues who invited me to publish work in progress in reviews such as *Agora, Ny Poetik, New Formations,* and *Radical Philosophy.* Parts of the material appeared, at an early stage of elaboration, as a long article in Swedish in *Tingets Imperium* (Natur and Kultur, 2000). The invitations to publish made this into a better book as did the comments on the texts made by Ingeborg Owesen, Lis Möller, Chris Bremers, Monique David-Ménard, Paul Moyaert, Veronica Vasterling, Ben Vedder, Stella Sandford and Peter Osborne, Renata Salecl, Christian Nilsson, Hent de Vries, and Paola Marrati.

The editors at Stanford University Press—Norris Pope, Tim Roberts, and Elizabeth Berg—offered crucial help in the final stages toward the realization of this book. Rachel Åkerstedt helped me with the proofreading. Finally, I am particularly indebted to those who read and discussed this manuscript simply as friends and colleagues, many of whom are already mentioned above, but also Karen de Boer, Tina Chanter, Carl-Michael Edenborg, Claudia Linden, Hans Ruin, Rudi Visker, and Ewa Ziarek. My gratitude to Philippe van Haute must be singled out, since he encouraged me to present this manuscript as a doctoral thesis at the department of philosophy at the University of Nijuugen. And all along, since the very inception of this project, Simon Critchley has been engaged in it, offering fun, love, and support.

Introduction

"What would have happened if psychoanalysis had chosen Antigone rather than Oedipus?"[1] George Steiner, who considers *Antigone* to be the most canonical text of the West, posed the question as a provocation, but to some extent we have seen a shift of interest toward this figure. Such a shift may not have taken place in the psychoanalytic clinic, where the notion of the Oedipus complex remains a defining concept. However, in theoretical fields addressing problems of desire and subjectivity, such as literature, philosophy, and social thought, *Antigone* provides us with a treatment rich in complexity and implications. Freud's notion of the Oedipus complex has proven to be an inadequate model for the understanding of femininity and feminine desire for many of those engaged in that issue from a social or political viewpoint, and Sophocles' tragedy about Antigone enables us to discuss some of the most pertinent questions concerning contemporary desire and subjectivity from new and thought-provoking angles. Discussing Antigone as an alternative paradigm of desire means a shift not only of focal point but also in point of view. Rather than isolating desire as an aspect of symbolic castration, Antigone relates it to ethics, politics, and the law, to the social sphere, the family sphere, and the public sphere. In contemporary thought, she has been made into a metaphor for individuation, ethical action, uncompromising desire, feminist revolt, and the collapse of heteronormativity. In short, Antigone allows us to confront the complexity of the concept of desire and to question the possibility of ever reducing it to a given, universal structure. Antigone, Lacan writes in *The Ethics of Psychoanalysis*, reveals "the line of sight that defines desire."[2] And one might argue that Antigone does indeed seem to provide us with the pattern for a complex, just like Oedipus—an Antigone complex. But rather than incarnating a structural model that can be transposed into the psychoanalytic clinic to define an alternative to Oedipus,

Antigone keeps us riveted through the enigmatic radiation of her figure, generating questions, problems, thoughts, and a fascinated interest that defies any attempt to extrapolate a model. We mentioned earlier that the Freudian notion of the Oedipus complex is insufficient to clarify feminine desire. But if we are to talk about an Antigone complex, then such a complex cannot be said to constitute an alternative symmetrically opposed to Oedipus that takes its point of departure in a feminine rather than a masculine model. This book introduces the concept of the Antigone complex not in order to define the function of feminine desire, but rather to illuminate that obscure and multifaceted object of desire that has fascinated generations of philosophers and theoreticians, as well as readers and spectators. The Antigone complex, then, refers not to an actual function of the feminine, but rather to the complexity introduced in any discussion of desire where the feminine is concerned.[3]

In the process of writing this book, I have come to focus on a very specific question that presents itself in the study of Sophocles' play. Departing from the figure of Antigone and reflections on the dynamics of tragedy, this book argues for a notion of desire that is intrinsically related to *ethics* rather than being reducible to structural, sexual, or social terms. Ethics is to be understood in broad terms: the comments I have made on *Antigone* and feminine desire approach the question of morality in diverse ways, but they all examine the question of how we should act and what values determine the guidelines for action. I wanted to introduce an Antigone complex not only because it offers an interesting figure of female identification, but also because it allows for reflection on the intrinsic relation between desire and ethics that has been given particular attention in philosophical, psychoanalytical, and literary discourse related to femininity. I am not making an ethical argument, nor do I attempt to define what kind of ethics we ought to elaborate in relation to desire. I am rather attempting to show that the analysis of desire is intrinsically intertwined with the formation of ethical values. *Antigone* serves as a focal point, and I have restricted the scope of the book to theories related to the figure of Antigone, a narrowing that has helped reveal the point where desire is intertwined with ethics. This focal point helps show some of the ways in which feminine desire has been depicted in some distinctive modern philosophical projects.

Generally considered an enigma, feminine desire is often figured either as an excess or as a deficiency in relation to ethical norms. Above all, it is a provocation and a challenge because it cannot be adequately represented within a social and cultural order in which norms and values have been erected. Whether feminine desire is regarded as mysterious or simply indecent, ironic, or intrinsically conflictual, a dark continent or a symptom of *jouissance*, modern thinkers have tended to view it as touching the limits of the community. Referred to as negativity, lack of being, or the real, femininity becomes a margin or outside in relation to ethical and social norms. In this perspective, it is a "gap" or deficiency in the moral edifice that serves to illustrate either moral weakness or the failure of the individual to identify with laws and norms. Unlike male desire, the feminine does not strive for social recognition or power. A kind of purpose—devoid of desire, properly speaking, since it is indifferent to the various projects and kinds of subjectivities that come with individuals who define themselves in a social framework—is found in the domain of sexuality, or in the "natural" family domain, which is considered to be situated outside of a universalizable value system and to concern itself with love and care. A typical tendency exemplified by some of the philosophical texts considered in this book is to consider metaphysical (if one can talk about the desire to know and name metaphysical desire) and social desire as masculine, while sexual desire is feminine. In the process, ethical and political concerns are detached from the lower sphere of sexuality and desire. Ethics, in other words, is presented as a domain of values—of good and bad, right and wrong—that characteristically can be reflected upon independently from issues of desire. Such detachment becomes problematic, however, if one looks more closely at the way desire and ethics are intertwined in the analysis of *Antigone*; the tragedy is for its modern reader a kind of remainder in which the sphere of ethical values can no longer be considered separately from subjective and seemingly contingent investments of various kinds. The example of Antigone overshoots and problematizes any attempt to fully detach dualities such as the ethical and the natural, social desire and sexual desire, masculine and feminine, and singular and universal.

It is not the aim of this book, then, to show that the feminine plays the role of an excluded or hidden outside, but rather to present ways in which feminine desire has been theorized as a problem intrinsically intertwined with ethical issues and the very texture of the social fabric itself. I have come to regard such theorization of feminine desire as interesting and productive.[4] Rather than criticizing the position of the feminine as marginal and enigmatic in these contexts, I would argue that it is precisely in being problematic and enigmatic that femininity functions as a revelatory power, allowing a theorization of desire that is philosophically rich. Because of its association with sexuality and eroticism, the feminine has been denied an impact in the social or structural register. At the same time, however, the feminine challenges the idea that desire is restricted to social or metaphysical goals.

The theoretical framework deployed throughout this discussion of desire is inspired by French psychoanalyst Jacques Lacan, whose *Ethics of Psychoanalysis* is the subject of the final chapters of the book. The knowledgeable reader will no doubt notice that Lacanian figures of thought are present throughout the book. I have not, however, applied an orthodox or a "proper" Lacanian analysis in my conclusions concerning the relation between ethics, desire, and femininity. All in all, I have striven to move away from Lacanian terminology, and there are many aspects of Lacanian theory with which I do not agree. For example, I have not put much emphasis on Lacan's ideas on sexuation, or on his notion of fantasy, as presented in the discussion of the *objet petit a*, which may seem surprising in a discussion of sexual difference. One reason is of course that the *Ethics of Psychoanalysis* does not discuss these notions. Above all, however, I wanted to stress other aspects of Lacan's thought for philosophical reasons. While some premises of Lacanian discourse have been useful, others have been left out and still others modified. The modifications have been worked out in accordance with concerns introduced by, above all, Heidegger's ontological investigations and feminist theory. For example, I have decided to focus on the "Thing" as the cause of desire, rather than the formal *objet petit a*, because the Thing is a concept loaded with philosophical connotations, which therefore demands a more thorough investigation of phenomenal experience and ontological relations. In his discussion of the Thing, Lacan clearly shows that the origins of desire cannot be reduced to a discursive sign, although the signifier is the "home" of the Thing. I take it to be presented as a cause of desire not entirely compatible with the *objet petit a*, which introduces another logic in Lacan's theory. Whereas the Thing is the focus in a theory of sublimation, *objet petit a* leads Lacan to underscore the role of fantasy. From Simone de Beauvoir—who represents a feminist position that necessarily challenges or maybe completes Lacan's analysis—I retain the idea that although desire is never determined by biological sexual differentiation, it must always be thought of as attached to a corporeal or embodied "situation." Moreover, I have taken Beauvoir's critique of psychoanalysis to heart and decided to go with her elaboration of and challenge to Claude Lévi-Strauss's theory of exchange. Therefore, I emphasize aspects in Lacan other than those inspired by Lévi-Strauss.

It may seem like a paradox that the first chapter of the book, on Mary Wollstonecraft, does not mention Antigone. It was necessary for the sake of the overall argument to show how the philosophical discussion of feminine desire was introduced through a discussion of ethics and morals. Mary Wollstonecraft's fictive depictions and philosophical reflections on the issue are, to my mind, an underestimated contribution to the philosophy of desire that should not be ignored. The issues of desire, ethics, and sexual difference were placed on the agenda at the end of the eighteenth century and the beginning of the nineteenth century. Wollstonecraft's *Vindication of the Rights of Woman* (1792) was written as a response to male philosophers who argued that women were incapable of following moral norms and laws. Her argument is that women are morally responsible but prone to self-deception because they are raised to consider themselves as erotic, frivolous objects. Wollstonecraft's book is the only place where fantasy is examined, and it plays a crucial role in her argument. In her last, unfinished novel, *Maria or the Wrongs of Woman* (1798), Wollstonecraft shows the destructive power of fantasy for women who are not raised to trust their senses. Feminine desire may lead to self-destructive turmoil, in which women are unable to detach themselves from fantasies that keep them fettered to a position of social and sexual submission. Rather than proving them morally irresponsible, however, the fact that they succumb to their fantasies rather than to the violence of a repressive, male-dominated society shows that women have to be considered autonomous moral subjects in that they are the cause of their own deception. Interestingly, the arguments made or perhaps implied by Wollstonecraft can be connected to a contemporary discussion of this theme in the work of the Marquis de Sade. Much has been made of the implicit contradiction *and* relation between Sade's fantasies of submission and Immanuel Kant's making of an autonomous moral subject; this connection has been explored by, for instance, Simone de Beauvoir, Theodor Adorno, and Jacques Lacan. Wollstonecraft, however, has been left out of the discussion, although her writings deal with the same paradoxical interconnection between the morally and politically autonomous subject and the unconscious production of desire that works against such autonomy. Introducing her in this context has been necessary not just for the historical grounding of the argument; I consider her work to be a better example than Sade's for giving a nuanced and complex presentation of the paradox.

The second chapter presents G. W. F. Hegel's considerations on feminine desire, with special focus on his reading of *Antigone*. I also bring up his brief comments on Aeschylus's *Oresteia*, because they introduce questions of feminine desire that will arise in conjunction with *Antigone*. In his reading of *Antigone*, Hegel gives femininity a problematic status in terms of social consciousness and moral capacity. Hegel separates natural desire from social desire, using "natural" as a code for a feminine sphere external to the universalizable values of the community. The natural sphere includes the bonds of both familial love and sexual desire. Hegel's problem is how to retain the "good" aspects of the natural sphere and involve these in the social construction of ethical life, while cutting off the chaotic sexual aspects of the family domain. Both the higher and lower aspects of the natural sphere are represented by feminine desire, which is thus intrinsically conflictual for Hegel. Feminine desire, in his view, represents a deficiency in the community, something that is not working in the symbolic institution of ethical life. This is figured especially by the feminine figures of tragedy, Clytaemnestra and Antigone. These women represent a feminine sphere that is impossible to transpose into the domain of the ethical order. However, the fact that feminine desire becomes a deficiency, outside, or remainder in Hegel's philosophy—when it is not considered an impossibility—is not necessarily the result of a flawed and prejudiced male point of view. Social conflicts are formed and acted out not only in the community but also *in* the subject. The chapter highlights contemporary views on Hegel in which he is considered to present a logic from which modern subjectivity can be thought. Feminine desire can be considered, in such a perspective, not as society's outside but rather as a potential model of modern subjectivity as such, an opening toward new forms of subjectivity.

The third chapter discusses Martin Heidegger's reading of *Antigone*, which in many ways could be considered a response to metaphysical tendencies in social anthropologies such as Hegel's. Discarding metaphysical determinations of the human condition that are thought outside of the ontological conditioning of Dasein, Heidegger is suspicious of all arguments that give a positive definition of sexual difference, and therefore does not have an argument on feminine desire at all. Categories such as feminine and masculine are not even introduced. Rather than discussing problems of sexual difference, he is interested in the conflict between beings and being, a conflict at work in his discussion of *Antigone*, although it is introduced in a more thorough manner in his early work, where it is also shown to be related to sexual difference. Heidegger avoids issues of sexual difference in order to focus on "neutrality" as a more fundamental condition of

Dasein; sexual difference is a potentiality and not a social or cultural determination. Sophocles' text, which received Heidegger's attention in the 1930s and 1940s, is considered to exemplify a tragic violence inherent in the human condition as such. Tragedy does not follow a development or unfolding properly speaking, but rather returns to a liminal point that was present from the beginning. In this way, Antigone introduces a figure that we will examine as an ontological analysis of feminine desire, although the concept of femininity is never introduced. Heidegger's understanding of Antigone is only implicitly sexualized: he avoids the categories of "sexual" and "natural" that were part of Hegel's reading, and the concept of desire never figures in the discussion. Instead, Heidegger focuses on the temporality of Antigone's fate: her quest is directed not toward an object, but toward an impossibility that can be described as an evasive origin rather than an end, which is inscribed in her being as the very premise through which the unraveling of that being will take place. In Heidegger's ontological analysis of Greek Dasein, however, Antigone is distinctly colored by a feminine trait, and the "natural" sphere of love, desire, sexuality, and death presents itself as a subtext in his understanding; in fact, without intending to sexualize the text, Heidegger ends up offering us an ontological analysis of feminine desire.

The fourth chapter introduces the concept of an Antigone complex properly speaking, and argues against structuralist tendencies in psychoanalysis. Freudian psychoanalysis, as is well known, relates the question of feminine sexuality to an Oedipal structure, in which it becomes problematic at best and deviant at worst. If we take Freud's Oedipus complex as the basic model representing the development of desire in the male child, then we find a relatively coherent relation between subject and object: the subject is denied its primary (maternal) object by a prohibitive paternal law, and replaces it with others. From the point of view of the girl, however, there is no coherence between the development of her identity as a woman, her desire, and the objects of her desire. In fact, as many feminists have pointed out, the enigma surrounding feminine desire from a Freudian point of view is how it can develop at all, given that femininity is inherently prone to melancholia and depression. The perspective provided by Antigone, Oedipus's daughter, therefore has the advantage of shifting thought altogether from the problem of how to fit femininity into the Oedipal structure to another kind of analysis altogether. Antigone is not symmetrically opposed to Oedipus, nor is she complementary. Antigone's desire is not directed toward a replaceable object, and there is no evolutionary logic of displacement and compensation to its movements. Moreover, her desire does not originate in a prohibitive law that correlates with a social and cultural structure. But it is precisely because it does not originate in this way, because of the dissonances and deficiencies that certainly abound in the Antigonean examples, that another kind of thinking of desire is allowed to emerge.

Simone de Beauvoir's feminist critique of the structural assumptions in Freud's psychoanalytic theory of feminine desire is a necessary point of departure for approaching this issue. In her call for an ontological analysis of sexual difference, Beauvoir shows a need to rethink the question of feminine desire, so that the point of view of identity in the social sense is replaced or completed with an ontological analysis of sexuality as a project and a measure of finitude. Showing why it is necessary to discard certain Freudian assumptions, Beauvoir's suggestion that woman is the "Other" does not imply a complementarity to the male sex, but rather implies that she occupies an empty space in the patriarchal order. Her argument presages some basic features of Jacques Lacan's notion of feminine desire, showing why the feminine is an "empty" or impossible space in the so-called symbolic order of sexual difference. Although Lacan never introduces anything like an Antigone complex, and although he never distances himself from Freud in the way that Beauvoir does, Lacan clearly shows that feminine desire is irreducible to the structural logic implied by Oedipus. Lacan makes "woman," or *la femme*, into the sign of a constitutive lack in the symbolic order: an object of fantasy constructed around the fallibility of the system itself. Feminine desire points to the limits of the symbolic order: feminine enjoyment, or *jouissance*, reveals the lack in the structure upholding desire as such. Lacan's argument is that Antigone becomes a model for the ethical subject because she follows her desire, unraveling the cause of desire as singular, irreversible, and impossible to suppress. Rather than excluding such psychoanalytic concepts from the ethical domain as unclear or irrelevant, the example of Antigone calls for an ethics accommodating a subject of desires and drives. Lacan's "ethics of the real" shows that neither metaphysical support, nor religious beliefs, nor social structures can suffice to explain the motivation behind an action that seems driven by a desire that can never be reduced either to a purpose or a goal. The kind of desires for which psychoanalysis resort to an "ethics of the real" have their origin in an aspect of the subject that is impossible to sublate or transform into a normative suggestion. Antigone's desire is formed around a cause that can never be dissolved, a foreign aspect intrinsic to her being. Rather than being reduced to an example of femininity and marginalized in terms of the social and cultural (which are usually considered to condition sexual identity and desire), Antigone is paradigmatic not just for feminine desire but for all subjects. One may note that in Lacan's reading a shift has taken place with regard to the tradition that tells us women are morally inferior to men: rather than regarding Antigone as deficient with regard to ethical norms, he regards her as "extra-ethical." Precisely because her actions appear to lack aim or intent, there is a serious ethical question to be asked concerning her actions. One must ask whether they reflect what she must do or what she ought to do: they reveal desire as lacking aim and object, and by comparison Lacan argues that a truly ethical action from a psychoanalytic point of view—an action motivated by an ethics of the real—must be considered in the same terms. Desire, as well as the truly ethical action motivated by an aspect wholly foreign to moral considerations, originates in an impossibility internal to human subjectivity as such, not in a goal or an object external to the subject. With Lacan, we remain within the parameters of the tradition, which has set up an intrinsic relation between feminine desire and a deficiency in respect to social and ethical norms, but Lacan reverses the relation between ethical values and normativity, and thereby the philosophical denunciation of feminine desire; the ethical is no longer complicit with values found in the social and culture sphere.

In the fifth chapter, I take as my departure Judith Butler's reading of *Antigone* and her critique of the naturalization of normativity in family politics. Perhaps the first philosopher to observe the subversive aspects of an Antigonean model in comparison to an Oedipal one, French feminist philosopher Luce Irigaray has shown that feminine desire must be analyzed in an order entirely different from the patriarchal order. In the hope of recuperating aspects of feminine being that have been hidden from or buried in the patriarchal order, we may well turn to Antigone to understand the sensitive relation between mother and daughter, which has been perverted by patriarchy, and we may offer her example to introduce another kind of genealogy of female kinship. The problem with Irigaray's reading, however, is a wish to find an unambiguous model of feminine desire. In this way, the interpretation remains stuck in the grid she is criticizing. Picking up the thread of Antigone and arguing against structuralist assumptions pertaining to kinship and the relation between kinship and desire, Judith Butler uses the example of Antigone to question the heteronormative basis of society and the "origin" of the subject in a certain interpretation of the incest taboo. Antigone points not to an intelligible origin, but rather to a state of confusion. The issues she forces us to confront are situated at a limit where the question of origins and the question of family bonds are political; in order to make sense of her claim, we have to negotiate the way we consider kinship as a prepolitical foundation of a political community. While I agree with Butler's critique of Lacan's conception of the symbolic as a naturalized version of a normative order, I would like to propose a reading of Lacan that explores the domain he calls an ethics of the real, which would support her attempt to politicize human bonds rather than considering the real as a mere downside of the symbolic/social order. Working through the notion of feminine desire as it relates to an ethics of the real rather than accepting it as a deviant behavior in relation to the moral norms of society, as many philosophers have up to and including Freud, allows us to consider desire as irreducible to discursive and social analysis. In the *Ethics of Psychoanalysis*, Lacan questions the traditional psychoanalytical concept of an object of desire with a discussion of the Thing as a cause of desire. The meaning of desire must be sought in the moment of its inscription rather than in its objects or aims. In this discussion, Lacan shows that the psychoanalytic theory of objects as good or bad must be rethought in the same manner as philosophy has approached the problem of nihilism, which demanded an investigation into the production of values such as good and evil, thus overcoming the confusion between metaphysics and social normativity. More importantly, the contours of an ethical argument can be seen to take shape in Lacan, where psychoanalysis contributes to an understanding of desire as a motive, and therefore as relevant to ethical questioning. One way of understanding Lacan's famous description of psychoanalysis as an ethics of the real is to contrast it with a normative position in general terms, or any notion of what one *ought* to do (which is the normative consideration) as opposed to what one *must* do (an ethics of the real). Although Lacan may well agree that the kind of moral values that are of use to us in everyday life belong to a sphere in which psychoanalysis is of little concern, it would appear that some actions that are especially important to us and that carry weight are colored by what psychoanalysis calls desires and drives. Without suggesting a theory of ethics properly speaking, psychoanalytic research into the function of desire gives us a perspective on these actions and their place in the life of the subject.

Although my argument is philosophical, I should add that I wanted to use examples from film and literature to enhance my discussion of the Thing. I have found very few *positive* or encouraging representations, at least in contemporary literature and cinema. As soon as feminine desire becomes the leading theme of a story, women tend to perish or kill their lovers or themselves.[5] Feminine desire may no longer be considered a dark continent or an enigma, but it is still depicted as a devouring, threatening, or self-destructive force. There is no intrinsic reason in feminine subjectivity that would explain why women would be closer to devouring and threatening forces than men, or to death, for that matter. But these images confirm that the Antigone complex continues to live on and that the challenge of depicting feminine desire is as pointed as ever. I have settled for citing two films that seem to complete one another in a curious way: Jane Campion's *The Piano*, and Elfriede Jelinek's *The Piano Teacher*, which was transposed into the cinema by Michael Hanneke. These two films challenge and transgress the traditional codes framing women's sexuality in our culture, and both approach that fearful darkness called the Thing without withdrawing into safer realms. They show how the Thing is present in the origination or direction of desire as a foreign and destructive entity, interestingly portrayed in both these examples as the cold dead weight of a wooden piano.

To conclude: in introducing an Antigone complex, this book does not attempt to say anything about what feminine desire actually *is*, or how one should talk about it. The fact that Antigone has been widely used as a representative of the feminine does not mean that her actions should be seen as producing a coherent set of issues concerning femininity. Indeed, in contemporary thought—in the arguments of Martin Heidegger and Jacques Lacan, for instance—one also finds a tendency to avoid casting Antigone's predicament as a specifically feminine one, opposed to and marginalized in a patriarchal order. Instead these writers regard the example of Antigone as symptomatic of the enigmas surrounding human existence and identity as such. Irreducible to structural, social, or sexual terms, the analysis of her desire calls for the profound understanding of an alterity that is irreducible to the social sphere; for Heidegger, such alterity would be time, for Lacan the real. And this is precisely what the Antigone complex is concerned with—the pressure of an unfathomable alterity in our daily lives. As I will attempt to show in this book, the insistence of such an alterity is that of feminine desire itself.

Morality and the Invention
of Feminine Desire

Feminine Desire and Modernity

What is feminine desire? Contrasted with the political and ethical project of modernity, it has been made into an elusive object of speculation in literature, art, philosophy, and psychoanalysis. Unlike its masculine counterpart, feminine desire is rarely depicted as social engagement. Sexual rather than political, narcissistic rather than ambitious, it aims to satisfy sensual appetites and not the need for recognition and emancipation. While men strive for empowerment and change, women seek immediate satisfaction of the senses. The feminine, or so it goes, is a fluid language of sensuality and pleasure, a promise of soft, maternal eroticism in its domesticated form, or a threatening force of triumphant enjoyment or polymorphous perversity in its untamed version. Lingering between poetry and subversion, it has been depicted as mysterious, exhilarating, subversive, and titillating: a mythical object of excess and exaggeration, the dark hole of modern reason.

Even before psychoanalysis engaged the question of feminine desire, it was considered an enigma in the philosophical tradition. Modern philosophy makes it into a very particular problem—namely in relation to *ethics*. In the enlightenment debate, there is a discursive link between lack of morality or virtue and feminine desire. Women are judged either as "pure" or too sexual, too virtuous or too promiscuous. Whether excessive or insufficient, they do not fit the moral standard. Failing to incorporate virtue by way of their frivolous nature or their lack of education, women fall outside of the ethical community because their femininity prevents them from participating in the first place. While the moral subject is declared autonomous from the late eighteenth century on, it is still compromised by a moral weakness that is coded as feminine. In his essay on the sublime and the beautiful, Kant announces that women are incapable of sticking to moral principles: "Nothing of duty, nothing of compulsion, nothing of obligation! Woman is intolerant of all commands and all morose constraint. They do something only because it pleases them, and the art consists in making only that please them which is good."[1] Failing to shoulder the freedom that accompanies the discovery of reason, women lack the capacity to apply reason to morality, although Kant will later declare this capacity to be universal. The above quote, however, cannot simply be said to be arbitrarily chosen when one looks at its place in a philosophical-historical thought, where weak, dependent women are described as pleasure-seeking and frivolous. The idea that feminine subjects lack moral reason returns in nineteenth-century thinkers. Displacing morality from the realm of reason to a social context, Hegel still regards women as creatures of pleasure and not reason; the laughing woman is the eternal irony of the ethical community. Kierkegaard, in turn, defined femininity in aesthetic rather than ethical terms. And Freud, who initiated the discussion on the enigmatic character of feminine desire properly speaking, regarded the female subject as having a weak super-ego, and therefore as a weakness in the moral development of the modern fabric.[2] The notion that feminine desire is too little or too much in relation to ethical values, an excess or deficiency in the community, or exists outside of the social context subscribing to those values is a commonplace, traceable to a modern philosophical discourse that continues from Rousseau to Sade, Hegel to Kierkegaard, through Freud and Lacan.

Although a depreciative view of the feminine body appears already in ancient metaphysics, it becomes a problem properly speaking when it is associated with desire, sexuality, and pleasure in the philosophy of modernity, where the conflicts of new forms of consciousness are defined. A nebulous concept, modernity could be considered in terms of a multitude of conflicts that defined debates from the late eighteenth century until the beginning of the nineteenth century. These conflicts concern slave and master, individual and collective, law and divine rights, religion and politics, rights and responsibilities, family and state, private and public, and a split between the sexes.[3] The idea that sexual difference entails a social conflict took on a particular significance in the upheavals of intellectual life of the late eighteenth century in Western Europe, at the juncture between enlightenment and romanticism. Writers such as Mary Wollstonecraft, Madame de Staël, Friedrich Schlegel, Bettina von Arnim, G. W. F. Hegel, and many others began to inquire about the status of women as subjects.[4] Wollstonecraft's influential *Vindication of the Rights of Woman* helped formulate many of the emancipatory demands that we associate with modern feminism. Her thoughts depart from a more or less misogynistic tradition, in which sexual difference was considered to be a conflict that impeded the recognition of women as able social subjects. Sexual difference was in turn mapped onto another opposition, which must be added to the list of conflicts formulated in the philosophy of modernity—namely, the split between the corporeal world of the senses and the moral world of reason. Both Wollstonecraft and Hegel argued on different grounds and from different perspectives that the sexes were brought up in radically different spheres and were unable to quite respond to each other. For Wollstonecraft, women could all too easily lose themselves to corporeal and inauthentic desires. Hegel split desire into two: on the one hand, he considered it a political weapon, pitting slave against master in the quest for recognition. Thus it was associated with struggles for power and domination, change and development. Feminine desire, on the other hand, was sexual and corporeal. In the split between social and sexual desire, ethical and political concerns were detached from what Hegel considered the lower spheres, and a feminine domain came into being that was defined as natural, in contradistinction to the social and political world of the spirit.

There are, however, significant exceptions to the idea that women are merely sexual and corporeal. While feminine desire was mystified and sexualized, and considered excessive and childlike in much of the philosophical tradition, an emancipatory potential was also identified and explored. For this reason, contemporary thinkers have been fascinated by the stories of the Marquis de Sade, who explored the intersection between the newly won freedom of reason and sexual slavery. Sade's fictional women incarnate this intersection, in particular his alter ego, Juliette. It is a strange fact, perhaps, that one of the most famous "female" autobiographies in the history of philosophy is written by a man, praising the *delices* of rape and humiliation. And this riddle becomes even more interesting—not least for the purposes of this book—when one looks at his pornographic stories as allegorical satires of the subject of enlightenment: how are we to understand our bondage under sexual inclinations and desires when we are declared autonomous and free? It is of course not by chance that Sade chose women as proponents of the inquiry into this mystery—all philosophers did. The difference with Sade was that he did it in order to point to a universal problem that was not reducible to women. Celebrating her freedom in the service of an enslaving fantasy—that of an endless use of pleasure—Juliette gives a whole new meaning to the old figure of feminine desire as excessive and immoral, and she does so in order to undermine the enlightenment belief in the intrinsic relation between reason and freedom.

Feminine Desire and the Shortcomings of Virtue: The Case of Juliette

Sade's most extensive work, *La nouvelle Justine ou les malheurs de la vertu suivie de l'histoire de Juliette, sa soeur*, is the story of two sisters, one of whom is a virtuous victim, the other her perverted and sadistic counterpart. Their lives are intricately woven parallels, producing a double-layered portrait of the workings of feminine desire. Together, the sisters are less mirrors reflecting one another than multifaceted proponents of a dialectics without teleological direction. While Justine suffers rapes and humiliations she is subjected to with great pain, Juliette thoroughly enjoys the same thing, whether it is afflicted on others or on herself. Sade's novels resemble the educational treatises for girls that were so popular in his time, a genre revisited also by Jean-Jacques Rousseau and Mary Wollstonecraft. One may in fact claim that the way he saw their respective fates is indicative of a dialectics between ethics and desire that Sade himself never saw to a conclusion, remaining content with widening the rift in the conflict set up by enlightenment philosophy. It is, of course, not by chance that female characters were used for this purpose. Juliette has been considered to be the most interesting figure in Sade's work by commentators such as Adorno and Horkheimer, Beauvoir, Lacan, and Angela Carter. Juliette is Sade's most political heroine. Moreover, she is Sade's alter ego. With her, a new, pornographic womanhood is invented that is as inhumane and powerful in its transgressions as the male libertine. Unlike Justine, Juliette takes an active part in her submission. Therefore, she does not commit the mistake of avoiding responsibility for her fate and acting like a victim.[5] A true Sadean female hero *enjoys* her own submission, as Angela Carter has shown.[6] Active heroines, like Juliette, are even more cruel than the men. Angela Carter has chosen to read the heroines as fictional proponents of emancipatory demands, claiming the "rights" of free sexuality for women. By enacting and countering the psychic fiction of female castration, Sade's novels are a powerful testimony to the potential subversiveness of feminine desire. Juliette is a true heroine of feminine eroticism, opposing repression through imitations of cruelty and abuse. Parodying through mimicry and exaggeration the conditions of power that regulate desire, Sade elevates her as a strong, perverted woman, thereby challenging a system where women had few constitutional rights. Describing sadists and masochists rather than masters and slaves, his work may seem a far cry from any struggle for emancipation. But the figure of Juliette points to an unexpected product of moral autonomy—the subversive potential of feminine enjoyment. Sade's superfluous aristocrats live in the delusion of unbound power and freedom. But, in fact, they are dependent upon the submission of others, tainted by struggle and dependency, humiliation rather than triumph. Enjoyment has nothing to do with self-interest or the submission of others to one's needs. Juliette displays a different logic of desire at work, where true enjoyment surpasses dependency. The victim is more free than the torturer because she does not need any object or any other individual to indulge her fantasy. Her perversion of feminine desire serves as a powerful subtext in Sade's writings, where moral autonomy as a consequence of the transcendentalism of reason is undermined.

Several authors have used Sade's debauched women to unravel what they perceive as the problem with the rationalism of the enlightenment. Identified by Kant, the modern subject is autonomous, rational, and free. Discarding the Aristotelian belief in an intrinsic relation between pleasure and the good, Kant refers pleasures to the domain of the pathological, which is dissociated from moral law. Kantian ethics presumes that the subject can prove its autonomy only by dissociating itself from desires and inclinations. As a consequence of this argument, the good can no longer be the equivalent of self-interest.[7] The selfish subject is at odds with moral autonomy, and we cannot use self-love as a measure of morality.[8] Needs and feelings, pleasure and discomfort, and all emotional conceptions of the good and the bad are examples of inclinations that must be considered separate from the definition of a moral sphere in order for its autonomy to be intellectually secured. Some authors, however—including Theodor Adorno and Max Horkheimer, Simone de Beauvoir, Maurice Blanchot, and Jacques Lacan—have turned to the writings of Sade in order to examine dimensions of ethical problems and subjectivity that are repressed in Kant. From their perspective, Sade's maxims reveal the flip side of the Kantian subjection to moral law. Kant's categorical imperative exhorts us to act in such a manner that the maxim of our will is raised into universal law.[9] Sade's writing is littered with phrases that read like travesties of this idea: "Let us take as the universal maxim of our conduct the right to enjoy any other person whatsoever as the instrument of our pleasure."[10] The question is why Sade's law appears to be a joke whereas Kant's moral law incorporates reason. Formally, the injunctions may seem similar. But on closer inspection, in a surprising turn of the logic implied, the parallels are illusory. Surprisingly, Kant's discovery of moral autonomy seems to unleash Sade's stories of unbounded enjoyment. Claiming the use of another to be a universal right is, naturally, absurd. Sade never really transcends the barriers of . solipsism; he just absorbs all forms of passion and pain into a machinery satisfying a hypertrophied self. The aim is to transcend every kind of conflict or rupture.[11] Sadean law is, as Blanchot has noted, absolute egoism. His libertine is not an autonomous being but rather a life of omnipotent delusion lacking the laws and limits that secure the autonomy of the moral subject. The desire of the libertine, consequently, is always returned upon the self and never directed toward an object.[12] The Sadean woman who takes pleasure in pain incarnates the most extreme example of the hypertrophied self. This is also why almost all interpreters have understood Juliette to be the alter ego of Sade. In *Juliette*, the abbess Delbène makes Juliette, Sade's cruelest heroine, into an atheist, by trying to convince her that nature is excess, and finite sexuality an invention of moral convention:

I go so far so as to repudiate a duty I consider to be as absurd as it is childish, commanding us *not to do towards others that which we do not want them to do towards us*. Nature advises us strictly in the opposite direction, since its only injunction is to *find pleasures, whomever we may harm*. Without doubt these maxims tell us that our pleasures may destroy the happiness of others; but should that make them less intense?[13]

The abbess goes to the heart of the matter: either you use others for the sake of your own pleasure or you identify with the position of submission. In Sade's fiction, accordingly, desire is organized hierarchically, in asymmetrical positions of enjoyment versus submission. These positions are, by the way, reflected in the social hierarchy of his figures. The cruelest men are always those with most power. The women lack power, and therefore both freedom and rights. Aristocrats, popes, and priors kill for their own pleasure, and their victims are always unremarkable enough to disappear without leaving a trace. Most of the time they are, of course, young, poor, and seemingly expendable. At second sight, however, the truly expendable class consists of useless aristocrats and priests, who may have the power to subject their victims, but only to enjoy a humiliating freedom. The Sadean orgy is a metaphor for a social hierarchy lacking legitimacy in the age of reason. Its participants are degenerate and isolated.

As Adorno and Horkheimer put it in the first magisterial essay on Sade and Kant, "Juliette or Enlightenment and Morality," Juliette is a cynical instrument of subversion. In creating Juliette, Sade imagines a heroine who, like himself, finds pleasure only in sacrilege and the destruction of Christian morality. Uninterested in emancipation, she does so with cynicism rather than revolutionary fervor. Although she may have understood everything, she still acts just like the rest of Sade's women, who are fountains of pleasure given to pointless enjoyment. Locked in an aimless pursuit of pleasure, women incarnate nature's revenge on reason. Like nature, woman is both irresistible and powerless. She is the object of man's striving for control, whether it be depicted in philosophy—the transcendental object of science—or myth.[14] Sade's stories about Juliette complete a development beginning with the Homeric epic. Odysseus_s conquests aim toward mastery of the unknown, incarnated in the song of the sirens. The sirens are, however, both luring and dangerous, an immanent threat. One can see the sirens as a metaphor for repressed sexuality. The more intense the repression, the greater the sexual pleasure. This means that cultural and social codes create the insistence of sexuality through their attempt to repress it. Adorno and Horkheimer draw the conclusion that "all pleasure is social," having its origin in the transgression of interdictions and norms. This does not necessarily mean that enjoyment is a conscious act of transgression. But it "owes its origin to civilization."[15] Adorno and Horkheimer assume modern man bears the mark of a distant memory of a "primeval era without masters and without discipline."[16] But while his homesickness, alienation, and disillusion produce a need to transgress the limits of his own subjection, he remains caught within a logic of subjection. In Christianity, woman incarnates the threat of the forbidden and impossible pleasures of sexuality. The cultural idolatry of women as virtuous and beautiful disguises their real position: "The emotion which corresponds to the practice of oppression is contempt, not reverence, and in the centuries of Christianity love for one's neighbor has always concealed a lurking, forbidden though now compulsive, hatred for women—the object which served repeatedly to recall the fact of futile exertion."[17] Women represent sexuality and bodily pleasures, which threaten to tear apart the project of enlightenment unless they can be controlled through cultural, economic, and intellectual institutions. Juliette does not challenge this fact—she takes advantage of it.

Adorno and Horkheimer's critique of the ideology of the enlightenment has rightly had an extraordinary influence. But there is a problem with their introduction of a gender perspective: for them, the subject is always male. In this way, their analysis is complicit with the structures of enlightenment thought. Odysseus represents the fragile emergence of self-consciousness through the domination of nature, both at a mythical and a transcendental level. The subject of enlightenment, in this account, clearly distinguishes between self and other. The other, as woman, nature, or body, is distinctly separated from the self, and therefore subject to control and domination. In this perspective, the patriarchal discourse of the enlightenment is one of strength and exploitation, a narrative without weaknesses or gaps. But if we cease to figure the subject as homogenous and one-sexed, and consider it castrated, marked by sexual difference, the perspective changes. The female figures that Odysseus needs to escape embody not just sexual pleasure or the lures of unknown nature but the *desire* of another, threatening to engulf or dissipate that fragile subject.[18] Rather than being coded and controlled like a scientific object, the feminine figure *escapes* the parameters of objectification precisely because she cannot be reduced to nature. In Sade's erotic parody, women undermine the structures of power they are supposed to support.

Adorno and Horkheimer read these women as a source of pleasure contained within the parameters of capitalism. But if we look at their experiences, most of them represent nothing but the enjoyment of *suffering*, which has very little to do with pleasure in the traditional sense of the word. Through the excess of their submission, and the enjoyment taken in their own suffering, Sade's women manifest a perverted exploitation of their position, which is precisely what makes them so worrying. They are not just unwilling and powerless victims or dominated objects, but they contribute more than willingly to their own humiliation. This tasteless feature of Sade's parody gives it its power: these women do not just represent something that can be controlled, although it can be dominated. They represent *another desire*.

Simone de Beauvoir is sensitive to this fact when she explains the absurdity of Sade's maxims from a gender perspective in *Faut-il brûler Sade?* (*Must We Burn Sade?* 1951). There is a hidden motive behind Sade's parody of Kant: the threatening presence of another subjectivity, another desire, another body. In order to understand these mechanisms better, we have to penetrate the Sadean night and consider how its solitary firmament is constituted. What Sade thinks of as "ethical might"—that is, unlimited freedom to use others for one's pleasure—is in fact nothing but "ethical night," Beauvoir points out. In Sade's world, we are never touched by the pain of others: "My fellow being means nothing to me: there is not the slightest little connection between him and myself."[19] The encapsulation in the world of nonrelation derives from anxiety. We know very little about Sade's sexual activities, Beauvoir notes, probably because he only wrote his fantasies down, without acting them out. He is more of a passive sodomite than a sadist, and rather the enjoying *Juliette* than the martyred *Justine*.[20] But he would never desire a woman. Sade hates the female organ and refuses to mention it.[21] His ideas of freedom may seem like a call to pursue pleasure under any circumstances, but it is a call founded only on false ideas of reciprocity. A suspicious gap persists between the call for freedom for ourselves and the inability to recognize freedom as essentially belonging to the other. What is so worrying for Sade is that we can never fully objectify or subject our neighbor. The real target of Beauvoir's lucid account of Sade, therefore, is not the lack of Sadean morality, but the fear of another desire. He is effectively a "grand moraliste" through his uncompromising questioning.[22] But his fantasies are formed around the denial of the freedom of the other, and intimately linked to the fact that the other is represented by the other sex. He believes himself to be strong and free. But Sade's fantasies are in fact symptomatic of someone who is locked inside a body that makes him not free but estranged and foreign to himself:

If he refuses to give the other an ethical recognition based on false notions of reciprocity and universality, it is in order to allow himself to concretely break through the carnal barriers that isolate consciousness.[23]

The fantasies of pain and death are, in fact, an acting out motivated by absolute isolation, an attempt to pierce the corporeal shell. Sade is a pathological example of what has been left out in enlightenment ethics. For Beauvoir, our freedom to act or engage can never be thought beyond our corporeal "situation." What comes out in Sade is nothing other than the failure of the enlightenment to comprehend the deep ambiguity of human existence, which resides at the crossroads between embodiment and reason.[24] Sade's body is not a project or a situation but an inapproachable thing that is unknowable even to himself. It is an object of science and reason rather than an invisible ground for projection, desires, and appetites. The foreclosure of sexual difference is symptomatic for a subject who has become estranged from his own body. The desire of the other sex is frightening because the body must either be denied or foreclosed.

"Kant with Sade": The Discovery of the Drive.
The Case of Justine.

In his comparison of Kant and Sade, Lacan joins Adorno, Horkheimer, and Beauvoir in confronting Kant's separation of desires and inclinations from the sphere of morality. Lacan deals with Kant and Sade in two works: *The Ethics of Psychoanalysis* (1959–60) and the article "Kant with Sade" (1964). In the Ethics seminar, the Sadean law is quoted in the following manner: "Lend me the part of your body that will give me a moment of satisfaction and, if you care to, use for your pleasure that part of my body that appeals to you."[25] It may seem as if we find ourselves turning back toward an infantile state of polymorphous perversity, a body of organs capable of infinite pleasure, but the significance lies elsewhere. Sade is fantasizing about becoming the victim of the enjoyment of the Other. Such a subject is defined as submission and lacks consistency other than that demand in itself. In Lacan's writings on Sade, it is clear that the desire or enjoyment of the Other is a category designating perverted behavior in the subject, but in itself, it is an empty formula, meaning very little beyond the fixation on some kind of fantasy.

"Kant with Sade" (1964) is a small text serving as a twin to the Ethics seminar (1959–60). It was intended as an introduction to an edition of Sade's work, but was withdrawn because of its incomprehensibility. The major difference between the Ethics seminar and the shorter essay lies in the fact that the injunction "Enjoy!" has turned into the pledge "Whip me!" In "Kant with Sade," the Sadean moral law takes a new form: "I have the right of enjoyment over [*le droit de jouir de*] your body, anyone can say to me, and I will exercise this right, without any limit stopping me in the capriciousness of the exactions that I might have the taste to satiate."[26] Rather than simply enjoying unlimited power, the subject presents itself as an object for somebody else's pleasure: anyone can say to me that they have the right to use me. What is pronounced in the law is therefore a fantasy of submission. The law is not designed to express any (false) reciprocity. The central message hidden in the form of the law is: "It is thus indeed the Other as free, it is the freedom of the Other, that the discourse of the right to *jouissance* poses as the subject of its enunciation."[27] The supposed limit-less freedom of the aristocrat has turned into what Lacan calls the freedom of the Other—which effectively means that he is submitted to his own law of seeking enjoyment. The effect is not limitless enjoyment but *too much submission*. Enjoyment is not transgression, as Adorno and Horkheimer hold. It is the extreme end of submission, the frozen fixation in fantasmatic servitude. Sade, who seems to tear down all barriers at one level, is more stuck in rigid norms than anyone else, more dependent on the laws he is feigning to transgress.[28]

In Sade's world, we are free to do whatever we want with whomever we would like to do it with, and we show solidarity with every form of use, every pedophile action, every rape. Every positive injunction, like the one given by Sade, shows us the limit beyond which freedom threatens to an-nihilate us, where no mediation is available. This shows that desire cannot simply be based on the exploration of human freedom. It must be based on an original *prohibition*.

"*Jouissons! Telle est la loi de la nature*," Sade's heroes keep saying: "En-joy! That is the law of nature."[29] An atheist with a developed belief in the disintegration of matter as the final end of desire, he makes an inter-minable state of infinite pain into the highest pleasure. Sade imagines a death of eternal pain. Saint-Fond, one of Juliette's friends, coins the term "molecules of evil" (*molécules malfaisantes*).[30] He believes in a God of re-venge, barbarism, injustice, and cruelty—*l'Etre suprême en méchanceté*.[31] The evil molecules lie beyond the temporal atoms of decay and death. In "Kant with Sade," Saint-Fond's fantasy of a life after death is figured as a grip of pain from which there is no return. It is a remarkable image, Lacan notes, where the hell sought by Sade the atheist returns in a form even more extreme than the Christian version. In a second death, the disap-pearance of the subject becomes double—not just a physical disintegration but a vanishing from memory and significance.[32] Sade's victims are always beautiful, as if beauty compensated for this. Foreclosing the pain of an original trauma, Sade creates an alter ego that escapes destruction in the guise of beauty.[33] That alter ego is Juliette. Through Juliette, Sade's anxi-eties are conjured to a certain extent. If Beauvoir sees that Sade, in his "ethical night," is driven by an anxiety released in response to the freedom of the other, which is manifested as feminine desire, then Lacan shows that the creation of Juliette covers his own fear of annihilation in the "molecules of evil."

Kant discovers the "purest" form of desire—the drive—while formulating moral law in its most universal form; getting rid of soft, human objects, he points to the "empty" determination of those objects.[34] Lacanian psychoanalysis begins with the slipping away of the object. It is not the object or the aim of desire that should be examined, but rather the *cause* of desire. A new term is introduced in this context: the *objet petit a*. The *objet petit a* does not stand for an object or another person. It stands for the cause of desire, which is to be found in the subject itself. The *objet petit a* organizes the subject in a structure of fantasies. What matters is not the content or aim of those fantasies, but rather the way in which they lock the subject in a particular founding fantasy or symptom. The cause in question is inscribed in a larger context: the symbolic Other, or the structure mediating any possible direction of desire.[35] "Kant with Sade" argues that Sadean fantasy is not directed toward possession of or concession to another person as an object of desire; instead, it originates in a fundamental lack or void. One could say, perhaps, that this lack or void is a flagrant lack of completeness or totality. In a religious society, such a totality would have been represented by God. But the tragedy of the modern subject lies, of course, in being left with that void. In Lacan's analysis, the secular order that installed itself with the French revolution had decisive effects on the way the symbolic order was integrated into the subject. In Sade's case, the disappearance of the Christian God left a void that caused a grueling anxiety, and the fantasy of a much more cruel and punishing God—the "molecules of evil," a big black hole. The Sadean fantasy is therefore a form of subjection, but it is not motivated by any kind of religious authority; instead it comes from the anxiety felt in the face of a void.[36] The aim of psychoanalysis is to "traverse" or unravel fantasies holding the subject in an unproductive grip of repetition. When the *objet petit a* is revealed, what appeared to have been the machinations of an evil Other becomes a cause situated in the subject itself. There is, of course, no higher power hidden in the path of our destinies. The fantasy of a diabolic force only serves to cover a void that then appears even more frightening. Together, Kant and Sade tell us something crucial about the psychoanalytical subject: *without the discovery of reason, autonomy, and freedom, no drive would have been posited.*

Lacan's drive is not considered eternal or archaic, as is the case with Freud, or Adorno/Horkheimer. The drive is a symbolic and modern invention dating from the end of the last century, in the junction between Sade's enjoyment and Kant's reason. The dualistic construction of Adorno and Horkheimer, where sexual pleasure constitutes "the revenge of nature," is theoretically untenable. Enjoyment does not originate in archaic worlds before culture. It is futuristic and repetitive, lacking both authenticity and aim. It has little to do with pleasure and more with an *excess* that the discovery of modern subjectivity has produced. *Jouissance*, or enjoyment, the most important expression of the drive, is a term that never appears in Freud. Freud describes the drive [*Trieb*] as a remnant or derivation of the constitutional biological condition of man. Touching the limit between body and language, Freud's drive is defined as "a concept on the frontier between the mental and the somatic, as the psychical representative of the stimuli originating from within the organism and reaching the mind as a measure of the demand made upon the mind for work in consequence of its connection with the body."[37] For Lacan, however, the drive derives from the rift between the corporeal and the linguistic domain. It is not just a corporeal phenomenon, but rather something that the symbolic, or culture, has helped to create. The origin of the drive is to be found at the junction where language cuts between corporeal needs and the excess of those needs, which no object can satisfy.[38] The impossibility of linking an object to the drive, or of founding the drive in a specific object or concept, shows its fictional character. The modern subject is therefore caught in the pangs between desire (which has an object) and *enjoyment* (which has none).[39]

Juliette may be Sade's most interesting character, but there are few Juliettes that we know of—women who in an aggressive and affirmative way take pleasure in abuse. What happens if we cease to read Sade's heroines as his own fictional alter egos—if we take his heroines not as codes for Sade's autobiography but as images of feminine desire, traces of another subjectivity? Sade's subversive potential may then be seen to lie elsewhere than in Juliette's affirmation of abuse, namely in the excesses of feminine *virtue*, which Justine manifests as a superior kind of enjoyment.[40]

Justine is not free; she incorporates the passive virtue of a good woman. She presents herself to the reader as pale and tearful. Bad things keep happening to her because of her passivity and her incapacity to protect herself. A far cry from Juliette's transgressive eroticism, suffering and martyrization have become her lifestyle. Her definition of virtue is, as Angela Carter has pointed out, first of all not to have sex, but if that proves impossible (and it will), then not to take any pleasure in it. She fears seduction because she fears "the loss of self in participating in her own seduction, for one must be willing or deluded, or, at least, willing to be deluded, in order to be seduced."[41] Justine may be virtuous in her resistance to pleasure, but it is a virtue that proves inefficient and useless.

Justine seems to incarnate the pathos of fruitless victimization. The emancipatory potential of her story, however, lies precisely in that pose. There is an intimate connection between, on the one hand, the breakdown of the *ancien régime* and the moral deficiency connected with it, and on the other hand, Sade's insistence on letting women be excessive in *virtue* as well as the most prominent explorers of forbidden pleasures. The hidden triumph of Sade's heroine is similar, in all its exaggeration, to the moral power of a saint. Justine takes no pleasure in immoral conduct. Instead, it is the excess of moral virtue that causes her excitement. The repetitive pattern of her misfortunes gives her away. Sade's *Justine* is the tale of a woman who gives in to pleasure in spite of herself over and over again, thus proving the vanity and hypocrisy of the moral values she embodies. She is constantly "deluded" into feeling pleasure. It is precisely Justine's inability to protect herself against the seduction she is desperately trying to avoid that makes Sade's satire both so ludicrous and so efficient. In the scene of her fall in the beginning of the novel, corrupt and experienced prostitutes try to lure her into the profession:

Continence is an impossible virtue for a woman, my child, do not ever imagine that you would be able to succeed with it. When the passions light your soul, you will see why it is impossible. . . . Do not be mistaken, Justine; it is not virtue they demand from us, it is only the mask of virtue and if we are able to fake it, they will demand no more. . . . What brings true happiness is nothing but the appearance of this virtue to which the ridiculous prejudices of men have condemned our sex.[42]

The Sadean analysis unmasks the appearance of women as virtuous rather than sexual. More important, however, is the revelation of the fact that the very appearance of virtue increases rather than killing their capacity for enjoyment. Madame Delmonse, who gives this speech, is the personification of this unexpected relation: the pleasure she takes in her prostitution is enhanced by the fact that she hides it from her husband, who still believes her to be as pure as snow.[43] Madame Delmonse's speech also gives us a key to Justine's character: Justine is also, although in a different manner, split between virtue and indulgence. Her claim to virtue is a poor disguise for the drives that force her into disgrace. "O well, madame," she cries to the prostitute landlady who takes her money and tries to persuade her to return to a vicious libertine, "I will return to him because you tell me that he respects me, my misfortune leaves me no choice."[44] But no logic in the story suggests that she is forced into prostitution through anything but her own desire to remain a victim. She tries to resist the fall into seduction, but she constantly falls. She falls so many times that it becomes obvious that *the suffering of the victim is compensated by the enjoyment she takes in the virtue of being a martyr.* Her torturers may well have caused her suffering, but they are unable to contain or control it. The *objet petit a* at play here could perhaps be identified as the repeated act of falling under someone else's control. Justine's transgression consists in the fact that she *enjoys her submission all too much.* The more she suffers without pleasure, the more virtuous she becomes, and the more she enjoys. This pious vindication is arguably a more troubling manifestation of the drive than that of an aggressive avenger like Juliette. Justine manifests a kind of enjoyment that her torturers are unable to control, which gives her enjoyment a certain quality of independence and autonomy. In many ways, she is a more "pure" figure of the drive than Juliette, if we are to follow Lacan: the void beyond the *objet petit a* or the cause of desire opens up through these endless unsatisfactory acts of submission. But she can hardly be made into an emancipatory figure of feminine desire.

Wollstonecraft's Ethics of Desire

While the connections between Kant and Sade on issues of desire and ethics are well documented, it is rarely noted that Kant and Sade were contemporaries of Mary Wollstonecraft. Wollstonecraft, like the Marquis de Sade, exploits and overturns a discourse in which feminine desire is depicted as the negation of moral freedom. To this day, philosophers focus more frequently on Sade's doubtful ideas on feminine desire than on those actually written by women. Wollstonecraft's complex figures of feminine subjectivity and desire remain surprisingly untouched outside of the feminist tradition, but there are interesting parallels between Sade and Wollstonecraft, in particular if one looks at the paradoxical production of autonomy and enjoyment as a simultaneous event. Both Sade and Wollstonecraft explore the relation between desire and freedom through the figure of women's sexual slavery. Wollstonecraft's last novel, *Maria or the Wrongs of*

Woman (1798), is filled with as much perversion, abuse, and blood as Sade's stories. But Wollstonecraft has an emancipatory ambition. Sade's alter ego, Juliette, celebrates her freedom as a subject of reason in the service of an enslaving fantasy. Wollstonecraft's women are also locked in a fantasy, but the implications of their enslavement to a fantasy that is only the product of their own minds are quite different. Because they are already slaves in an economic and social sense, their discovery that they are subjected to nothing but their own fantasy is liberating. Wollstonecraft has found stern critics among feminist commentators because she depicts women as weak, faulty, and full of self-deceit, and all those feminine shortcomings that men used to accuse women of in her time. This was, however, her way of showing that women are autonomous agents, and therefore capable of moral and intellectual responsibility. As social beings, women may well have been denied such responsibility and therefore behave as weak and irrational children. As moral subjects, however, they lack limits.

Wollstonecraft famously argued against Jean-Jacques Rousseau, who defined femininity as the successful outcome of the systematic education of girls, in which girls' natural inclination toward limitless enjoyment is stifled and replaced with humility and submission. Both men and women are endowed with a capacity for "boundless passion," according to Rousseau, but they have different means of resisting: men use reason, women restrict themselves through modesty or shame.[45] Women therefore lack direct access to the faculty that defines the freedom of the modern subject: reason. Their moral capacity is mediated by and dependent on men. Wollstonecraft opposed Rousseau, retorting that women must be educated on equal terms. The so-called moral inferiority of women is the result of repression. This can be proven by the fact that men, although they behave as irresponsibly as women, are always recognized as moral agents, no matter how much they seem to lack virtue: "*Men* have submitted to superior strength to enjoy with impunity the pleasure of the moment: *women* have only done the same, and therefore till it is proved that the courtier, who servilely resigns the birthright of a man, is not a moral agent, it cannot be demonstrated that woman is essentially inferior to man because she has always been subjugated."[46] The moral weakness of women is explained by Wollstonecraft as the result of a wish to arouse desire in others. In this way, it is directed toward passive and unproductive goals rather than empowerment and change. But she does not draw the conclusion that feminine desire is at odds with moral agency per se. In fact, while most moral philosophers of her time used the example of "feminine" behaviors to show that women were inferior as moral agents or not moral agents at all, Wollstonecraft's argument went in the opposite direction: it is *because* women are prone to irrational, immoral desires that they can be proven to be moral agents and educated as such—not the other way around. The arguments in *Vindication of the Rights of Woman* (1792) sketch a particular relation between moral issues and desire, aiming to show that freedom or independence can be achieved only if a balance is established in which "senseless" desire is overcome. Nevertheless, Wollstonecraft, like her predecessors, contributes to the coding of moral weakness as feminine. Failure to shoulder moral freedom is manifested, above all, by weak, dependent women. In her discourse, however, the assumption becomes loaded with an emancipatory potential: the failure to shoulder moral freedom becomes proof of autonomy rather than an argument against it. Freedom is precisely the capacity for failures, faults, and wrongs—a capacity abundantly manifested by feminine desire. In her overall political argument, which is intended to establish the need for justice for two equal subjects, man and woman, the autonomy of feminine desire becomes an intrinsic and necessary component.

The establishment of this moral domain, which belongs to the realm of reason, begins with the firm separation of ethical and social spheres. Wollstonecraft implicitly separates femininity from female persons. Using the term "femininity" to imply corruption to a lower domain of desire and self-interest, she makes it a synonym for indulgence governed by one's sexual definition. Femininity is a sign of self-deception and lack of authenticity.[47] Women often become too dependent on their own fantasies and ideals, which are projected on external objects: "Their pains and pleasures are so dependent on outward circumstances, on the objects of their affection, that they seldom act from the impulse of a nerved mind, able to choose its own pursuit."[48] Unable to separate authentic and productive desires (passions) from debilitating and infantile ones (appetites), women are epicureans searching for gratification rather than change.[49] However, Wollstonecraft assumes that women, although they are dependent and considered property, are not just coerced into certain kinds of behavior. The weakness of femininity that she complains about is the result of subjugation to an imagined authority. This subjection is, if not self-induced, then at least independent of actual social conditions. This is an important discovery. Women are not just victims of circumstance; as moral agents, they are also free. Wollstonecraft utilizes a range of expressions—many of them violent and demeaning—to prove that precisely because they are subjugated under an interiorized and imagined authority, and not an external one, women are moral agents. The weakness of femininity criticized by Wollstonecraft is a moral deficiency and not a natural one, and therefore it is subject to rectification and improvement.

Wollstonecraft's interrogations concern the effects of injustice not just on women but on the moral subject as such. The erratic behavior of women serves to explain the problems pervading social hierarchies dating back to feudalism. She has a political analysis and a reformative goal in sight, whereas Sade's revolution never goes beyond the philosophical bedroom. But Wollstonecraft does, like Sade, take an intense interest in feminine *suffering*. She does so to fortify her own political theory: justice requires a strong normative foundation based on reason. When women and men are educated and socialized according to reason, the symptoms of their dependency and repression will come to an end. The aim is independence, in economic, social, and moral terms. She puts forward the supremacy of reason—sometimes spoken of as moral law—which in her account serves as the only guarantee of independence. Her philosophy of reason has been criticized by feminists for its claim to universality and its incapacity to operate with gendered categories.[50] It must be remembered, however, that Wollstonecraft's claim to a sexually undifferentiated reason was a significant contribution to the elaboration of a notion of universality that included women. At that time, reason was not considered universal; it was gendered and identified as a male prerogative in her own time.[51] Women were therefore left outside of the moral discourse on reason.

Through her recourse to reason, Wollstonecraft can also argue that the problem which arises with erratic feminine behavior does not merely arise with the fact that women submit to "men," although she criticizes the fact that they are considered and treated as property. Women might have to obey a husband, brother, or father, but these men are only mediating agents subjected to the same irrational system. The problem with women is that they *submit to submission* itself, deceived by the empty authority of the civil hierarchy. It is this state that makes them prone to self-deception, victims of fantasy and false beliefs. Patriarchy may have encouraged women to become weak and needy, but the new science of politics will contribute to the creation of free and rational individuals of both sexes. Although the conditions of patriarchy may still apply, the discovery of freedom and universal rights will affect the self-perception of women. The immorality of women is the result of an oppression that can be traversed. Male power may have had a demoralizing effect on women, but there is no *causal* link between male oppression and feminine weakness.

One may therefore conclude that Wollstonecraft, like many male philosophers of the Enlightenment—including Kant—figures subjectivity as a kind of submission to a superior law, namely that of reason. Like Sade, she is interested in the perverse forms of such submission. The idea that subjectivity can be conceived of as a form of submission takes on two expressions. She differentiates between, on the one hand, an empty or useless form, the irrational and outdated hierarchies of the feudal system, and on the other, the moral subject's submission to the principles of necessity discovered by reason. The first is examined extensively both in her philosophical writings and in her fiction, where Wollstonecraft attacks the hierarchies of social *dependency*. These hierarchies are "empty" authoritarian structures lacking legitimate foundation. As such, they foster dependency and alienation. Using the example of women and soldiers, Wollstonecraft exposes moral weakness as an affair not of gender but of submission to "empty" authorities: "Every profession, in which great subordination for rank constitutes its power, is highly injurious to morality."[52] She compares the relation between the sexes, manifested through the empty hierarchy of marriage, with the hierarchies of the military, the church, and the state. Subordination under the "irrational strength" of institutions and hierarchies create useless individuals. The actual place of the individual in the hierarchy does not matter. In fact, the higher the rank, the more debilitating the subordination. Weakest of all is the king, incorporating and sustaining the emptiness of the irrational structure itself.[53] It is this, and not the contingent constituents, which makes the hierarchy an impotent system. Along these lines, women and soldiers can be compared—they are domesticated through the same means and for similar purposes. Forced to show subservience, they are kept in the dark—in the interest of blind obedience: "As for any depth of understanding, I will venture to affirm that it is as rarely to be found in the army as amongst women."[54] Well aware that her comparison between women and soldiers is unexpected and shocking, Wollstonecraft's goal is to make a point about ethical disposition, which is independent of gender and social status. Forced obedience under an irrational system produces not just hypocrisy but an extreme "sensibility."[55] Sensibility, a complex term in Wollstonecraft's writing, is aimed toward pleasure. It strives toward immediate satisfaction, which is also what makes it problematic—such satisfaction can rarely be achieved, and its inhibition creates debilitating fantasies. The autonomous or, as Wollstonecraft puts it, "independent" moral agent detaches pleasure and feelings from the moral sphere. The dependent individual, however, is incapable of separating pleasure from the core of his being: he lives in the realm of sensibility—the crippling need for constant satisfaction. The result is an alienated individual incapable of giving up an inflated search for meaningless pleasures. Such a person is dedicated to romantic love rather than friendship, emotion rather than respect, "inflamed" rather than "strong" passions—a disposition toward arbitrary feelings rather than conviction.[56] Her notion of passion has more to do with strong desires than with what are commonly called feelings. Passion is always an "auxiliary to reason."[57] It is no moral designator in itself, but it can help the moral project. Sensibility, however, does the opposite. It falls prey to a calculating or contingent perception of things, imprisoned in a faulty conception of the world, which makes it both unreliable and vulnerable. Feelings are hedonistic. A person prone to sensibility is morally weak or incontinent, because he is "blown about by every momentary gust of feeling."[58] Sensibility is the sign of a slave mentality, which holds its members in a steady grip of self-deception. They learn manners before morals, become vain, frivolous, conceited, and narcissistic. Both women and men can fall under the grip of self-deception, but only women are taught that their submission in actual fact gives them special powers and advantages. Therefore women are made slaves to their own senses, "because it is by their sensibility that they obtain present power," a power that of course is wholly imagined.[59] As has been shown in the comparison between women and soldiers, women are not the only group to fall. They are, however, the only ones to be systematically deceived through the systematic aesthetisization of childlike and irresponsible behavior. They lack education, property, legal rights, and political voice. And they are led to believe that lack of self-control and an uninhibited search for pleasure belong to the charms of "feminine" behavior. They are also led to believe that they will be able to exert a silent power through such charms. Women are brought up to prove nothing but their desirability. To help them escape such self-deceit, one would have to "teach them, in common with man, to submit to necessity, instead of giving, to render them more pleasing, a sex to morals."[60] In other words, teaching women to be docile, undemanding, and narcissistic only deepens the bad effects of an unproductive social hierarchy, in which the erratic idealization of a weak femininity undermines the moral capacity of women. The "sublime heights" of moral law must be made available to both sexes. Morally weak, women remain useless to the community.

Feminine Desire and Freedom: Wollstonecraft's Mary

In her fiction, Wollstonecraft shows the way in which a social and political order without legitimacy comes to undermine morality, and therefore the social fabric as a whole. Here a notion of sensibility is developed that implies more than uneducated frivolity. Wollstonecraft's women do not take pleasure in their abuse. Like Justine, however, they continue to fall into the traps of seduction, abuse, and violation. While their humiliation may be conditioned by their difficult circumstances, Wollstonecraft never blames their initial fall into such traps on external causes. She understands the social conditions that lead to their errors, but she does not simply explain their actions through these conditions. Even when her women are forced by economic difficulties and abusive husbands or lovers, their submission is ultimately independent of authorities or physical difficulties. This may seem surprising, as if she was saying that women should blame themselves or as if she were accusing women of failing to take responsibility. The title *Maria or the Wrongs of Woman* explicitly refers both to the *wrongs being done to women* and the *wrongs committed by women*. Sensibility is an exaggerated search for pleasure, which is bound to go wrong and turn into its opposite, hedonism. The path of pleasure-seeking easily reverts to suffering, because beyond pleasure lies a malignant power toward which some individuals seem to be driven without knowing why and without being forced. This is why women tend to be the cause of their own downfall—for example through following men who take sadistic pleasure in their submission. There are no obvious rewards to be expected, and yet they continue to fall into humiliation, suffering, and self-denial. Wollstonecraft, like Sade, depicts extremes of suffering so pervasive that they turn into *enjoyment*—the payoff of victimization and martyrdom. If we are to believe the Lacanian analysis of Sade, the flip side of autonomy and reason is a limitless capacity for enjoyment. And if we are to stick to the Lacanian definition of these terms, then Wollstonecraft, together with Kant and Sade, shows that *the discovery of the drive is a derivative of reason and freedom.* The drive is a fall into submission, forced by an imagined authority but effected by a subject that Wollstonecraft is eager to define as autonomous and free. The continuous fall of Wollstonecraft's women is futuristic and repetitive; it lacks both authenticity and aim, and it has little to do with pleasure in the frivolous sense. Feminine desire is the product of a pervasive and crippling fantasy, which ultimately has its origin in the continuous investment of women in their own submission. The story is in part based on experiences of Wollstonecraft's own life and was left unfinished on her table when she died in childbirth in 1797. Her famous relationship with Gilbert Imlay is depicted in the novel under the guise of Maria's involvement with a fellow prisoner. And like the heroine, Wollstonecraft tried to kill herself after he left. The women in her novel betray themselves and each other. For that reason, Wollstonecraft has also been accused of misogyny, of having inscribed a deep self-hatred into the feminist tradition.[61] But she does not simply blame her female figures for their failures; beyond the descriptions of female weakness, we may reconstruct another argument. It can be shown, contrary to most moral philosophers of her own time, that women are moral agents *precisely* because they continue to fall into humiliating forms of submission. Failing to claim a causal link between submission and outer conditions or make them victims of circumstance, she views them as moral agents. This is not in spite of the errors they commit, but rather because of them. Her refusal to make female protagonists neither particularly pure nor particularly virtuous is precisely the point, as she writes in the introduction to *Maria.* While male characters gradually acquire wisdom and knowledge through experience, women are "born to be immaculate, and to act like goddesses of wisdom, just come forth highly finished Minervas from the head of Jove."[62] Moral subjectivity, however, proves itself not through moral superiority but through deficiency and error. This is the point where Wollstonecraft's conception of the relation between desire and ethics differs from Sade's. Wollstonecraft's heroines are no parodies of reckless men, like the extraordinary Juliette. In fact, Maria's figure of subversion distances us from Juliette: it is produced not through aggressive appetite but through *sheer submission.* Martyrdom or suffering, so close to masochistic enjoyment, is the real transgression. While Rousseau feared that female lightheartedness and irresponsibility would fray the social fabric, Wollstonecraft points to a much more powerful figure of feminine desire. Its power lies in *the excesses of virtue,* in the giving up of the self, which she calls: "the epicurism of virtue—self-denial."[63] Woman's humiliation is compensated by an excess that the patriarchal system is unable to contain. Feminine enjoyment exploits the "void" inherent in the useless morality of the patriarchal system. Wollstonecraft's women may seem quite powerless, but there is another dimension to their experience. Sade's Justine is, as Angela Carter points out, unable to learn through experience, because she is unable to take responsibility for her own fate.[64] Wollstonecraft turns the argument around: women learn by traversing their positions as victims. What is fruitless victimization in Sade turns into emancipatory force in Wollstonecraft.

In *Maria*, the counterposition of Justine is represented by Jemima, whom Maria meets in prison. Jemima represents the unreflected fall into pleasureless victimization. She was born a slave, and has been unable to rise above it. Forced into making her living as a servant from an early stage, she is raped by her employer. When his wife finds out, she tortures Jemima; more cruel than a man, the wife incorporates the brutal truth that the wrongs of women pass from the stronger to the weaker. Jemima is kicked out. Eventually, she becomes a prostitute. There is no reward in that, not even the satisfaction of receiving money. In her own words, she "yielded to the desires" of the brutes she met, but with detestation and contempt. She has learned about the pleasures of seduction, "but I had not even the pleasure of being enticed into vice."[65] Jemima is the counterimage of Juliette, and like Justine, she takes no pleasure in her seduction. Instead, she attempts to escape through education. She takes a job as a servant, becoming the disinterested mistress of an older man, who is a scholar and a writer. Since she does not enjoy the respect women normally have, she is accepted in the company of his friends, and this company leads to her intellectual development. But there is no reward for her in this, no possible use for her intellectual abilities. He dies and she inherits nothing. Back in the streets, she is again made into a slave. A man takes her in, and she convinces him that his mistress must go. The woman in question kills herself. Again, the chain of cruelty stretches from woman to woman. Guilt-ridden, Jemima is unable to work and is eventually thrown into prison for prostitution.

Although Jemima represents the impasses of female dependency, she is not ultimately forced into submission. There is an economic link between her being thrown out on the streets and her life as a prostitute, but it is not a *causal* one. The domain of social conditioning may influence the moral one, but there is no causal link between moral degeneration and social downfall. Jemima commits the wrongs of women by repeating the cruelty of her employer. As Wollstonecraft points out in the introduction, she does not explain the misery of women through social conditions alone. Instead she chooses to depict an exaggerated subordination. While these women are the victims of unjust laws and social conditions, they contribute to their misery through an exaggerated relishing of self-denial.[66]

In the case of Maria, the intertwining of desire and subjugation is even more complicated. The plot is an extraordinary example of a feminine *éducation sentimentale* that counters the narrative of the morally perfected heroine. The story paints in graphic detail the inherent violence in the system of injustice, incorporating forced prostitution, lawlessness, degradation, and suicide as possible components of working-class and middle-class female life at the time. The plot is driven by the powerful metaphorical code of the prison walls, which serve as an image for female servitude. "Was not the world a vast prison and women born slaves?"[67] Sinking into apathy and melancholy, Maria discovers that her marriage to a heartless and selfish man has failed to give her the satisfaction she expected; instead it has "bastilled" her for life.[68] Unlike the safety it is supposed to procure, marriage is lived as a form of punishment that inflicts pain in addition to depriving women of their freedom. The "bastille" makes a drastic comparison with Sade possible. The heroines of both Sade and Wollstonecraft are victims of their own fantasies, reproducing, to a certain extent, the lives of their authors. Sade conjured up most of his narratives in prison and created his suffering alter egos from there. Wollstonecraft's imprisoned heroines also have a strong resemblance to herself. The metaphorical meaning of the "bastille" could be read in a double sense: the fact that they are slaves through the institution of marriage, made into property, also makes them victims of their own factitious sentiment.[69] They are slaves in a double sense: to the institution of marriage and to themselves. It is the second category that provides the most powerful motive in the plot. Maria escapes from the prison of an unbearable marriage. She is clearly *wronged*. After her flight, she is imprisoned for life in a real institution. Again she is *wronged*, through the instituted violence against women. But rather than freeing herself after the escape, she remains a victim. This time, however, she falls victim to the violence produced by her own fantasies. Wollstonecraft thereby shows an intrinsic link between the capacity for morality, or moral autonomy, or moral reason, as a domain detached from social conditioning in the absolute sense of the term, and the tendency to negate the capacity for judgment through repetitive and destructive fantasies of submission.

The first proof of Maria's autonomy is her initial infatuation with her husband. It is the result of her *imagination*—a faculty that is free. The marriage she desired, however, leads to a series of catastrophes. Her husband becomes an intolerable, greedy drunk. She is secretly sold to a friend by her husband, like a prostitute. She discovers the affair, but she is bound by her principles and has to remain in the marriage. Her only chance of escape is to get financial help from a friend. But her husband discovers the arrangement and takes her to court. From there, she is thrown into prison, which in Wollstonecraft's times served to keep undesirables off the streets, whatever their circumstances—she is *wronged*, again, violated by a systematic order of injustice. Whereas the story of her marital humiliation is extremely violent, the part where she falls in love with a fellow prisoner may seem sentimental. In fact, it repeats the marital subjugation in another form. Subjugation does its work not by outer force but through a complicated spectrum of perverted fantasies, inclinations, and feelings. In prison, Maria becomes a slave to the violence of her own fantasies, figured in the text by the screams of invisible fellow prisoners. Alone at night, she lies awake listening to their howls, a symphony of anxiety. She is awoken by the "dismal shrieks of demoniac rage, or of indescribable anguish as proved the total absence of reason, and roused phantoms of horror in the mind."[70] Of course, these howls are phantoms signaling the absence of reason, a sign of catastrophes to come. Just like the howling voices of the night, which are products of violence threatening the outer limits of the self, so the fellow prisoner she falls in love with represents such a limit. Darnford is a mixture of animal and genius, an unbound and threatening image of sexual desire with "untamed" eyes. Darnford is, Wollstonecraft lets us understand, a monster of her own imagination. Her love for him is partly produced by indulgence in Rousseau's *Heloïse*. Volatile and on the verge of madness, he is a fantastic image of the cause of desire Lacan calls the *objet petit a*—the sheer animality of her lover is an echo of the "demoniac rage" when desire both takes hold and threatens to disintegrate. Before she gets to meet him, she sees his books. Jemima tell her what he looks like:

"He sometimes walks out, between five and six, before the family is stirring, in the morning, with two keepers; but even then his hands are confined."

"What! Is he so unruly?" enquired Maria, with an accent of disappointment.

"No, not that I perceive," replied Jemima; "but he has an untamed look, a vehemence of eye, that excites apprehension. Were his hands free he looks as if he could soon manage both his guards: yet he appears so tranquil."

"If he be so strong, he must be young," observed Maria.

"Three or four and thirty, I suppose; but there is no judging of a person in his situation."

"Are you sure that he is mad?" interrupted Maria with eagerness. Jemima quitted the room, without replying.[71]

In typical fashion, Darnford turns into an agent of destruction as soon as they escape prison. He abandons her, not once but twice. Eventually he leaves her for another woman—as reflected in Wollstonecraft's own life. The prison stands for the submission that forces her to repeat the mistake of the marriage: succumbing to a man who has been constructed out of her own fantasies. His abandonment of her outside the prison continues the same metaphor. Even in a state of freedom, she is incapable of escaping the self-destructive impact of her own fantasies. Darnford flees, leaving her distraught. And even though the novel implies that this chain of events may have actually taken place, we have reason to wonder if there ever was a "real" Darnford beyond the volatile fantasies of subjugation. Maria is captured in the product of her own fantasy, "bastilled" not in marriage but in her own repetitive act of submission. The point is, then, that it is actually marriage that has imprisoned Maria for life. It has imprisoned her because even outside of the institution of marriage, she remains caught in the logic of degeneracy and ethical illegitimacy that it has installed. Maria is imprisoned for life, for even after escaping her husband, she keeps falling into the position of victim. Sacrificing the morally distorting objects of her desire, she can face her own freedom only in the void that lies beyond it. It is typical, perhaps, that the novel remains unfinished, a fact that only heightens the impression that it is oscillating at an impossible limit between the fantasy of freedom and the subjugation that comes at the price of moral autonomy. Only Wollstonecraft's notes for a planned continuation remain. They read like an endless list of sufferings: separation, miscarriage, reunion, miscarriage, death of close friend, finds child, loses child, finds child, suicide attempt, decision to live on—(a decision that Wollstonecraft herself did make, only to die in childbirth).

Feminine desire thus becomes much more than a question of frivolity and lack of seriousness in Wollstonecraft's writing. It has very little to do with pleasure in the sense of polymorphous perversity. Maria's desire ends in a state of submission to the defining fantasy of a cause that is supposed to be a product of free imagination, but ends up having quite another impact. It is of course not by chance that the fantasy creation of an animal lover such as Darnford—on the limit between sainthood and the nonhuman—is created in the bastille. The bastille, here, is a metaphor for an imprisonment that is the paradoxical product of an autonomy that remains both impotent and uncanny. Beyond the deceit of his erotic powers lies a great danger: the dark abyss of freedom. Thus it is clear that Maria is not subjected to any man, or any law, but only to the machinations of her own desire.

Wollstonecraft's failing women may seem to only conform to what is expected of them. But beyond their overzealous willingness to comply, their self-absorbed and narcissistic search for pleasure, and their easy slippage into humiliation and abuse, their freedom emerges, but not because they are masochistic or self-denying. Behind the frozen sexual fantasy of Darnford lies the void in which the autonomous moral subject presents itself—not through freedom of choice, but through an excess of subjection. In the writings of Mary Wollstonecraft, feminine desire becomes a paradoxical sign of moral autonomy.

2

Sexuality Versus Recognition: Feminine
Desire in the Ethical Order

Natural, Ethical

In German idealism and the literary romanticism of the early nineteenth century, femininity was less a social and moral issue and more a metaphysical one. Still, the question of feminine desire is very much an issue in a discussion of subjectivity and desire that raises points that are still of interest to contemporary theory. As I will try to show in this chapter, at least three kinds of desire were considered, and a philosophical concept of femininity was developed in connection with these. The German word for desire, *Begierde*, was not used in the texts that I discuss, but since I have chosen to infer my points from a theoretical point of view that emphasizes the role of desire in human subjectivity, I hope to show in what way such inferences could affect the reading of these texts in turn. The aim of this chapter, then, is to indicate the ways in which the marginal and marginalized concept of femininity could be seen to indicate a conception of desire in Hegel's philosophy that is irreducible to the socially determined forms of subjectivity, including gendered forms of subjectivity, that are identified through what Hegel calls the universal. Identifying a subtext in a philosophical argument is a dangerous task, naturally, not least because Hegel's philosophy of desire is of a complexity that must at all times be respected. But as several commentators have remarked, including commentators working in feminist philosophy, Hegel's reflections on femininity remain an enigmatic and perhaps even problematic element in his theoretical edifice. But while this chapter aims to examine the intertwining of the feminine and the (un)ethical in Hegel's thought and to suggest how such an intertwining could be understood, I must point out that my ambitions are restricted to this point alone, and that I leave more systematic investigation of Hegel's thought to other scholars. Therefore, I will limit my questions on Hegel's notion of desire to concern his texts on tragedy or to those aspects of desire than can be referred to social issues and issues of sexual difference, leaving aside the epistemological project of *Phenomenology of Spirit* (1807), where desire is an endless process of consuming sensory objects in the production of self-consciousness.

The first two kinds of desire that would be identifiable through the theoretical grid I am applying concern the relation between the sexes. Here a split can be observed between low, "natural" or sexual desire and a higher kind incorporated in marriage, where erotic love and spiritual friendship merge. Natural desire, which is coded as feminine in Hegel's phenomenology, for instance, is regarded as potentially disruptive, and a possible threat to the community of law and order. While some intellectuals at the same epoch tried to raise the sexual or natural aspect of feminine desire to a higher sphere by advocating that the spiritual bonds of love and friendship in marriage exist in harmony rather than in contrast with erotic excitement,[1] Hegel envisioned love as a "living whole" bridging the gap between a higher and a lower form of desire.[2] In his readings of tragedy, however, the feminine is linked to both a lower domain encompassing sexuality and other corporeal appetites, and a higher, more spiritual one where it is purified of the lower aspects of sexual content. Hegel also describes a third kind of desire: a desire for recognition that is determined in and by the social order, the world of norms and rules, the political and legal community. He codes this form of desire as masculine, and marginalizes the feminine in relation to the social. The question of femininity and sexual desire will be considered later, in my discussion of *Antigone*; what interests me here is the "natural" or sexual appetite, which has nothing to do with recognition. In Hegel's comments on *Antigone* and the *Oresteia*, tragic women stand for the "natural" domain of human life, to which love and sexuality belong. A simple interpretation indicates that such a desire stands for those sexual needs that must be controlled within a cultural and social order—through marriage, for instance. When sexual needs are controlled, the natural sphere becomes ethical and connotes a loving and benevolent feeling between members of a family that keeps the family together—the family bond. Femininity is congruent with impulses in the "natural" domain: passion, sexuality, and love. Part of these impulses is transferred to and protected by the universal domain of legal rights. The problem, however, is that the natural domain is tainted by instincts and passions that are "inorganic," as Hegel puts it: destructive and dangerous. A separation has to take place between a "good" natural domain and a chaotic or inorganic one; otherwise the "good" practices of the natural domain cannot serve the transformation from practices to universal rights. The problem with feminine desire, therefore, is that it incarnates a tension between the ethical domain and that which can neither be included in it nor controlled through it.[3] Hegel included sexual conflict in tragic discourse and identified feminine figures such as Clytaemnestra and Antigone as disruptive threats to justice and law. He noted that both Antigone and Clytaemnestra refer to a divine order in their claims to be tools of a higher justice that the human order fails to recognize. And both have to be excluded from the community in and through the process they set in motion with these claims, negotiating the universal order of the state and the domain of protection on the one hand, and love and the family on the other. We again confront a philosophical discourse that makes feminine desire a problem specific to ethics, although Hegel discusses these issues as aspects of the living fabric of ancient society rather than the social norms of modern morality. As we will see, however, the enigmatic status given to feminine desire in Hegel's text deserves to be highlighted, not least because the feminine is closer to contemporary theories of subjectivity than to a social definition of women's actual role in society.

The *Oresteia* is the first tragedy to be considered by Hegel, in *On the Scientific Ways of Treating Natural Law* (1802–3). But although Hegel rarely comments on the ancient texts in an extensive manner, one may well argue that he builds his arguments around them. The essay on natural law is one such example: although the direct comment on the *Oresteia* only takes one page, one may observe that the conflicting mechanisms of the tragic text have been transposed into the philosophical argument. Many terms of the dialectic defined here return in another form in the *Phenomenology* and are used in the reading of *Antigone*, although the objectives of the texts are quite different. While the *Phenomenology* is a cultural and spiritual history of different modes of consciousness, the earlier text examines the development of ethical life in modern society and the evolution of concepts such as justice and morality. In both works, Hegel begins his argument in the ethical order, or *Sittlichkeit*—the order of social relations and customs in a finite, historical community where people are "free," not constrained by laws foreign to their habits and customs. The ethical order is prepolitical, constructed on the basis of harmony and consent. And yet it is already marked by a deficiency, something that is not working.[4] Although it seems to make up a totality, the ethical order carries with it an inherent tension between its status as a community made of customs and habits, and the abstract and universal concept of a state. Tragedy shows how the deficiencies of that order bring it to a dramatic split and force a renegotiation of the ethical order.[5]

Women in Tragedy

Hegel's choice of the *Oresteia* is, of course, motivated by the mythological installation of justice that takes place in the tragedy. The *Oresteia* depicts the institution of a legal system, the moment when the ancient custom of revenge is replaced by the legal rulings of a court. The law sets a limit to the impure, erotic, and violent powers that are in play. These forces stem primarily from the excessive figure of Clytaemnestra, who represents an unstable notion of justice that will continue to haunt the community as long as it cannot find a system to neutralize the forces associated with it. Both Clytaemnestra and her husband, Agamemnon, are agents of an excessive violence that undermines the fragile order of habits and customs governing the forms of social interaction in the society in which they live. The triggering event that releases that violence is Agamemnon's ritual slaying of his daughter, Iphigenia. She dies like an animal, like a "goat for sacrifice" (*Agamemnon* 233), blindfolded, a hand put over her mouth to silence her screams. At Agamemnon's homecoming, the scorned Clytaemnestra takes great pleasure in her revenge:

> As he died he spattered me with the dark red
> and violent driven rain of bitter savored blood
> to make me glad, as gardens stand among the showers
> of God in glory at the birthtime of the buds.
> (1389–92, trans. R. Lattimore)

Clytaemnestra declares herself to be an agent of *dike* or justice. Raising the axe, her hand is "struck in strength of righteousness" (1406). She makes herself into a defender of women, complaining about their exposure in a society where men rule. But just as the sacrifice of Iphigenia is depicted as the perversion of a ritual intended to appease the gods, so Clytaemnestra's slaying of Agamemnon displays an excess of violence. Instead of celebrating the homecoming husband and war hero with a bath, she drenches him in a pool of blood.[6] Defending a line of heritage passing from woman to daughter, which patriarchy has destroyed, she says that Justice, or *dike*, is a woman, a daughter of Zeus: "Her wind is fury and death, visited upon those she hates" (*Libation Bearers* 950–51). In other words, the archaic form of justice she represents is feminine, and therefore dark and unpredictable. This is a significant fact to keep in mind, not least in the last part of the trilogy, which forces revenge to succumb to jurisdiction. While aspiring to justice through his own actions, Orestes identifies the tragic pollution with Clytaemnestra: "I killed my mother not without some right, / My father's murder stained her, and the god's disgust" (1027–28). The horrifying Furies, monsters from the underworld, seek revenge on Orestes the mother-murderer. But Orestes escapes their revenge through the court of the gods, symbolizing the installation of *dike* in the city. The court rules in favor of Orestes, and the Furies become protectors rather than torturers. Justice is protected through the domestication of the feminine principle of revenge and fury. But the originary demand for justice is feminine and therefore unpredictable. *Dike* is never fully subject to human control; it is not a logical or absolute construction, and as Vernant has pointed out, it is a matter of degrees. Even at the end of the play, justice remains undecidable, although the scenic closure implies a mythical installation of justice.[7] Even though the instinct for revenge has been condemned as illegitimate and damaging, the threat has not been undone. Other claims to justice can still be brought back into play. This means that the social and political institutions of justice can never be wholly removed from the elements of undecidability that forced its installation in the first place.

Feminist critics and historians have analyzed the *Oresteia* as a central text of Western misogyny, some of them inspired by the German historian Bachofen, who in 1865 presented the thesis that Greek tragedy serves to conjure the traces of an original matriarchy, the object of a patriarchal overtake of power. Tragic conflicts elaborate a violent shift of power. There may be more or less substantial truth to this hypothesis. When it comes to the space of tragedy, it would in any case have to be made into a symbolic issue rather than a historical one.[8] A woman from Athens was owned by her father or brother and married off in her early teens to become the possession of her husband. She was expected to stay within the home and was virtually invisible in the city. Ironically, in Sparta, which did not have democratic rule, she was more free, participating in the economic running of the city.[9] But Sparta produced no tragedies, and Athens did. One of the curious facts we have to respond to, even if we chose not to believe in the myth of an original matriarchy, is that the strength of the heroine in Attic tragedy contradicts the oppression of real, historic women. If women were invisible in ancient Athens, and if democracy and tragedy were an affair for free men, why were so many tragedies about women? The question is not why female characters are flawed or even evil, but why they appear at all, given the male dominance in Athenian society. How can a feminine subject be represented in a society dominated by men, which renders her politically and socially invisible? Can we really use the testimony of a tragic play, written and performed by men for other men, to reveal something about feminine desire? Clearly the thoughts, feelings, and experiences of real women have disappeared under the projections of male fantasies. Women become screens of projection and are portrayed as troublesome, dying unheroic deaths through hanging or suicide. Or they are sacrificed in a pattern determined by their value as objects of exchange within a patriarchal economy; death thus becomes a punishment for their threatening sexuality. The female heroine is the product of a society dominated by men, a threatening fantasy of the Other. But Greek literature, however dominated by male writers, lets female "countercultures" shine through. Alternative interpretative strategies allow us to discern the feminine subject buried in patriarchal society, according to Adriana Cavarero, whose hermeneutical project consists in "stealing" female figures from their original context and investigating "the traces of an original act of erasure contained in the patriarchal order, the act upon which this order was first constructed and then continued to display itself." Cavarero's archaeological search points to an original matricide, providing us with a reversed Oedipal complex at the root of the degradation and disempowering of women in ancient Greece. The sons kill their mothers, symbolically or literally, because her desire threatens their freedom.[10] Simone de Beauvoir, among many others, characterizes the trilogy as a mythical description of the origins of patriarchy. Set between feminine chaos and the male order of *polis*, the *Oresteia* reflects an ancient mythological universe from which the threat of the feminine must be eliminated. Only a patriarchal organization of the *polis* can contain natural, divine, and human forces alike.[11] The myth of an original matricide has been carried over into psychoanalytic theory, where Melanie Klein has revealed the mythic (and misogynist) origin of the maternal image. The image of the mother is irrevocably split between good and bad. Dependency on the mother is accompanied by persecution fantasies, and unconscious fears of being devoured, torn up, and destroyed by her. These fantasies are the result of an initial aggression directed against the mother: a maternal super-ego. Representing a persecutory maternal super-ego, the Furies make it necessary to kill the mother in turn.[12] Clytaemnestra is, unlike the Amazons, not an open threat, as Froma Zeitlin has observed. She is a threat from within.[13] As such, she represents that other desire, or power, as Zeitlin puts it, that tragedy is intended to suppress. The Dionysian play with appearances, disguises, and lures is not just a mimetic unraveling of truth, but also a dialectic in which feminine desire becomes the void around which fantasies and appearances are constructed. Perhaps the tragic space itself, and its play with illusions, concealments, and revelations, could be regarded as the conjuring of an "inner" enemy of the *polis*.[14] There is, of course, no such thing as an authentic image or representation of femininity wholly uncontaminated by male desire. But the reverse is also true: there is no tragic conflict that is wholly uncontaminated by female desire. This is made visible, above all, in the divine dimensions of tragedy.[15] The abyss of human desire is opened by the interferences of divine contingencies. The female characters are closer to it and more prone to become the agents of a divinity that is as scornful as it is inadmissible in its demands on human life. Clytaemnestra is a bloodthirsty scorned wife, slashing her husband in rage under the influence of deadly *ate* (the Greek word for tragic misfortune), because she represents the prepolitical, a mythical sphere in which the legal order of justice has not yet been introduced in a human context. Antigone evokes divine laws rather than human ones and opens the gates of a bloodletting. Inverting the norms and procedures of the society in which it originates, the symbolic space of divine power exceeds the ethical order. The divine may be seen as a lack or failure in the ethical order, and in tragic texts it is often opened by women. Transposed into the context of modern philosophy, one may say that it is the interferences of a divine sphere in a human one that open up for reflection the excesses of ethical life. Modernity has striven in vain to contain these excesses. Some of the most pressing issues in ethics and desire present themselves through feminine figures of excess.

Maternal Love—Maternal Revenge:
The Impasses of the Natural Sphere

In his early texts, Hegel argues for a transition from the ethical in the form of existing customs to the ethical as an abstract imposition through the law, rather than the other way around. In *On the Scientific Ways of Treating Natural Law*, the ethical order is considered to be prepolitical, constructed on the basis of harmony and consent. Tragedy shows, however, that this order is fraught with deficiencies, which will force a split and produce new conflict. Since it has its origin in the same order, tragedy shows the diremption of the absolute with itself, the conflict between a supraindividual order of law and jurisdiction, and the contingent interests of individuals. The transition from a "natural" order, which Hegel identifies as the unstable rule of desires and drives, to a civil society of legal codes and laws must proceed through a complete transformation of ethical life, which *begins* in the universal. The logic of tragedy corresponds to that of the development of consciousness itself: the limits of the universalizing concept (justice, for instance) are made visible by its violation. Only through a universal legal system can a moral subject properly speaking begin to develop. Desires for personal possessions, vengeance, and power belong to a natural sphere overcome by the installation of ethical consciousness. Tragedy shows the need for a universal order to contain the destabilizing factors of the natural sphere. The aim is to separate the kind of desire that can be associated with ethical self-consciousness, a consciousness mediated through moral norms, from the natural sphere of particular interests and inclinations. In his early work, Hegel uses the term "nature" to designate reality as a whole, whereas in *Phenomenology of Spirit* it is identified with spirit's "Other"— raw, physical nature. In his work on natural law, however, "nature" refers not to the raw physicality of nature but to the sphere of the prepolitical, which is fraught with emotion and passion. Morality can only be deduced from the principles of negation through which the ethical sheds the natural aspects excessive to it: Hegel operates with a distinct table of antinomies in which the universal is set against the particular, and the human against the divine, or the excess Hegel calls the inorganic (*aorgisch*). The idea that the absolute surrenders itself to suffering and death means that it must always sacrifice part of itself to the chthonic powers, recognizing its intrinsic involvement with such powers: one may say that the ethical realm emerges from suffering and death. At the same time, suffering reveals that which is intrinsically foreign to it. As we have seen, the divine space of tragedy is the domain in which the dangerous excesses of the divine are acted out. Identifying these excesses as "inorganic," Hegel recognizes that tragedy always revolves around that which is intrinsically foreign to it. The purge of the inorganic opens the modern dynamic of a *Tragödie im Sittlichen*, a tragedy in the ethical order: "This is nothing other than the enactment, in the ethical realm, of the tragedy which the absolute eternally plays out within itself—by eternally giving birth to itself into objectivity, thereby surrendering itself in this shape to suffering and death, and rising up to glory from its ashes."[16] One should perhaps stress, as Christoph Menke does, the fact that this expression, "Tragödie im Sittlichen," does not simply imply a dialectic between particularity and universality, but rather the way such a dialectics always demands the sacrifice of *Sittlichkeit* itself. Menke reads Hegel as a "pan-tragic" philosopher in the sense that he is radically antimetaphysical, showing not how history develops toward a certain goal or totality but rather how the failure of achieving such a totality is inscribed in the reflection of history itself.[17] The institution of universality demands that ethical life must be abandoned. This is why Hegel's reflections on tragedy are in fact reflections on modernity, substituting politics and jurisdiction for the destiny determined by the gods. Given this background, it is interesting to examine Hegel's tragic readings for what they reveal about the subject. The subject of tragedy is split in and through itself because it can never be fully separated from the universal order in which its demands arise. The suffering of the protagonist is inseparable from the ethical order, just as his downfall can be generalized as the downfall of the ethical order itself. Although Hegel would perhaps not recognize feminine subjectivity and desire in this context, he still observes that it is precisely through the feminine that the tragedy's most demanding sacrificial logic is played out: the demands of Antigone and Clytaemnestra, representing forces that are as irreducible to the definition of social desire and the demands of recognition as they are intrinsic to the social fabric.

Two orders clash in natural *Sittlichkeit*. On the one hand, there is the order of physical needs, pleasure, and desires—the dimension of life itself, which will always occupy a central place in the life of the individual.[18] The domain of ethics is concerned with both negative and positive feelings, such as the drive for self-preservation, love, hate, sociability, and so on.[19] On the other hand, there is a need to regulate such desires—a system identifying the rights of the individual through law rather than affirming them through custom. Tragedy's divine space is thus invested with a surplus of passion and wrath, and it is this surplus that Hegel identifies with inorganic forces and desires. Hegel realizes that the fragility of natural law depicted in the tragedy—its lack of symbolic support—is due to the fact that the natural domain is contaminated by what he calls the "inorganic." The forces that threaten the fragile balance of a natural order must be suppressed or contained by law; otherwise the community would vanish. The inorganic includes not just what is foreign and external to the individual, but also what is foreign *inside* him—such as an excessive desire for revenge, or a passion out of control. Clytaemnestra incarnates inorganic forces, an undifferentiated domain of instincts lacking qualities that could be taken up in the normative order; these forces evoke suffering, passion, and wrath.

Much has been said about Orestes' amnesty from punishment in the court of gods as a mythic installation of a legal system. Hegel considers it a transformation from a natural to a legal system, which will allow ethical life to develop. The question is how the separation of the "inorganic" forces of passion and rage from the bonding forces of the natural sphere, love, and protective instincts between family members will take place. Such a separation is not only difficult but perhaps in the end quite impossible to perform, since these aspects of the natural domain are incarnated by a femininity which in itself is unstable—unpredictable, terrifying, vengeful. The "bad" thing about the inorganic forces is therefore not necessarily that they stand for corporeal needs, inclinations, and passions, but that they produce collisions and conflicts. The natural is not merely chaotic. It is also inclined toward love, pleasure, and well-being. As such, it stands for another kind of femininity, a maternal and protective one. Clytaemnestra is a defender of love and family blood ties, whereas Agamemnon violates these bonds.[20] The problem, however, is that her defense of these blood ties—Clytaemnestra's furious demand for justice—can only manifest itself through a violence that is linked in Hegel's mind to the inorganic aspect of nature. Particular instances, such as demands for revenge, must be overcome in order for ethical life to develop in a reflective and conscious manner. Violence, from this point of view, is not exerted by the universal on the particular. It has nothing to do with an individual being who is repressed or coerced to conform by the community. Instead, violence is exerted in the opposite direction—the individual confuses and violates the fragile human order in which the demands of justice must originate. The *Oresteia* is a perfect example of this logic.

Clytaemnestra's revenge shows how fragile a "good" natural order is without support from a universal system. As long as individuality manifests itself through contingent demands, as it indeed does in tragedy, it will necessarily violate ethical life. Manifesting itself through force or violence, the difference between the particular and the universal cannot simply be described as a dialectic; rather it is found in tragic eruptions of conflict through which the ethical is continuously sacrificed.[21]

The most poignant moment of such a sacrifice occurs toward the end of the play, when Clytaemnestra's avengers, the fearsome Furies, turn into Eumenides, guarantors of welfare and protection for Orestes, the mother-murderer. This could well be considered a moment of catharsis and peace. For Hegel, however, such an interpretation misses the point. The vengeful Furies represent a demand for justice that must be purged from inorganic passion to create a universalizable concept of justice. Inorganic desire for vengeance must be detached and replaced by an ethical consciousness that cannot exist in the form of singular, subjective demands or passionate opinions, be they malevolent or benevolent. The transformation of the Furies into Eumenides signifies not a passage from evil to good, but rather a process in which the inorganic is separated from a natural sphere that can be idealized as good. In Hegel's reading, the Eumenides represent not justice but another nature, the "good" nature that the state wishes to protect and preserve in a system of justice. This means that justice comes into being not through the elimination of the Furies, avengers of a matricide, but through the submission of the natural to the legal, of the particular to the universal. The most important figure of the play is therefore Apollo, who simply declares Orestes' offense to be less serious than Clytaemnestra's, not on the basis of tradition or feeling, but on the basis of principle. The benevolence of the Eumenides stands for a justice that is differentiated and split, while Apollo negotiates right and wrong, good and bad, on the basis of nothing other than the *need* for a principle of justice that is unequivocal. Apollo, unlike the Eumenides, is a God beyond diremption and conflict. The conflict between the Eumenides and Apollo is therefore more important than the transformation of the Furies into the Eumenides.[22] For justice to prevail, the inorganic aspect of the demand for justice—wrath and the desire for revenge—must be suppressed and contained in the universalization of the law.[23] This calls for the uplifting of all natural forces, including the Eumenides, into the ideal order of Apollo. At the same time, however, the call for a society based on principles rather than ethical instinct is bound to evoke conflict, not only in the social fabric but also in subjectivity. This problem is demonstrable in Hegel's consideration of the feminine figures that are supposed to protect the family bonds internal both to the state and to the legal system that is supposed to serve as a continuation of ethical life. Femininity is at the same time foreign and threatening to the universality the latter must necessarily represent.

In his text on natural law, Hegel does not distinguish the family as a specific entity that is withdrawn from conflict. Uncontrollable forces operate in and through the family. Ethical bonds, such as love and care within the family, are much too unstable to stand on their own. They will be tainted by a dangerous fragility unless they are bound by a principle of justice beyond nature or feelings. Such a principle acquires its strength and support from the good side of nature, which it represents—the love and intimacy of the family. But love needs the support of the law in order to survive; otherwise it will be tainted by the inorganic threat of passionate demands. Another way of putting it is that ethical life in the absolute sense emerges only through the negation of the inorganic order to which lower desires or appetites belong. Ethical norms must be structured around the elimination of unregulated desires as such. This problem is incarnated by the feminine figures of tragedy, who point to something that is not fully working in the ethical order, a discrepancy and a deficiency. The problem, however, is that this discrepancy continues to have its effects *after* the universal order is installed.

Axel Honneth, who has used Hegel's text to develop a theory of intersubjectivity as a model for the social function of laws, has pointed out that in the text on natural right, Hegel preserves an intersubjective dimension that is absent from the *Phenomenology*. In other words, he places a lot more emphasis on the social impact of the natural sphere, which is where intersubjective relationships are formed through love and care. In the *Phenomenology*, the universal and public aspect of the ethical order, including laws, is imposed in a violent and conflictual manner on a community. In the text on natural law, however, the law is not imposed as something coming from the outside; rather it is considered to be developed out of customs and relations already in place. The universalization of such a notion of justice does not create a gap or tension between family and state, or within the natural sphere of the law as we see in the *Phenomenology*. A modern legal system, which is what Hegel is trying to get to, assumes that functioning relations of intersubjectivity already exist. Its function is to protect these relations of intersubjectivity, not to upset or manipulate them. What remains unclear, according to Honneth, is what these functioning relations are like, and how they can be negated into universal validity or transformed into universal laws.[24] Honneth argues that what is most important here is not the content of the law, but its function. When the good and loving side of the natural is fixed in the ideality of a universal ethical order, then this order fulfills the function of a loving and protective mother. In the words of Hegel: "The child . . . is nourished at the breast of ethical life, lives at first in the intuition of that life as an alien being, increasingly comprehends it, and so becomes part of the universal spirit."[25] Honneth argues for a conception of the law in a similar vein. The law, Honneth argues, should fulfill the same function as what Winnicott calls a "good enough mother." Therefore, there is a direct link between the maternal nourishment of a child and the spriritual nourishment of the individual by the state. In Honneth's account, love serves as an introduction to the social order. It gives the individual self-esteem and self-respect. And it teaches the citizen to esteem and respect the values that ought to be assured him or her through the juridical system: justice, rights, and so on. But this means that these values are assured through the spirit and culture of the law rather than through interferences in everyday life. The law that gives its citizens rights, thereby recognizing him or her, is continuing the work of the "good enough mother." A good law places certain demands on its citizens, but it recognizes the autonomy and responsibility of those citizens. It does not strangle its child with too many demands. It does not demand to be loved back. But it gives its "child" the recognition of an autonomous, ethical agent. The consequence of the argument is that a citizen should be able to identify with its laws in the same way that a child identifies with its "good enough" parents. Otherwise the protection and care they offer does nothing for them, and the project of making these citizens into autonomous and responsible beings fails:

The only way in which individuals are constituted as persons is by learning to refer to themselves, from the perspective of an approving or encouraging other, as beings with certain positive traits or abilities. The scope of such traits—and hence the extent of one's positive relation-to-self—increases with each new form of recognition that individuals are able to apply to themselves as subjects. In this way, the prospect of basic self-confidence is inherent in the experience of love; the prospect of self-respect in the experience of legal recognition; and finally the prospect of self-esteem, in the experience of solidarity.[26]

Rather than incorporating a natural good, then, a universal legal system can do nothing but protect it. This means that there will remain a tension between intersubjective relations and the intimate sphere in which they are determined, on the one hand, and the universal order of the state, on the other hand. Ethical life can only be realized through a universal principle that considers any desire that is particular as a violation of its principle. In this way, the natural sphere always constitutes a potential threat to the universal order, even if this threat only concerns the expression of love and benevolence. As tragedy shows, the most destructive forces in the community are those that cross the line between family and state—like Clytaemnestra's demand for vengeance of the violation of family bonds, and the feud that follows. The image of youth feeding at the breast of universality as a maternal principle conflicts with the idea that this breast is also the home of inorganic forces that threaten to shatter the loving image of the mother. Although some kind of sublation of the inorganic is achieved when the formal machinery of justice is put in place, the question of how the universal and the natural are to cooperate remains unsolved. There is no elucidation or sublation of the kind of tragic violence that originates in the transgression of the barrier between family and state: terror may be domesticated, but dread and doubts remain as long as one relies on a natural domain to provide us with a model on which ethical life can be built. The balance between the system of universality, which can only present itself as negation, and the particular demand of the individual for justice and rights is always threatened. Hegel's problem is how to *bury* threatening aspects of natural desire—representing the violence of particular demands for justice, for instance—while keeping good aspects of the natural sphere accessible. Distrusting the natural goodness of the protective Eumenides as a guarantee for law and order, Hegel assumes that a universal idea of justice operates through negations and universalizations. As such, it may be able to protect the natural sphere and the healthy intersubjective relations that are at work in it. But no intersubjective relationship can ever define the universal system, not even in the form of love and benevolence. This is, ultimately, why the expressions related to femininity and the feminine sphere of the family, whether they be depicted as vengeful hatred and excessive desire or as maternal instincts and other caring relations, are kept outside of the sphere of universality for Hegel.

Antigone and the Conflict between the Sexes

From the beginning of the nineteenth century, when Sophocles was rediscovered, a large number of interpreters—Hölderlin, Hegel, Schlegel, Kierkegaard, and George Eliot up to Lacan and Irigaray—have made *Antigone* into the symbol of a fundamental ethical conflict: how are we to relate the city to the family, the universal to the particular?[27] Hegel has rightly seen that this question is intrinsically related to the question of sexual difference.

The tragedy, which revolves around the question of whether Polynices, an enemy of the city but also Antigone's brother, is to be buried or not, is an example of the kind of catastrophe that is released when the boundary between the sphere of the city and the sphere of the family is broken. The divine—or the ancient customs of religion, which Antigone stands for—contributes to the *miasma,* or contamination, of the community.[28] When Creon proclaims his law, that Polynices is not to be buried, we know already that Antigone has transgressed the proclamation. Antigone is then caught trying to bury the body a second time, at which time Creon asks how she dares transgress the laws, and Antigone answers:

> It was not Zeus who proclaimed that edict to me, nor did that
> Right who dwells with the gods below lay down such laws for
> mankind; and I did not suppose that your decrees had such power
> that you, a mortal, could outrun the gods' outwritten and unfailing
> rules. For their life is not of today and yesterday but for ever, and no
> one knows when they first appeared. (450–58, trans. A. Brown)

If Antigone stands for divine law, the unconditional love of the family, Creon stands for the human law that he has instituted with the *polis* in mind. He wants to do good for the city. Even if ancient customs demand that the family bury the bodies of the dead, these ancient customs must be forgone for the good of the city. Creon believes he is capable of creating a more perfect order. Thus he transgresses into the domain of the divine and the unwritten laws, believing that he is capable of restoring balance on his own. He thinks he knows the nature of justice and believes himself capable of introducing a universal principle of the good.[29] The fact that he is challenged by a woman incites him to commit such a transgression. But while Antigone accuses Creon of hubris, he accuses her of the same crime:

she thinks she knows justice, too. The actions of Creon are intertwined with those of Antigone. Creon accuses Antigone of a crime—hubris— that effectively applies to himself. But Creon succumbs, and Antigone's principle pervades. She is more than a static character positioned against Creon's erring but human behavior. Both sides are dependent on each other, their actions dependent on those of the other. But Antigone's crime is a product of Creon's law, her reverence for the dead a mirror of Creon's disrespect for life, her inability to love the living a reversed image of his disrespect for the dead.[30] Antigone's crime belongs to the divine sphere of excess, even though she is human: she believes that *dike*, justice, belongs to the nether world, or that it dwells "with the gods below." If Creon fatally mistakes human for divine law, it is the other way around in her case. Her action originates in the nether world, a sphere ultimately governed by death. Caught between two deaths, she is unable to participate in life. She is as cold as ice, Creon complains to his son; to embrace her would be like embracing a stone. She wants to marry someone in Hades (639–54)! Antigone's beauty corresponds to her pain. Her descent into the zone between two deaths is only a consequence of her distress. She has been dead for a long time, she tells her sister, even before she made the final choice (559–60).

If we remain within the parameters of ritual, Antigone's deed is easy to explain. But it carries with it an excess. Her crime is not in transgressing contingent laws; rather she refuses her duty to submit as a woman. Antigone is *autonomous*, a law onto herself, which means that she causes disruptions. In Athenian tragedy it was easier to depict women than men as autonomous in this sense, often with the result that they had to die.[31] Antigone transgresses the laws she is expected to follow *as a woman*, as Ismene reminds her: "Therefore we should listen to such orders, and those that are worse" (63–64). Challenged by Antigone, Creon says that he will not let himself be ruled by a woman (524–25). Antigone and Ismene should behave like women and not be "let loose" (578–79). Chaos would ensue: "We must on no account be beaten by a woman" (680). Fearing effeminization, Creon goes too far.[32] He thinks his own son weak, held under the spell of a woman who acts too much like a man. The chorus points it out to the public: Creon believes he is capable of controlling the powers of love. Thus he will lose his son to the same death to which he has condemned Antigone, and his own lineage will be destroyed.

Antigone's refusal to act like a woman, however, is not a political stance, as was Clytaemnestra's. It is spurred by love or desire, which is exactly what makes it dangerous: *Eros* is the god of ruin. Her brother is irreplaceable:

> My husband being dead, I could have another, and a child by
> another man if I had lost a child; but, as my mother and father
> are hidden in the house of Hades, no brother could ever be born
> again. Such was the law by which I singled you out for honour;
> but to Creon I seemed to be doing wrong in this and acting as a
> reckless criminal, my own brother. (909–15)

Antigone is prepared to die: "I shall bury him since it is beautiful to die doing such a thing: I shall lie by he whom I love who loves me, I—the villain sanctioned by the gods" (72–75). The Greek original tells us that her death, in these circumstances, would be *kalos*. *Kalos thanatos*, a beautiful death, usually refers to the honorable death of a warrior and is intimately connected to manliness. In Athens, women could not aspire to the social "beauty" or excellence of an honorable death.[33] The fact that women were excluded from such ideals makes Antigone's gesture all the more subversive. She considers her death to be an act of courage, an impossibility for a woman. Moreover, as will be made clear later in the play, she considers herself to be dying in the name of justice, thus causing the city to become polluted.

It has often been pointed out that Antigone does not act like a woman.[34] It has less often been observed that Creon does not act like a man. Arriving at the grave, he sees Haemon embrace the dead body of Antigone. Haemon kills himself, as does Creon's wife, Eurydice. Greek custom makes it the task of women to care for the dead. But Creon finds himself alone. His pain is as strong as that of a sister, or a mother. He ridiculed the "feminine" sensitivity of the son, but in the end his own wailing turns into the sign of an unbearable suffering, which no catharsis can silence or purify. Such a suffering traditionally belongs to the female mourner.[35] Gender roles are both overturned and intertwined when Creon stands with his dead son in his arms, wailing like a woman. The opening scene of the play, where Antigone holds her dead brother in her arms, is repeated by Creon, a repetition that figures an excess which the tragedy fails to contain. The reversal shows that sexual difference is a fluid concept in tragedy, but a dangerous fluidity that contaminates the city after limits and barriers are broken.[36] When Creon is told that someone has strewn earth over the body and performed the rituals of burial, he condemns both the unknown perpetrator and the chorus—the city—who place themselves on the side of the ancient customs respected through the burial. At this point, the chorus scans "Hymn to Man," the third chorus of the tragedy. We will analyze it in detail later; here it is enough to point to the fact that the end of the song provides yet another key to the tragic interlacing of Antigone and Creon: only the one who respects *both* the law of the land and the divine rights of the gods is allowed citizenship. He or she who pursues only one of these principles must be excommunicated. Antigone cannot choose anything else: her brother is irreplaceable. The uncompromising posture criticized by the city is a gesture that defends the *unique* value of the brother. Creon, on the other hand, shows disrespect for the singularity and the divine, failing to balance their claims to universality. Elevating his own law in the place of ancient customs, he bares his misunderstanding of *dike*. Both Creon and Antigone are enemies to the city, the foreign elements through which the ethical order is sacrificed.

Sexual Difference in the Ethical Community

In Hegel's reading of the *Oresteia*, femininity is identified as inorganic and destructive, as well as maternal, loving, and caring. In his reading of *Antigone*, the distinction between a teleological or "good" nature, on the one hand, and a chaotic or inorganic one, on the other, is downplayed. There is no longer any need to elevate "natural" desires into the ideality of communal law through a separation between "good" and "bad" nature. Instead, the conflict is between "natural" desire in the family domain and the universal claims of a public domain. The function of universalization makes it possible for the community to construct a normative order in and out of itself, without regard for the particular. The universal order would include and submit the family, rather than accepting dependence on the particular relations that govern the family. Hegel wants to submit the natural sphere of the family to an order of norms and rules that would be universally valid for the members of the community in its entirety. The question is how this will be made possible without a violation of family bonds, without a dangerous disruption between the so-called particular interests of the family and the universal pretensions of the order of the community as a totality. The ethical order is dependent on mutual cooperation between the family and the state.[37] This is where Hegel's reading of the *Phenomenology* becomes crucial to his negotiation of the problem. Although the discussion of *Antigone* concerns a state of *Sittlichkeit* that is no longer

instituted, the conflicting relation between family and state remains problematic for the modern state, as can be seen in the *Philosophy of Right*.

Antigone's actions, while justified from a subjective viewpoint, cause
an irreparable rift. Her engagement may seem justified, but it is invested
with a surplus, and it is this very excess that makes Hegel respond to
Antigone as a symbol of feminine desire, in a way quite different from
Clytaemnestra. Although Hegel does not explicitly comment on Antigone's femininity and he denies her desire, he clearly understands that the
action revolves around sexual difference and difference is irreducible to social status—which comes to the fore in the discussion of femininity. Femininity is situated at the margins of self-consciousness, but it nevertheless
plays a crucial role in its development. And if the categories used for the
interpretation of *Antigone* are influenced by the *Oresteia*, it is largely in a
negative manner. Clytaemnestra's love turns impure, threatening, and violent. Antigone, however, represents a higher form of purity. Rather than
being detached from the ethical order as a chaotic and threatening sexual
force, Antigone is elevated above it. Hegel's reading takes its place in the
long line of interpretations disassociating Antigone the sister from sexual
connotations. The lack of sexual references is part of the fascination, and
the notion that Antigone's desire is pure is an important factor in the
analysis.[38] Antigone is the starting point from which a dialectics of tragedy
must be thought—somewhere between the natural (which cannot be uni-
versalized) and the ethical (the domain from which a universal principle of
justice can be claimed).

The ethical community is controlled by two aspects. One is universal—valid for all members of the state. The other is divine law, resistant to
universal claims and governed by natural good, such as love and intimacy,
even sexuality, which has its place in the family. The family, a "natural ethical community," may threaten to disrupt the claim to universality.[39] The
private bonds between family members have to be separated from the function of the state. But the relation between family members can be ethical
only insofar as the bonds are not merely based on feelings. The family is
submitted to duties mediated through the state: only the state gives the
family the recognition it needs for the natural bonds to function. Family
and state are mutually dependent. The family depends on the life of the
community, which in turn grants it a certain recognition and a certain freedom. If this recognition, and thus this freedom, is removed under society's
regime, the family revolts. Referring to divine law set against human law,

Antigone becomes an instrument in restoring the balance between family and state. The fact that Antigone follows the unwritten laws of the gods means, for Hegel, that she follows the bonds of love. Antigone's action is not consciously ethical—she is excluded from the public culture in which individuals are raised to self-consciousness. Men are part of the family and the state, while women, as wives and mothers, lack access to recognition in the state. This is why they lack desire, properly speaking. Although the relationships of mother and wife must be looked at as relationships of individuality and therefore of desire in the natural sense, that desire tends to be negated through the contingent relation of the particular individual to the universal order. Rather than affirming and following desire, whether it be natural or social, women are dedicated to their task as guardian of the family, fulfilling their tasks of reproduction and raising children. Lacking the free and conscious status of the male individual, the desire of a woman is therefore negative in kind. Paradoxically, although women are supposedly the guardians of the natural domain of care and love, they are devoid of the kind of desire that attaches one individual to another. The relationships formed by woman are based not on feeling but on the ethical demands imposed by the universal, and therefore reflect the function of the family in the ethical order.[40] Hegel does, however, also distinguish a specific kind of desire that does not fit into any other category, natural or social. The relation between brother and sister is, in Hegel's view, devoid of sexual or natural desire; it is free and unaffected, or "pure."[41] The only objective of a sister's desire is sisterly duty. This argument seems incoherent with its premises. The evacuation of natural desire from this relation serves a rather interesting purpose in the argument. The brother/sister relation comes to constitute the limit of the "naturalness" of the family, the point where the family becomes ethical. Brother and sister are constituted as opposites: they have symmetrically opposed functions. The brother is expected to leave the family and the sister to remain in it. But at the same time, they remain singular in their opposition. Unlike other functions in the family—father, mother, son, daughter, and so on—brother and sister incarnate both the singular and the universal. In Derrida's account, they constitute a model for sexual difference as such, where two individuals are both representative in terms of their sexual identity and irreplaceable in terms of their position vis-à-vis each other. This means that Hegel's system is tainted by an undecidability that fails to dissolve.[42] What Derrida does not discuss, however, is that the factor of instability introduced through the tragic logic originates in a desire that must be considered feminine, whether we look at it from the point of view of Clytaemnestra or of Antigone, both tainted by the inorganic contamination between maternal protection and sexual threat. Moreover, in Hegel's reading, the other sex becomes both a natural and an ethical category, thus undermining the differentiation between the two. Antigone's love for her brother is an ethical rather than a natural or sexual love. By linking sexual difference to the social sphere in this way, Hegel shows that it is neither natural nor given. Or rather, nature may have marked the sexes differently, but the primary function of sexual difference is the realization of the ethical.[43] The biological aspect of sex and sexual difference is therefore subjugated to the social sphere and ultimately *defined* by such an order. The difference between the sexes is determined through their negative relation to the ethical order—they are both lacking in relation to it. In this way, the line between a natural sexual desire and the universal aspect of the ethical sphere is blurred.[44]

The sister wins recognition through the dead brother, not as a result of a perverted death drive, but as a keeper of *the value of her brother's singularity*. His singularity becomes part of the social and cultural memory through the rituals of the funeral, which are the family's task in general and a sister's in particular, the sister being the keeper of divine law. The weight granted by Hegel to the funeral is connected with an implicit idea of something that could be called the second death: the idea that there is something beyond physical death, which is pure disappearance, oblivion, and disintegration. The second death occurs when the living obliterate the memory of the dead, when death is neither sublated nor singularized through the funeral ritual. The dead body is an empty form of being, prey to the appetites of the nether world. Through the burial, the family rescues the singular value of the dead individual from annihilation.[45] His memory detached from a disintegrating body, he is made part of universal memory, history, and culture as a singular being. Calling on divine laws for support, Antigone makes Creon's refusal to bury Polynices look self-sufficient and tyrannical. He violates her family name, together with the ancient laws. What Hegel does not mention, however, is that he also violates her right to *protect the sphere of the natural*, where sexuality resides. Antigone's relation to the ethical order is impossible to determine; Creon's inability to determine the status of her femininity as natural or ethical points to a deficiency in the ethical order, which is incapable of containing femininity. The feminine is a remainder that will not be enclosed in the absolute, neither in the tragedy nor in Hegel's system. This is of consequence not only for his discussion of Antigone, but also for his discussion of self-consciousness in the ethical order itself, just as we have seen in the "Tragödie der Sittlichkeit."

Antigone shows that consciousness in the ethical order always remains split, in and through itself, between the demands of particularity and the laws of universality. Making the singularity of her brother into the very object of her claim to justice, Antigone shows that an order of justice with a claim to universality can be instituted only at the cost of a loss that will continue to haunt the development of consciousness: a tragic remainder that will put the universal claim into question, a remainder that leads Hegel to the famous argument about woman being the eternal irony of the community.[46]

The Feminine as Deficiency

Hegel's reading of *Antigone* has been widely criticized for excluding the feminine from the ethical order and reducing the function of women to the family sphere. But at the same time, many critics have pointed out that the exclusion of femininity may well open up for a view on subjectivity, which serves as a subtext in Hegel's writings on tragedy. Through their insistence on the interests of the home and the individual, women show a disconcerting lack of respect for the universal order: this is the laughing female irony. The state acquires legitimacy by subjugating the family. But the family is likely to keep a certain independence, which perverts the claim of the ethical order to universal validity. Woman is society's "eternal irony" in her refusal of every absolute universalization: she laughs at the public order to which she will never have access. She not only will in some way always remain outside of the community, but she will threaten to dissolve it in her perversion of it—a perversion that we may understand as her challenge to the order of universality, but which is also connected to her audacity in representing a form of desire that must be considered a challenge to the social form of desire, which Hegel talks about in terms of recognition and which is supported by the dialectic.[47] Placing woman on the side of intuition, nature, and the unconscious, Hegel denies her access to recognition and self-consciousness. The desire for recognition is figured by the struggle to the death between master and slave. Feminist critics of Hegel have pointed out that he disqualifies women from even entering the competition.[48] Defining the conditions of ethical consciousness and recognition in the ethical order, the dialectic between master and slave depicts a meeting between forms of consciousness that are equally marked by alterity in relation to the other. Self-consciousness, says Hegel, can only be won through a reciprocal relation of recognition, where two subjects recognize each other as mutually recognizing each other. As stated in the figure of the struggle between master and slave: "Self-consciousness exists in and for itself when, and by the fact that, it so exists for another; that is, it exists only in being acknowledged."[49] And so Hegel argues that self-consciousness does not belong to an individual, rather it exists as a split between two terms, the self and the other, mediating the possibility of self-consciousness for each other: "Each is for the other the middle term, through which each mediates itself with itself and unites with itself; and each is for itself, and for the other, an immediate being on its own account, which at the same time is such only through this mediation. They *recognize* themselves as *mutually recognizing* one another."[50] In Hegel's argument, self-consciousness is irrevocably split and produced by a desire that originates in someone and is directed toward the mastery of an other, causing a displacement where the goal of desire moves from the other as object back to oneself, thus constituting the self as an object for the other. Such a desire can never be achieved or fulfilled; instead it is maintained in and through the loss of self that such a displacement accomplishes.

As observed by Simone de Beauvoir, the obvious problems with such a symmetrical model of desire for recognition is that it holds death as the sole determination of human finitude. From a feminine point of view, subjectivity is not necessarily determined that way. Beauvoir introduces the term "natality" for that through which the feminine conditioning of finitude must be thought. Protecting life, woman is unwilling to risk her own—a disposition that would automatically exclude her from the dialectics of social recognition in Hegel's account.[51] Other feminists have observed problems with the dialectics of recognition and criticized Hegel's reading of Antigone using that grid. According to Luce Irigaray, Antigone is not given access to the conditions that would allow her to recognize the alterity of the other. Emerging from the space of negativity itself, and lacking knowledge of or access to the ethical order, the trace of alterity gains no hold in her own mind. No feminine self-consciousness develops. For this lack of knowledge, she is punished, denied access to the ethical order, and sacrificed. For Irigaray, therefore, the most problematic aspect of Hegel's model lies not in the fact that women are excluded by a patriarchal order,

but in that they effect their own exclusion.[52] Kelly Oliver defines the logic
of the phenomenology as a continuous process of eliminating the feminine. Man consumes or "eats" the feminine, and then re-creates it to his
own mind. The unconscious appetites that consume man are defined as
feminine, nature, the nether world, and so forth. These elements cannot be
brought to consciousness. Instead, they constitute a threat to male historical self-consciousness: "Man consumes woman so that he won't be con-
sumed by mother nature."[53]

In sum, the point of these critics is that *there is no confrontation* between feminine and masculine desire. Self-consciousness reflects itself in another consciousness, passing from the *an-sich-sein* to an *an-und-für-sich-sein*
through a conflict or collision. The feminine is, however, never allowed to
constitute a pole of consciousness in such a collision. Given that Hegel's
whole system revolves around the notion of confrontation, there can be no
space in which the feminine might show itself or from which female self-
consciousness might emerge. Relegated to a femininity defined as the negativity of nature, sexuality, or the nether world of appetites, women are denied access to an emancipatory space. For feminine self-consciousness to
emerge and for feminine desire to become an emancipatory force rather
than just a sexual force, it would need to be assessed as a term in the social
dialectic of recognition. But since woman is disqualified from that conflict,
she is incapable of constituting herself in relation to another consciousness.
In other words, feminine desire remains at the level of sexuality and lacks
emancipatory potential. In this way, the model of self-consciousness and social recognition that has been drawn in the master-slave parable of the *Phenomenology* is in line with the suppression of questions concerning feminine
desire that we have seen in Hegel's readings of tragedy's feminine figures.

But is it not a mistake to insert terms like "desire" into the understanding of the tragic action, since desire presupposes a modern idea of reflexivity and interiority? Or to treat the tragic characters as if their sexuality and identity would be even remotely similar to modern ones? Hegel is
well aware that it must be questioned to what extent a desiring subject can
be observed in the ancient texts at all.[54] The citizen in general and women
in particular are identified with institutions such as the family and the *polis*, their laws and customs. Antigone and Clytaemnestra act according to
the place they are given in the family or rather the house identified with
that family, the *oikos*. As such, the fact that they lack self-consciousness in
Hegel's description is not only the result of exclusion of femininity in

Hegel's philosophy but an effect of his historicizing of consciousness. If they provide a form of resistance, it is not conscious, because the feminine tragic agent has nothing to do with modern self-consciousness. The feminine tragic subject is, as we have seen, exposed not as a self-conscious agent but as a deficiency in the community.[55] And so the question ought not to be what kind of gendered conflicts can be discerned in the historical background of tragedy, but rather how feminine subjectivity can be represented at all in a space that clearly does not allow women a role as agents or subjects of ethical consciousness. In Kierkegaard's words, ancient tragedy lacks the moment presenting the subject for-itself—the individual is never detached from his or her institutional functions. Tragedy lacks the moral consciousness that, in the words of Kierkegaard, "reflected [the tragic hero] out of every immediate relation to state, race, and destiny [and] out of his own preceding life."[56] It is a misunderstanding to transubstantiate the tragic into a model of subjectivity because "our age has lost all the substantial categories of family, state, and race." In a Christian form of consciousness, the individual is left to himself or herself, becoming the creator of his or her own guilt and pain, which "nullifies the tragic."[57] Kierkegaard rewrites *Antigone* as a modern drama of guilt: anxiety about the hidden family secrets throws her into a reflected state of ambiguity and pain. In ancient drama, however, guilt is involuntarily transferred through external factors, such as heritage. It would seem as if such a lack of interiority and reflexivity would cancel any modern notion of subjectivity. Hegel is quite aware of this. He does not make Antigone into a conscious, modern heroine. He makes her into an impossibility in and limit of the community. In the process, he provides us with the sketch of a form of subjectivity that is *not* defined as the self-consciousness of the social agent, but rather as a desire that finds satisfaction and recognition neither in the ethical order nor in the modern form of universality. Such a subjectivity cannot be considered the equivalent of the historical woman of the Greek community; rather it is brought to another level in Hegel's argument. It is, if one likes, the margin, the fault, the deficiency that opens up the gap in the social fabric of any historical community. We have stumbled upon a possible figure of feminine desire.

Seyla Benhabib has written an important essay that may help us look further into these concerns. Situating Hegel in a historical context where his views on gender relations seem conservative and crass, she points to the fact that his reading of *Antigone* is more than a historical account of women in the *polis*; it is a response to the emancipatory demands made by women in his own time. Hegel, as is well known, rejects the utopian vision of erotic and spiritual egalitarianism promoted by romantics such as Friedrich Schlegel, and the demands of women are caught in the process.[58] The inscription of those demands, Benhabib argues, constitute the path on which Spirit's detachment of alterity moves ahead: "There is no way to disentangle the march of the dialectic in Hegel's system from the bodies on which it treads."[59] What Hegel calls feminine irony—the laughing voice of women, who will not be included in the ethical order at the cost of submission to its annihilating movement of universality—is a trace of female demands for justice, not just in ancient times, but in Hegel's own. Hegel's reading of *Antigone* conveys the traces of an alterity or femininity that does not fit within the description of *Sittlichkeit*. Ironically, however, it is the unintended irony or remnant of that alterity that has come to make up the most important legacy of Hegel's dialectic, in Benhabib's mind: "The vision of Hegelian reconciliation has long ceased to convince: the otherness of the other is that moment of irony, reversal and inversion with which we must live."[60] The more interesting way to read Hegel, then, would be *against* himself, as Seyla Benhabib suggests, and to retain the fractured moments in which an alterity comes to show itself, which are more interesting for our perspective on modernity. Christoph Menke has argued, in opposition to Benhabib's critique of Hegel, that Hegel does more than marginalize the feminine in his reading of Antigone. On the contrary: he considers the outsidership of women in the ethical order to constitute an originary model of modern individuality, through their ironic, reflective position. The ironic subject challenges old definitions of virtue and makes it possible to renegotiate them. Irony is not just an empty reflection—it is based in freedom.[61] Such an interpretation is not altogether impossible to join with Benhabib's, who retains the ironic moment in Hegel as a possible model for modern subjectivity. She does not suggest that this is a conscious gesture by Hegel, as Menke does, but both would hold that Hegel somehow makes women into individuals rather than products of suppression. The problem with Hegel's exclusion of feminine desire from the development of self-consciousness is, as we have seen, that it becomes a concept lacking emancipatory dimension. But we may choose to read Hegel against himself and make his notion of femininity into an unstable and uprooted form of subjectivity rather than just another symbol for excess and irrationality. Even if Hegel describes feminine desire as chaotic, inorganic, and anarchic, the feminine is not reduced to a mere negation of self-consciousness. Feminine desire is a tragic remainder or resistance of ethical reflection, but not the end of it. Rather the feminine principle has the pivotal role of releasing the ethical subject on its journey from a natural habitation in the ethical order toward a modern, split consciousness, which no longer mourns the *Sittlichkeit* that has been sacrificed in its path.

For Hegel, tragedy does not make women die, kill, or vanish as a manifestation of (patriarchal) society's desire to dominate. The question is why their dying, killing, or vanishing appears to be motivated by a cause *internal* to tragedy itself. The divine sphere incorporates passion and infatuation, and it is no coincidence that Hegel focuses on tragedies depicting what we might call *sexuated* heroes: Clytaemnestra, Oedipus, and Antigone. Desire is identified not with the striving toward possession, power, and control, but with fallibility and failure. The split and insufficiency of the tragic subject is, as Hegel rightly saw, intertwined not only with social and political conflicts but also with sexual themes. Tragedy shapes the contours of another desire, opening the negative space of failure and insufficiency, which makes it impossible to regard the ethical order as a totality. It calls the ethical codes of the society it represents into question, and the problems surrounding these codes are to a large extent provoked or overthrown by a feminine presence.[62] From this perspective, feminine desire stands for an interesting principle of otherness, the limits of self-consciousness, a claim to justice that points to a problem in what Hegel calls the ethical order, something that is not working. The split between the ethical order as a normative system of universal validity and the singular claims it fails to include can never be overcome. In tragedy, this split is sexuated. Men have access to the order of justice, whereas women are excluded from it. This is a problem in the *polis*, and it necessitates a renegotiation. Feminine desire is in fact impossible to subjugate to the universalizable concept: it points to a resistance irreducible to male consciousness. *Sittlichkeit*, or the ethical order in Hegel, shows its limits only through the negativity and violence that is directed against it, a violence incarnated by tragic women. Both Antigone and Clytaemnestra point to a *deficiency* of and in the ethical order, of which the inorganic volatility of feminine desire is but one aspect, albeit a crucial and symptomatic one. It may well be that the feminine itself is excluded from a consciousness that can only be male in Hegel's account.[63] Nonetheless, the feminine represents a kind of deficiency that points to the fact that the community can never come to peace with the demands of sacrifice, made by the dialectics itself. Hegel negotiates the fact that Antigone's deeds carry an excess in relation to the ethical order. Feminine desire, in fact, points to a deficiency produced in the gap between the process of universalization and the intersubjective bonds between individuals which no normative order seems capable of containing, a deficiency that *cannot* be closed. Whether she is considered to be pure, ironic, or overly sexual, the feminine is riveted to that deficiency.

3

The Purest Poem . . . : Heidegger's *Antigone*

Challenging the Metaphysics
of Sexual Difference

The philosophical discourse on femininity is heavy with metaphysical baggage. Aristotle's *Metaphysics* describes the feminine principle as an equivalent to the dark and bad.[1] In Hegel's history of spirit, the feminine is a discourse of the carnal, emanating from the nether world and excluded from self-consciousness. In this perspective, getting rid of feminine desire as a concept altogether would not seem to be a loss. But would the remedy be to conceive of a discourse beyond sex or gender? To reject questions of sexual difference because they appear to be restraining for philosophical thought? At a first glance, this is what Martin Heidegger seems to be doing. Unlike German Idealism and its inheritors or psychoanalysis, Martin Heidegger finds no mystery in femininity. He rejects sexual differentiation altogether in his consideration of the fundamental problems of philosophy, inventing a term that per definition is gender neutral: *Dasein*, or being-there.

But Heidegger's reluctance to speak about gender is not simply due to negligence; it is part of an ambition to purify the ontological description of Dasein. Strangely enough, this is an interesting project from a gender perspective. It does not so much invite us to ignore sexual difference as show us a way of conceiving of sexual difference beyond a structuralist or metaphysical point of view. Heidegger's invitation to reconsider the question of sexual difference takes us beyond a fixed idea of desire and sexuality as either natural or socially constructed. He reveals sexual difference as radically contingent. Its philosophical impact has little to do with what it *is*, and more to do with what it *can become*. Freed from metaphysical baggage, sexual difference—and therefore femininity and feminine desire—is considered a potentiality rather than an essence.

Although Heidegger is reluctant to speak of themes connected with love, sexuality, eroticism, desire, and sexual difference, this does not mean that sexual difference is left altogether untouched. In a 1928 lecture, *Metaphysische Anfangsgründe der Logik im Ausgang von Leibniz* (*The Metaphysical Foundations of Logic*), Heidegger explains his reasons for wanting to analyze the subject of philosophy beyond sexual differentiation. The term Dasein is chosen primarily because it refers to the temporal and finite condition of a speaking being, where all philosophical questions have their origin. But the term is useful also in other respects, not least because it can be employed to avoid distinctions that belong to the history of metaphysics, such as man-woman or subject-object. Heidegger's determination to avoid such descriptions is of course part of an attempt to leave behind all properties that are irrelevant to the analysis of Dasein as a finite being. Dasein replaces the subject, and the relation to the object is replaced by care. This means that man's engagement in the world cannot be disassociated from the world itself: the world that he is building, constructing, and speaking is projected as meaningful on the basis of his interaction with it. Therefore, there can be no concept of desire in Heidegger's analysis of Dasein; this would presume a subject in which desire originates and a series of objects to which it is attached, the kind of dichotomy he is trying to move away from. Moreover, categories such as sexual difference are not only irrelevant to this project, they may even threaten to interfere with it because they presuppose the kind of dichotomy he is trying to eliminate. Dasein functions on two levels: on one level, it is determined by lack, loss, and negativity; on another, it is involved in the world through manifest properties and relations, properties belonging to masculinity and femininity, for instance. The distinction between these two levels is what Heidegger calls ontological difference. Ontological difference exists between the ground of being as such (*Sein*), which has a transcendental status in early Heidegger, and beings (*seiende*).[2] Being is what makes beings possible, for instance through the negativity or nothingness that brings forth appearances. These appearances are made manifest in Dasein's different modes of existing, and include sexual difference. While human practices would be inconceivable without biological, social, anthropological, cultural, and sexual determinations, the task of philosophy is to move beyond the contingent nature of these relations. As an example of such a contingent relation, sexual difference is subordinate to the ontological conflict between being and beings, where all the important questions concerning Dasein are posed.[3] There is not much point in asking questions about femininity and feminine desire. When we have come far enough in our ontological analysis, Dasein transcends sexual differentiation. It is not involved in the world through desire, drives, or sexuality. In *Being and Time*, Heidegger shows that it is engaged through care, a category that has nothing to do with sexuality.[4]

In the 1928 lecture series, Heidegger explains that the "neutrality" of Dasein does not refer to simple indifference. The fact that Heidegger is uninterested in the philosophical question of sexual difference does not mean that Dasein could ever exist in a sexless form.[5] In its facticity or in its corporeal condition, its thrownness or its being with others, Dasein is sexually differentiated. Heidegger is not simply telling us that there is a neutral person in all individuals, a person who transcends sexuality and corporeal needs. Nor does he tell us that it is possible to isolate a neutral form of being beyond biological sex and sexual identity, or even that we should strive to do so; every Dasein exists in a state of thrownness (as man or woman, for instance) that he or she cannot detach from his or her being. But the ontological question of Dasein ought to be considered in a state of *metaphysical isolation*, where what is proper to it is to be found beyond such manifestations. Because he is interested in the potentiality that foregoes the principle of sexual differentiation, Heidegger wants to consider Dasein as gender neutral. If we look at Dasein in a state of metaphysical isolation, issues of sexual difference must be disregarded in favor of questions concerning the principles of differentiation as such. It is in order to get to these principles that Heidegger insists on the gender neutrality of Dasein. Heidegger's argument that Dasein is gender neutral contains in itself an argument on difference as such.[6]

One may deduce from these considerations that sexual difference is submitted to more primordial categories. Neutrality is a principle of differentiation rather than the idea of an abstract, nondifferentiated body.[7] Neutrality makes possible the production of differences. This is the most interesting aspect of Heidegger's discourse on gender: the philosophical importance of sexual difference has little to do with sexuality or biology, or even with the sexual identity of the individual. Sexual difference becomes a philosophical topic only in context, in the meaningful commonality and plurality of *being-with*, or *Mitsein*. The notion of *being-with* (*Mitsein*) is not particularly well worked out in this context, but it is pivotal for the way Heidegger understands sexual difference.[8] The being-with does not simply refer to Dasein as a form of plurality. It has to do with the way these Daseins are organized, not only as social beings in a community, but also as sexual and embodied beings living together. In the community of the being-with, some features of Dasein are actualized while others remain hidden. Gender is a meaningful category of difference only if we look at the way it functions in a network with other differences.

The notion of sexual difference as a form of plurality rather than a dualism, as a potentiality rather than nature, challenges certain ideas within the metaphysical tradition. The idea that sexual difference is necessary for procreation, for instance, is ignored. Moreover, the idea that sexual difference originates in an originary split is refuted. The latter could easily lead to the essentialist assumption that difference is symmetrical, that the sexes match one another and that the split may be bridged. In the Platonic tradition, for instance, the two sexes are considered to emerge from the same body. In Heidegger's view, the notion that sexual difference is a split is a devaluation, because it would mean that sex is a lack or deficiency rather than a potentiality. But if one thinks of sexual difference as a potentiality, one can never fully explain the function of sexual difference in a positive manner, or in a way that would make sense of the function of the sexes biologically, socially, or metaphysically. Men and women are not considered to complement each other physically, socially, and spiritually. Sexual difference is an organization of embodiment, and not a lack.[9] It organizes the way we conceive of ourselves as corporeal and sexual beings. It presents us not with an essential bond that ties us together but rather with an antibond that encircles and confirms our differences.

Thus it is not the actual manifestations of sex that are important, but the fact that Dasein only exists as plurality. Sexual difference is a form of dissemination (*Zerstreuung*) or manifolding of humankind. But sexual difference is considered to be a potential plurality present *in each individual Dasein* rather than a difference that is merely instituted between individuals.[10] Positing Dasein as a potential form of dissemination may seem to challenge sexual dualism in the same way as contemporary queer theory does, for instance, when it opposes the dualism of heteronormativity, allowing speculation on a possible manifolding of genders or a third sex.[11] Heidegger does not, however, promote cultural and sexual diversity. He wants only to move beyond cultural and biological issues that threaten to divert us from the real issues of philosophical analysis.

The being-with concerns not the manifestations of the manifold, or of difference, but the meaningfulness of differentiation as such. *Being-with* makes differences such as biological sex meaningful because it implies a complex web of relations and determinations. In this web, sexual difference has a direction and a function. Certain possibilities are actualized—such as masculinity and femininity—while other possibilities remain hidden. The analysis of differences is, however, secondary to the analysis of Dasein's metaphysical neutrality. The question is what makes such a complex net possible. The being-with presumes an ontological neutrality of Dasein that one may perhaps speak about in terms of openness. The principle of differentiation refuses to fix Dasein as one given sexual principle. Dasein has an open character, and it lacks an essential sexual determination. This is what makes the being-with possible. Dasein's plural condition has this openness or neutrality as its precondition. One may (as we will see in the readings of *Antigone*) consider Heidegger's insistence on Dasein's neutrality as a means of keeping open the question of the foundation of the community. The insistence on the neutrality of Dasein makes it possible to conceive of the being-with as a network of differences that is forever changing, grounded not in metaphysical principles but in openness and indeterminacy. The openness of Dasein helps *shape the bonds of the community as such*, although it seems to constitute a kind of antibond. There is no essential trait keeping us together, no perfect fitting of our differences that would in any way make us complement each other. We are thrown in a movement of dispersal, and our differences are manifestations of that dispersal and not given, unchangeable ties.

Sexual Difference as Decomposition

The daring theories of sexual difference as potentiality and productivity that Heidegger presented in his 1928 course are not sustained in his work in a consistent manner. In 1928, Heidegger is very careful to point to the fact that sexual difference is neither a split nor a state of fallenness. But in the interpretation of Georg Trakl's poetry in *Unterwegs zur Sprache*, concepts such as splitting and decomposition find their way into Heidegger's language. "Geschlecht," the German word for gender, has several meanings. Looking at its etymological roots, Heidegger's interest in it is motivated by the fact that it connotes not only sexual difference, but also filiation and humankind. It is a word split between its connotations of dispersal on the one hand, and of unity on the other. Trakl, foreshadowing the atrocities of World War I in his poems, writes about the possibility of "Ein Geschlecht."[12] The discord of the word "Geschlecht" is softened by a poetic reference to unity, although Geschlecht is itself suggestive of dispersal. Heidegger notes in his reading of Trakl "the curse of the decomposing *Geschlecht* consists in the fact that this ancient *Geschlecht* has been dispersed in the discord of the *Geschlechter*. . . . That *Geschlecht* is 'foreign' and it follows the stranger."[13] That which is foreign is *in* the stranger, an alterity one may interpret as death, although it could also be the mark of sexual difference, as we see in the reading of Trakl's "Geistliche Dämmerung." Typically, Heidegger turns to a poem colored by the fantasy of a beautiful dead woman as the most poetic figure of all.[14] The poem depicts a nature scene embedded in darkness and night, lit only by the moon. It ends with the sound of a "moonlike" voice, that of the sister, piercing the night.[15] The text has, as Heidegger rightly sees, clear autobiographical undertones. The dark waters evoke the drowning of Trakl's sister. The text depicts a relation where brother and sister become interchangeable and intertwined. He imagines her staring at him in the mirror of dark waters. That which is foreign to him and in him is detached and made visible. Identifying with his sister, he sees himself as foreign to himself, marked by her death. But death is not the most disturbing dimension of this poem, according to Heidegger. Death is rather a remedy for another split—the decomposing function of Geschlecht, or sexual difference—and introduces an alterity that is even more frightening than death. When the sister's death becomes his own death, the split is overcome. Death is reconciliation, whereas the disturbing alterity of sexual difference is split and decomposing.

Heidegger does not mention, however, that the voice of the dead, invisible sister is also the voice of desire. It is as piercing and as inescapable as that of the Sirens in Homer's *Odyssey*. It is the voice of another desire, demanding to be heard. Is it perhaps the case that the falling apart of humankind is *introduced* by a femininity made visible or audible?[16] Is the discord or decomposition of sexual difference the effect of such a demand? These questions are not raised, and so the alterity that could have been interpreted as sexual, threatening femininity is reduced to death.

The scene in Trakl's poem depicts an encounter with an alterity that could be called uncanny in the Freudian sense. For Freud, the uncanny is another word for the anxiety of castration, which presents itself in fantasies or images that speak of the fear of death or the fear of mutilation.[17] Although the uncanny is a different notion in Heidegger, it can be understood in the Freudian sense in the text. Heidegger's reading evokes a phenomenon noted by many feminist philosophers and literary historians: the fixation on death is a complex strategy to cover the disturbing facts of sexual difference and femininity. The death invoked is not only the death of the finite human body, but also the death of castration, the sexuation of the subject. In philosophy, woman is often a Vorstellungs-Repräsentanz for death, Irigaray writes, using the Freudian term for a trauma represented in a sublimated form. A representation "of the death drives that cannot (or theoretically could not) be perceived without horror, that the eye (of) consciousness refuses to recognize."[18] The displacement of fear of castration toward fear of death is a powerful subtext in the Western tradition up to Freud. The experience of the uncanny gives rise to anxiety, but it reveals nothing about the world. The rejection of heterogeneity and difference is in fact the symptom of a death that, in a manner of speaking, already has taken place—castration, the splitting of the subject that comes with the mark of sexual difference. Castration is the symbolic mark of a constitutive lack and femininity its most worrying manifestation: there is nothing to see, no phallus. The kind of fear that derives from exposure to mutilation, splitting, and nothingness hides another, deeper fear caused by the feminine lack of a phallic organ. Fear of death is secondary to the fear of castration, which institutes the alterity of sexual difference, and of femininity.

Invested with a completely different meaning, the uncanny is a key term in Heidegger's analysis of anxiety in *Being and Time*. Through anxiety, Dasein is thrown back upon itself and exposed to itself as neither quite belonging to the world nor quite separated from it. Through the mood of anxiety, Dasein is exposed to itself as constitutionally homeless.[19] The uncanny unravels the truth about the human status of finitude; it throws Dasein back upon itself in all its endeavors of thinking, creating, and poeticizing. Thus it is not the experience of anxiety that retains Heidegger's interest, but rather the alterity inherent in Dasein when it is thrown back upon itself as a "seeking that at times does not know itself."[20] If we are to follow Heidegger, that which is foreign in man is death, and sexual difference is irrelevant to the question of alterity. And yet there is an intrinsic relation between death and femininity in Heidegger's lectures—death and sex at times seem interchangeable. In the uncanny, there is an unspoken link between femininity and death.

The Tragic Mode of Dasein

The last question is motivated by Heidegger's comments on tragedy. It is, interestingly enough, precisely when we turn to tragedy that these issues return, and they do so notably in a reading of *Antigone*. Just like in the poem by Trakl, the theme of sexual difference is ostensibly removed from desire and sexuality and "purified" through a pair of siblings, a brother and a sister. According to Heidegger, who thereby aligns himself with a desire seen in many other interpreters, Antigone incarnates poetry in its purest form.[21] She is Dasein unraveled in its homelessness, thrown back upon itself. The tragic impossibility that lies at the core of her being is exposed. But in the text itself, it is difficult to link this tragic exposure to the idea that Antigone is "pure." Sophocles sees Antigone as tragic not because she is pure, but because she is contaminated by a sexual transgression that underlies the text. Heidegger's ambition to qualify Dasein as neutral proves difficult, for tragic Dasein, death, and sexuality are intrinsically intertwined. Heidegger is silently suppressing the reference to the latter. And yet, just like in the poem by Trakl, we encounter an uncanniness in the text through Heidegger's reading, an uncanniness that cannot be fully detached from the call of feminine desire. The figure of Antigone reveals an impossibility inherent in Dasein as such because she is a woman. In this way, she participates in the formation of that figure in modern philosophy that we call the *Antigone complex*: the desire of a woman is used to reveal an impossibility inherent in Dasein as such. If Antigone is "pure poetry," it is, at a closer glance, because the tragic impossibility that lies at the core of her desire is exposed.

Heidegger refers to *Antigone* twice: first in the 1935 *Einführung in die Metaphysik* (*Introduction to Metaphysics*) and then in the 1942 *Hölderlins Hymne "Der Ister"* (*Hölderlin's Hymn "The Ister"*). His reflections on tragedy are quite extraordinary, not least because of his insistence on almost entirely disregarding the tragic action and claiming that not much is happening at all, either on stage or in the viewer. His interest in tragedy is theoretical and relies on the temporal and historical character of truth, rather than on the praxis of moral values. Such an understanding sets him apart from the Aristotelian tradition, where tragedy is considered a form of moral learning, serving a clarification of emotions and self-reflection.[22] Heidegger has no interest in tragedy's moral message. Instead, he argues that it shows us the function of unconcealment. Tragedy constitutes a form of unraveling, where the end shows us something that was already present in the beginning. But there is no significant development taking place that would teach or show us something new. There is no actual learning to be had from tragedy. And there is, strictly speaking, *no point in the tragic action itself.* It has nothing to do with lived experience: "In the Greek tragedy virtually nothing occurs. It commences with the downgoing."[23] But, at the same time, tragedy cannot be reduced to a logic of necessity or fate. It commences with the downgoing because art shows something and points to something that seems to have always been there. Through his interest in Greek art, Heidegger is trying to show that it can not be reduced to metaphysical teleology, moral edification, or an experience of pleasure.[24] For the Greeks, art was a form of unconcealment and thus a form of truth.[25] Oedipus discloses what he is through the gesture of poking out his eyes; he can no longer escape the blindness that is at the core of his being, or the illusions that have guided his life. Oedipus is "the embodiment of the Greek being-there [Dasein], who radically and wildly asserts its fundamental passion, the passion for disclosure of being, i.e. the struggle for being itself."[26] Blinding himself, he becomes *what he already is.* This does not mean that he has attained insight or reached a higher level of truth. He manifests Dasein's understanding of itself as imperfect and finite. And there is no hidden promise that life will become better or clearer once his suffering is traversed.

This notion of tragedy has very little to do with praxis, with ethical and political insight. And yet Heidegger does have an idea of what it means at the level of community, although his understanding of it diverges from the German metaphysical tradition also on this point. Hegel shows us that the logic of tragedy points to a movement of negation serving to restore peace and order in the community, an affirmation of bonds through the sublation of conflicting elements. Heidegger, however, altogether avoids reading the conflict between the characters in the play—and this allows him to avoid an analysis of their social and sexual function. The essential in tragedy takes place in language, not in the destiny of the characters, and consequently the focus is on the ambiguities of Sophocles' choral odes. The insistence on reading the choruses, where not much is happening at all, is a radical means of questioning the notion that tragedy can convey some kind of ethical or political knowledge. What tragedy does is rather to poeticize Dasein as engaged in the world—in the conflicts between being and appearance, the authentic and the inauthentic, unconcealment and concealment. Those conflicts should not be transposed to or translated into another domain. They are anterior to or more original than those that could be claimed as a kind of knowledge in the practical domain. These conflicts are thematized not in the theatrics of the play but in its language, where Dasein expresses its own possibilities and limits. Greek tragedy is an art form that gives witness to the kind of finitude to which Dasein is exposed, coming to a truth about itself only through the radical questioning of its own capacities. In tragedy, Dasein presents itself *as* finite: violent and transgressive, but also vulnerable and finite. Both modes are closely related to the function of the community and not only to an individual Dasein. While Hegel explained the conflict of tragedy through the loss of given communal values, the framework that constituted the bonds of the community, Heidegger rather welcomes such a loss as an opening. The search for foundation opens a lack of ground and a need to establish a foundation elsewhere than in the values one has become accustomed to applying.

The difference from Hegel becomes clear: in this perspective, tragedy has nothing to do with conflicts between laws, social codes, and ethical norms. It is a poetic creation or re-creation of an original loss, a moment that gives the dignity of nonfoundational foundations to the bonds of the community. The move away from dialectics is performed in order to situate the conflictual orders of tragedy on a more primordial level. *Polis* is not an order that can be momentarily left in disarray and then arranged in a new fashion. Tragedy does not enact a split that could be remedied through new institutions and concepts. It opens, rather, a split that was already there, the ontological difference or split between being and beings that makes differentiation and movement possible. The *polis* is a site of language, art, culture, and other human practices. What we think of as modern politics is just one example of these practices. Reading Sophocles is a way of keeping the question of the *polis* open, since tragedy is a "poeticization" of the political.

As Philippe Lacoue-Labarthe has pointed out, it may well be that Heidegger fits into a certain tragic paradigm of German philosophy where the Greeks are used as a model of great art that the Germans hope to recapture.[27] Heidegger, like Hegel, Hölderlin, and Schelling, celebrates the tragic mode as an art form that allows us a privileged insight into the essential issues of philosophy. The project to produce great German art would then expect an authentic mode of the Germanic to present itself, which would mean that the question of being would present itself with the same directness and openness with which Greek Dasein presents itself in Greek tragedy. Given the political context in Germany in the 1930s, the widespread critique of Heidegger for this theory may be justified.[28] Even though tragedy lacks political or ideological purpose, and the notion of authenticity has nothing to do with the search for roots or origins—but rather of a lack of origins—the search for a space proper to the "Germanic being" of art makes Heidegger's readings of tragedy into the vehicle of another project. Here the political becomes just another word for a people's singularity, translatable into art, language, and thinking.

The link between Heidegger's insistence on making Dasein "neutral" and the political project is obvious. Continuously asking, searching, and questioning its existence, Dasein encounters the limit of its own finitude. Insisting on the poetic character of this limit, and the fact that all that is important in man's being is to be found beyond the social and sexual dimensions, Heidegger consequently poeticizes what cannot easily be referred to the sexual domain. But as we will see, his extraordinary understanding of certain founding moments in the play will allow us to reverse this reading and reintroduce sexuality. We might even find that Heidegger helps us to come to an understanding of the sexual moments in spite of his refusal to engage them openly.

"Hymn to Man"

Introduction to Metaphysics introduces us to what will become the major pursuit of Heidegger's work. Using Sophocles' texts as a vehicle, Heidegger reverses the relation between Dasein and truth: the disclosing of truth or the coming into being of truth is no longer an active pursuit undertaken by man, but rather takes place in and through him.[29] Such a concept of truth—or unconcealment—emerges from the texts of Parmenides and Sophocles under the eyes of a reader who is prepared to follow Heidegger's notion of tragedy as a poeticization of truth. Sophocles shows us the conflict between the realm of appearances or things and the realm of truth or the process of unconcealment. The truth of man's being consists in the exposure to the violence inherent in his own manner of engaging in the world. Man is tragic because his path to truth cannot be disassociated from a certain violence released in the process.[30] The desire to know, to conquer, and to construct is inseparable from violence. This violence is manifested through *techne*, the knowledge through which man comes to engage truth rather than appearances, and work his way beyond manifest appearances to an understanding of their organization, meaning, and function—this is the process of unconcealment. *Techne* is, however, not intellectual knowledge, but a knowing of the manner in which the function of unconcealment may come to be. *Techne* cannot be thought without the inducement of a certain violence. *Techne* wrestles with the construction and organizing of a world in which man is exposed to the finite character of his world and confronted with the necessity of overcoming it. The Greek notion of art, and tragedy, is such a *techne*.[31] It manifests a tragic structure of unconcealment, where the striving for truth through science and culture exposes man to the limits of his being.

Techne, as knowledge, is intrinsically intertwined with the violence through which the dimension of the uncanny opens up. Dasein is uncanny, or *deinon*, because it is detached and uprooted, thrown back upon itself, exposed to itself as neither belonging to the world nor separated from it. The second chorus shows how *techne* or man's capacity to create art, politics, and culture opens the violent dimensions of man's constitutional homelessness and uprootedness. One may perhaps talk of the uncanny as a violence through which man is exposed to the limits of his being. But only art shows us a truth that can be immediately associated with uncanniness itself.

The political also belongs to the domain of *techne*. It is colored by an aesthetic dimension, a fact that has inspired a lot of criticism.[32] Heidegger shows us that *Antigone* opens the question of the political through the uncanny dimensions of the play. Heidegger's notion of the political is not politics in the proper sense of the word—not an open space of discussion, deliberation, and decision, of plurality and collectivity. *Polis* is not a social structure, but a transient and transitional space, the site of *techne*—of building, constructing, and thinking. It is a site in constant motion rather than an order. *Polis* is "the swirl [*wirbel*], in which and around which everything turns," a site where the very lack of foundations for belonging in being are laid open, and where Dasein encounters the limits of self-understanding.[33] It is the opening of a negative space in the community that constitutes the bond between the various forms of Dasein which inhabit it, a space that must be kept open for the community to continuously renegotiate its values and its bonds. That negative space, which in Heideggerian language could also be called the question of being, forces us to reconsider the technocratic foundations of the modern community, where the political has become a formal rather than a philosophical issue.[34] We may conclude, then, that tragedy tells us something essential about the alterity on which the community is constructed. The Greek texts show us a *polis* that can only constitute a community on the basis of a continuous questioning of what is inherently foreign to it. There is no essential trait keeping the community together, no fitting of functions, no ethical order or harmonious whole. Its limits are not constituted by what is foreign to it in the sense of external to it: what is foreign to it is to be found in that which is the most familiar to it. *Polis* is a swirl constructed by the impossibility of establishing a ground for belonging. If tragedy has anything to do with the political, then, it concerns not the way in which the order of the community is constructed, but rather the question of belonging itself, a question that precedes any kind of social or political formation and any kind of collective bond. It precedes, therefore, the construction of the *polis*. The question of what is foreign to it has to be determined on grounds that relate to Dasein's ontological status. It is rarely discussed, however, to what extent one may introduce the issue of sexual difference here. Heidegger would never draw the conclusion that the feminine is foreign to the community on the basis of sexual difference. Nevertheless, Heidegger identifies Antigone as the foreign moment in Sophocles' tragedy. Looking closer at his argument, the fact that she is a woman is decisive.

Heidegger's unwilling sexuation of Dasein takes place through his understanding of one of the most enigmatic passages in the play, the so-called "Hymn to Man," the second *stasimon* after the introductory *parodos*. Man, the chorus sings, is the most remarkable of all beings, to *deinon*:

> Wonders are many, and none more wonderful than man.
> This being goes with the storm-wind across the foamy sea,
> moving deep amid cavernous waves. And the oldest of the gods,
> earth the immortal, the untiring, he wears away, turning the soil
>   with
> the brood of horses, as year after year the ploughs move to and
>   fro. (332–41)

As everyone who has followed the philosophical debate on tragedy knows, the first line, *polla ta deina*, is ambiguous. It can mean wondrous, marvelous, strange but also uncanny. The ambiguity refers to the ambivalent stature of man. Man has "strong power": he uses it for his own survival, is master over the animals, hunts, fishes, rides, plows.[35] But this power also makes him fearsome.

In Heidegger's ontological categories, the uncanny refers to an overpowering force that is awesome even in silence. At the same time, it refers to the violence exerted by someone disturbing the peace, which for Heidegger is the very definition of Dasein's capacity to think, create, and organize the world (*techne*). The chorus reveals an originary split in the human condition: man is cast out through an original act of violence, of which he is both the maker and the object. There is no conception of any original unity, nor of any desire to restore such a unity. Man is *unheimlich*, or uncanny, because of the violent conflict that defines his being. He is the strangest of all beings because he is homeless, cast out, estranging himself through the acts of violence that are his means of engaging in the world. This is the tragic predicament of his fallenness: he violently subdues nature, expanding his knowledge and building his world, and thereby widening a gap that in turn generates even more violence.[36]

Dasein will always be subjected to the order or jointure of *dike* (*Fug*). *Dike* is commonly read as justice, but Heidegger changes its connotation in order to apply it to the balance between the overpowering and the overpowered—man and nature. Presumably, it is conceivable that such balance could be found. But tragedy shows us that the order or jointure is challenged by man: this is the reason behind his tragic downfall. Tragedy shows us a disaster that "governs and waits in the conflict between violence and the overpowering."[37] Here we see that man incarnates the gap between the overpowering and the overpowered. Human existence *is* tragic, because human beings, as the most *deinon*, bring disaster upon themselves through their propensity to respond with violence to their own constitutional exposure. Dasein is "to be posited as the breach into which the preponderant power of being bursts in its appearing, in order that this breach itself should shatter against being."[38] Dasein is, in other words, fundamentally and irrevocably split. Man comes to "nothingness," the chorus reads; he is *aporos* in spite of the fact that he can go everywhere—he is *pantoporos*.[39] The words do not present an opposition, but rather indicate the capacity of man to open up possibilities and techniques that will eventually conceal their own ground. Capable of fantastic machinations, man loses himself in the appearances produced by his own capacities. He strives toward the limit of his being. He is always trying to expand his powers. Responding to the overpowering forces of nature, he comes up with clever schemes and constructions, showing an extraordinary capacity to think and create. But these fantastic machinations always hit upon something disruptive, threat-ening, uncanny. Man is the strangest of all beings because "without issue on all paths, he is cast out of every relation to the familiar and befallen by *ate*, ruin, catastrophe."[40] *Ate*, in Heidegger's reading, is the tragic disaster that awaits all human beings when they try to overcome their own limits and are tragically crushed in the process. The limits of Dasein are, in this way of looking at it, the other side of his extraordinary capacity. Moreover, the extraordinary capacity becomes a product of a final limit, which man strives both toward and against.

All that cancels out the aporia between the overpowering and the overpowered is man's being toward death, the only disaster he cannot over-come, as the chorus declares. Death is that *which one cannot escape*, as the chorus tells us; it is the limit of exposure.[41] Death is not just a moment when life ceases to be. It is an end that is always present in whatever proj-ect man undertakes. The experience of the uncanny, and of anxiety, when Dasein is thrown back upon itself as finite and limited, constitutes a kind of eclipse. But rather than simply making him weak, man's exposure to death and the tragic vulnerability that comes with it make him terrifying. To summarize, then: Greek Dasein is violent, it is a Dasein of *techne*, a Da-sein that hunts, chases, constructs, stopped only by death. This appears to be a very masculine Dasein. But then Heidegger has stopped with one cho-rus and obliterated its follow-up in the "Hymn to Eros."

"Hymn to Eros"

Heidegger's analysis could in fact be paired with a chorus that ap-pears later in the play, in the "Hymn to Eros." If Heidegger sees Dasein as uncanny because it is marked by death, then the "Hymn to Eros" presents erotic desire as uncanny. Death, for Dasein, is that *which he cannot escape*. But so is, we learn later, erotic desire. What Heidegger does not mention, however, is that *deinon* is picked up again and altered in the fourth chorus, "Hymn to Eros." What man cannot escape is no longer death but love:

> Love, unconquered in battle, Love, despoiler of wealth; you
> who pass your nights on a girl's soft cheeks, who range across
> the seas and through shepherd's lonely dwellings; no immortal
> can escape you, nor any short-lived men; and your possessor
> runs mad. (781–90)

No mortal can escape the madness of Eros, as unconquered and threatening as death in the second chorus. The madness and strife in the wake of Eros is a disease as incurable as death. The hymn is sung while Antigone is led toward her grave, and makes up one of many moments in the tragedy when Sophocles' language moves in an ambiguous space, mixing infatuation and destruction, inside and outside, feminine and masculine, life and death. Love and death are intrinsically intertwined, their cause unclear but their effects similar. Eros, like death, is the tool of *ate*, the inevitable ruin that Heidegger has told us reveals the uncanniness of man. Aphrodite, the goddess of love, is the goddess of destruction (800). Haemon, the primary tool of this logic, chooses death rather than life without Antigone. Antigone disregards the goods of life: husband, children, love. There is a perverted desire for death in her actions, a desire caused by the dead themselves, as she complains further on in the text:

> Ah, the calamity of a mother's bed, the ill-fated mother's
> incestuous embraces with my father—from what parents was
> I born, their wretched daughter! To them I go thus, accursed,
> unwedded, to share their home. Ah, my brother, maker of a fatal
> marriage, in your death you have destroyed me while yet I live.
> (863–71)

Antigone's distress is in fact caused by *contamination.* The dead have infected the living: her brother Oedipus has, through the fatal marriage to his mother, also destroyed his daughter/sister. The disease of death—for which man has not found a cure—is transformed into the disease of Eros. Antigone's desire is *caused* by the dead, thus the limit between life and death is undecidable. Sophocles returns to this trope in other tragedies: in *Ajax*, for instance, the death that overpowers Ajax is a contamination from the dead to the living. *Antigone* could be described as a continuous process of contamination, breaking down and reorganizing the codes of differentiation between love and death, wedding and funeral, heroism and madness, power and weakness, woman and man.[42] Death is not a projection, but something that has already taken place. You, my dear brother, Antigone says, even though you are dead, you have killed me who am alive. The dead want their Antigone, who returns to the bridal chamber of the cave. The *deinon* is evoked by her figure, because she is contaminated by someone who is already dead. The tragedy brings the origin of this contamination back to the most harrowing manifestation of feminine desire: a criminal and excessive example of a maternal embrace. Antigone's sight when she is arrested by the corpse of her brother is *deinon*, says the chorus—she is like an animal or a ghost giving up:

> A piercing cry, the shrill note of a bird, as it cries
> when it sees, in its empty nest, the bed bereft of nestlings.
> (424–26)

The uncanniness of Antigone is the desperation of a bereaved loving mother. Here we are brought back to the chorus, which tells us that the ruin of the family has its origin in the maternal bed. The mother is "ill-fated," her sexuality the cause of disaster, or *ate*. The text rings with the Homeric sense of *ate*, infatuation: Iocaste is blinded.[43] The punishment of the house of the labkakids begins with erotic blinding. If we read the second chorus together with the fourth, the uncanny dimensions of man may be seen to consist in the intertwinement of death and love, through Antigone and her chiasmic vacillation between cold death and hot passion, and through Creon's failure to correctly estimate the force of the divine powers of love. But the origin of the contamination is feminine. In the last part of the tragedy, Creon finds Haemon in Antigone's grave, embracing her dead body. Curiously, the embrace is described as a *peripeteia*, the same word used by Aristotle to describe the tragic hero's fall from fortune to misfortune.[44] Indeed, the embrace of Antigone's dead body—a "corpse enfolding a corpse" (1240)—mirrors her embrace of Polynices' rotting corpse and signifies the victory of Eros over human law. The tragedy leaves a destitute Creon holding his son and wailing like a woman. Transformed into a mirror of Antigone, Creon incarnates an excess that the tragic form fails to bind—a desire impossible to escape, because it is attached to death. Such is feminine desire.

Here we find a radical transformation of the masculine, "heroic" image of Greek Dasein as a conqueror and a virile producer of knowledge. In the last images of the play, when Dasein becomes what it already is for Heidegger, the function of unconcealment can no longer be equated with a virile kind of uncanniness or violence. What makes man both vulnerable and terrifying, what makes him uncanny, is, in the last verse, the fact that he incarnates the fatal contamination between desire and death, a contamination that Greek tragedy figures through its feminine characters. Greek Dasein, then, is hardly neutral in the unconcealment of its being; it is sexual, embodied, and feminine.

The Purest Poem . . .

Heidegger's second reading is from 1942, in *Hölderlin's Hymn "The Is- ter."* It to some extent repeats the *Introduction to Metaphysics*, for instance on the ambiguities of Sophocles' language. In 1942, however, the main is- sue is that of historicity and the belonging of a people. The question of *techne* is replaced by an interrogation into the relation between belonging and being. The uncanny dimension of being is revealed in the community or *polis* rather than through the overpowering forces of nature. Conse- quently, Heidegger's interest is transferred from the first strophes of the second chorus to the last, where the question of the foreign is raised. The question of belonging is reflected in the call to the Germans to become "more Greek than the Greeks," although the call is intended not to urge the Germans to embrace a mythical foundation of origin, but rather to cre- ate a notion of the singular and historical character of the German peo- ple.[45] In Heidegger's mind, such a notion of singularity and historical des- tiny is not the same as the ideology of blood and soil, *Blut und Boden.* It means, rather, that the German people have to recreate themselves contin- uously beyond the alienation and deceit of modern capitalism. The di- mension of uncanniness, therefore, brings us back to the language and lit- erature in which the question of belonging is exposed.[46] His reading of *Antigone* has been criticized for its rhetoric of authenticity.[47] But although the rhetoric is deeply ambivalent, the aim is to analyze the bonds formed in and through language, questioning an essentialist illusion of origin and identity. Belonging cannot be defined in a positive or affirmative way, in terms of a mythology of origin. The recreation of roots entails a recovery of the alterity inherent in one's heritage: only by exposing that which is for- eign to it can the singular character of a people begin to emerge.

Heidegger's second reading of *Antigone* argues against the techno- cratic foundations of the modern state. The state had, in his mind, become too Hegelian, too totalitarian, too convinced that it could do good for everybody. The closed state is for Heidegger, who was a member of the Na- tional Socialist party, not Hitler's Germany but the modern, democratic, capitalist state, which has forgotten the issues fundamental to the commu- nity. His rhetoric can be regarded as a critique of the modern democratic state, because of its inability to keep open the question of being and be- longing. Reading tragedy is a return to issues of belonging and nonbe- longing. The dimension Heidegger strives to unravel is that of the prepo- litical, a bond that precedes the formalized and structured organization of the community. *Antigone* is a poeticization that brings us back to this domain. Reading tragedy is a way of keeping the prepolitical open. This time, however, the question of the prepolitical is moved from the battle of nature to the hearth.

The notion of tragedy is the same as in the *Introduction to Metaphysics*: not much is happening at all, and nothing comes out in the end that was not already there in the beginning. It is not particularly important what the characters are doing, or how they relate to each other. The text resists a dual or dialectical understanding: "The two main figures, Creon and Antigone, do not stand opposed to one another like darkness and light, black and white, guilty and innocent. What is essential to each *is* as it is from out of the unity of essence and nonessence, yet in a different way in each case."[48] One would expect Heidegger not to resort to the same categories that Hegel used in his description of Antigone, but to overcome the categories of divine and human, feminine and masculine, natural and ethical. Using Antigone as a symbol of the prepolitical, however, he ends up referring to bonds that Hegel would describe as natural: blood ties and love.

When the function of being is revealed in such terms, it is difficult not to read through the grid of oppositions between nature and culture, woman and man, the foreign and the homely, although the question of being is intended to shatter such distinctions. So does Heidegger's discussion of belonging and nonbelonging really manage to unravel a truth in the text that lies beyond social and sexual categories, or is it a construction that uses the very categories he wishes to avoid? This issue takes us back to the complex discussion of sexual difference referred to above. Heidegger's reading of *Antigone* is an attempt to unravel Dasein in its purest form, without determinations such as gender. But the interpretation of the Antigone figure nevertheless brings us back to the question of whether sexual difference can be subordinated to ontological difference, and whether the truth of Greek Dasein can in fact be disassociated from sexual desire.

Repeating the problems of the first reading, the text stresses the uncanny, something in man that is strange or Other to himself, an alterity inherent in the human condition, which is brought to the fore through his capacity to speak and create.[49] A people understands itself as singular and historical in a language that poeticizes its being or names it. Poetry reveals the uncanny or homeless dimension of Dasein. Poeticizing means naming, and naming for Heidegger is an endeavor concerned with the dimension of being that is spoken of here in terms of being at home: being something, being named, being at home in language. Man is always seeking to define that which he is or seeking a home in language. In the process, he is thrown back upon himself as what is most uncanny—or *unheimlich* in German (literally, un-homely): "The uncanny means that which is not 'at home,' not homely, within whatever is homely."[50] The Ister course explores the constitutional homelessness heard in the word "uncanny" itself, connoting the alterity inherent in Dasein as a form of "seeking that at times does not know itself."[51] The uncanny presents itself in a moment when man encounters something other or foreign to him and gives a measure of his finite capacity.

The foreign is not simply someone who is excluded from the community, but rather a negativity or lack inherent to it. The origin or foundation of the community can never be defined in a positive or affirmative way. The foreign opens up the question of origin and belonging. The foreign, and the uncanniness that follows it, has nothing to do with sexual difference, according to Heidegger, as we have seen, but if we explore the layers and the blind spots of his reading, it appears anyway.

Not only does it matter what *deinon* means. It is an equally important question of interpretation *whom* the chorus points to as being *deinon* or uncanny. The key is given in the last lines of the chorus:

> Respecting the laws of the
> land and the right of oaths sworn by the gods, he is a man of a
> lofty
> city; cityless is he who recklessly devotes himself to evil. Never
> may
> he be a guest at my hearth or a sharer of my thoughts, who does
> these things. (368–78)

The first line, *noumos pareiron cthonos*, is most often translated as respect of the laws of the land. Sophocles' ambiguous language, however, makes possible a reading in which "cthonic laws" would refer to divine laws: citizens should revere both human and divine laws. Therefore, both Creon and Antigone are lawbreakers. So who should be expelled from the city? The text relies on Sophocles' means of suspension. Not clearly pointing out the object of the wrath of the gods, or who is guilty of the final bloodshed, the chorus directs the audience's eyes toward both Antigone and Creon as being denied the status of neighbor and excluded from the community. "Never may he be a guest at my hearth," the Theban elders say, providing Heidegger with the next keyword in his reading: *estia*, or hearth.

The most foreign is revealed in the most intimate dimension of the community. We are thereby brought back to the ambiguity of the term *deinon*. The uncanny, as we have seen, reveals the limit of belonging, of home or hearth. Exposing the boundaries of the community, she or he is uncanny who shatters the illusion of belonging. Man, says the chorus, is *upsipolis* and *apolis*. He is both belonging and not belonging to the community or *polis*.[52] He has a tremendous capacity for overstepping the boundaries he has created for himself—what is most foreign to him is also that which is most intimate to him.[53] Being shows itself not in the overpowering forces of nature, but through the disruptions and disturbances of what is seemingly natural and familiar. In spite of the ambiguous status of who is uncanny in the text, Heidegger relates uncanniness to Antigone. Linking the first strophes of the chorus to the last ones, Heidegger concludes that the whole tragedy is in fact a poeticization of Antigone. She incarnates the purest poem itself, which means that she incarnates the uncanny.[54]

Antigone is uncanny or foreign because of her pursuit of the impossible. She is up against something that one may call the impossibility of her desire. There is no sense in acting beyond our limits, says Ismene: "A quest for the impossible should not even be begun" (93). But Antigone is in conflict with all human possibilities because she takes as her "all-determinative point of departure that against which nothing can avail."[55] She is, in this regard, inhuman. This point of departure is death. If, for all other human beings, death is a limit or endpoint that makes their projects on this earth meaningful, Antigone makes it into a goal in itself. Antigone desires a *kalos thanein*, a "beautiful" death. Her beautiful death, Heidegger says, coincides with the tragedy's function of unconcealment.[56] The most poetic moment of the text, in which the alterity at the "hearth" of the community is to be found, coincides with her burial. Here the tragedy turns toward its own beginning, where, in Heideggerian language, being is unconcealed. In other words, this is the moment when Greek Dasein discovers the limits of its finitude. For Heidegger, this has to do with language, thinking, and creating: it has to do with the tragic form itself, through which Greek Dasein poeticizes and discovers the limits of his being. Antigone is tragedy's "supreme uncanny."[57] She poeticizes the unnameable extremes of existence: death and blood. Heidegger does not identify these natural bonds with being, but they are indicative of its function: they serve to present us with that which is most foreign in that which is most familiar to us—that which is the most "Heimlich" turns out to be the most "unheimlich."[58] "Blood" connotes family ties: Antigone brings us to the domain of the prepolitical, the natural, and the mythical. She takes us to the hearth, the bonds of the family. But what is closest to us is also what is the most foreign to us, because Dasein is not simply naturally at home in its family or its hearth. As an image of sheer poetry, and in poetizing the link to her brother through her death, Antigone disrupts and challenges the naturalized representations of belonging. Through this function, she discloses the lack of origin around which tragedy turns.

We have to go beyond the construction both of natural bonds and of social bonds in order to see what constitutes a condition of belonging. Pointing to what is foreign to the *polis*, tragedy shows us that the question of belonging can only be posed in a domain we could perhaps call antibonds, which encompasses what cannot be integrated into the community. The antibond is incarnated by Antigone's death—the poeticization of the "supreme uncanny." Making death into a supreme political statement, she shows us that the prepolitical is to be situated not in original bonds, but in an original question of belonging that precedes every social formation. Antigone points to a gap or hole around which the community is formed, which is *internal* rather than external to it. The prepolitical is linked to a site, but this site cannot be reduced to the family hearth. Instead, it points to a question of belonging that must be constantly renegotiated. This question of belonging can only be understood through language.

It is at this point that Heidegger's mixture of poeticization and political reasoning becomes problematic. He transforms politics into a question of culture, of the singularity of a people and their language, and thus forecloses the possibility of thinking the political in a modern, pluralistic society and state. This is a point that deserves a much longer comment, but in this context, the way in which Antigone becomes a symbol for the foreign, the uncanny, and the prepolitical is more interesting. Aestheticizing not only the sphere of the political but also the sphere of the prepolitical through his reading of Antigone, Heidegger presents us with a subtext on sexuality that is difficult to disassociate from his understanding of Greek Dasein.

What Heidegger Can Teach Us about Feminine Desire

Let us return, then, to the issues brought up at the beginning of this chapter. Does Heidegger's vision of Dasein as "neutral" liberate us from the

metaphysics of sexual difference? Does his reading of *Antigone* present a
Greek Dasein for us where all the important issues can be found in the
questions of language, time, and space that define Dasein, transcending
sexual difference? In the second reading, Heidegger tells us that Antigone
incarnates the "supreme uncanny" because she opens the space of nonbelonging through her death. Death is supposedly neutral. But at the same
time, the question is how we are to detach her death from her feminine position. Antigone belongs not to the political but to the prepolitical, which
for Heidegger does not just refer to mythology or a primitive state. The
prepolitical is rather a communal space that cannot be reduced to a state or
city. As a woman, a sister, and someone who is close to divine law (or to
passion, feeling, conviction, and so on) rather than human laws, Antigone
is the very incarnation of the prepolitical.[59] Antigone represents, after all, a
kind of "natural desire": death and blood. "Blood" stands for family ties, as
we have seen. But it also stands, as pointed out in passing by Heidegger
himself, for passion.[60] And if we look at Antigone's "beautiful" death, the
moment of unconcealment, it is in fact motivated by Eros: "I shall bury
him since it is beautiful to die doing such a thing: I shall lie by he whom I
love who loves me, I—the villain sanctioned by the gods" (73–76). The
chase after the impossible is not just forced by her search for her own origins, or by her own being through her return to death. It is colored by the
blood of sexual desire. In the text, one cannot separate the violent uncanniness of death from sexual conflict. Antigone opens a foreign aspect *internal* to the community of Greek Dasein. But she does so not as a neutral
being, but as a woman.

As a poem about the disruptions and disclosures of being, Sophocles'
text stands and falls with the identification of Antigone as tragedy's
"supreme uncanny." She discloses the split in *polis*. Through this quality,
she incarnates the pure poetry of the uncanny. Antigone, like Oedipus, is
a pure figure of Greek Dasein. As in the case of Oedipus, the tragedy shows
her becoming what she already is. Antigone herself *is* the uncanny, shut out
from the hearth for showing the gaps in its foundation but at the same
time disclosing the nonbelonging integral to any concept of belonging. As
such, Antigone, like Oedipus, represents a pure figure of Dasein that gradually unfolds in the text. In Sophocles' text, however, this pure poetry is
the result of a contamination: the mortal, finite body cannot be distin-
guished from the loving, sexual body. Beneath an ostensibly neutral discourse on Greek Dasein, a sexuated subtext can be discerned. Heidegger,
like Hegel, views the play as turning around the excessiveness of her deter-

mination—a desire that the text shows us to be intrinsically linked to her femininity. Heidegger's language is soaked in presumptions about femininity. The dimensions that are imagined to reveal being—the chase after the impossible, pure poetry, blood ties, and passion—and beings—(sexuality, femininity, and so on) are the product of a thought that is already steeped in the metaphysics of sexual difference and not an undoing of this tradition. *Deinon, ate,* the limits of one's being, and so on are in the end submitted to the themes of femininity, sexuality, and desire. It is, effectively, very difficult to leave out these issues from any lecture of *Antigone,* and it is difficult precisely for the reasons Heidegger gives: Greek being is violent and uncanny. Sexuality is intertwined with the tragic process as such. It is interesting, however, that Heidegger, even though he wants to overcome the conflicts of sexual difference, effectively manages to illuminate the dimensions of eroticism and sexuality through a powerful subtext in his reading. In the Greek world of *mythos,* to which tragedy belongs, the mortal body is always a sexuated body. Although Heidegger claims to identify a pure dimension of Greek Dasein, femininity, eroticism, love, sexual difference, and sexuality form a silent presence in the background.

Let us return to the other issue brought up in the beginning of this chapter: can Heidegger teach us something about feminine desire, in spite of the fact that he denies issues of sexual difference a place in his ontology? If we relate the "Hymn to Man" to the "Hymn to Eros," an interesting picture emerges. Whereas Hegel's attention is focused on the ethical order of the community, making sexual difference a major issue in his reading, Heidegger removes all social, sexual, and legal contextualization of the tragic conflict in order to propound a more original vision. There is no direct consideration of the dialectics surrounding the ethical issues of the play, or any consideration of how these ethical issues have been gendered or determined by the sexual collision as it is figured in the play. The conflicts of tragedy that are of interest to Heidegger belong to what he calls in his course on logic the metaphysically neutral aspects of Dasein, which transcend the manifestations of gender. His ambition to read Sophocles at the level of ontology may seem both abstract and reductive. But at the same time it would be wrong to claim that he simply attempts to transcend political and ethical issues altogether. His questions are situated at another level: what creates the bonds of the community, what makes the political possible, what grounds the possibility of an ethics? At this level, Heidegger's suggestion that sexual difference has to be subordinated to other categories must be questioned.

Antigone is pure poetry because she opens up this foreign aspect through the question of belonging, and she opens it up because she is a woman emerging from what is most familiar and natural to any question of belonging—the hearth. It would, of course, be an exaggeration to state that Heidegger has modeled Greek Dasein after a feminine position. But his analysis of tragedy is colored by a subtext in which we encounter what is foreign in and to the community as feminine desire. Although Heidegger was unable to go beyond the metaphysical baggage he wanted to undo and remains indifferent to questions of sexual difference and feminine desire in this context, but at the same time he manages to transcend the presupposition that femininity is either natural (determined by an ethical or biological essence) or constructed. In reading Antigone as a figure of Greek Dasein, Heidegger indirectly shows that femininity is a tragic position because it is more exposed to the element of foreignness that determines all philosophical questioning, and it is more exposed because feminine sexual desire is inseparable from destruction and disaster in Greek mythology.

A picture emerges that could serve as a substitute for a theory of feminine desire that Heidegger never had. His views may well be engaging also for a feminist theoretician trying to explore sexual difference in a manner which is neither reductive nor simplistic, because this is a sketch that is as interesting as it is provoking: from a Heideggerian point of view, feminine desire is not teleological, it is not determined by a goal in terms of an object or in terms of feminine duties. It is not determined by biological functions, and it is not made up of natural bonds that ascribe different functions to the sexes, as Hegel would have it. But it cannot be reduced to a social or cultural construction either, or to the logic of a social and historical structure that gives it a certain place and function in the community. Feminine desire is rather a pure or naked figure for the kind of impossibility that is found at the heart of Dasein: a striving after something impossible, because it is a striving after something that realizes itself only through that which is most foreign to Dasein, through death. In this sense, feminine desire is a figure that is not about femininity in terms of sexual or social status, but rather about a foreignness that shatters the ground of neutrality on which the being of Dasein is supposed to stand. The feminine opens up a foreign aspect internal to Dasein, and a foreign aspect internal to the community. It is Antigone, rather than Oedipus, who provides us with a clear image of what the uncanniness of being actually means, and it is Antigone rather than Oedipus who shows that ontological questioning necessarily involves a foreign aspect, not least in the question of the political. Communal bonds are constructed in contrast to something that cannot be integrated in the community. In the case of Sophocles' *Antigone*, this is feminine desire itself—the chase after the impossible—which stands for this antibond or excluded factor, which provokes the communal bonds to take shape. Perhaps femininity is neither substance, nor social, nor sex for Heidegger, but merely this necessary element of foreignness that allows for Dasein to perceive of itself as ridden with an internal conflict that makes it both more interesting and more enigmatic than if it had been marked by a sexuality and a desire the meaning of which was clear to it, pure and simple. In that case, there is a link stronger than Heidegger wants to admit between feminine desire, at least as it was depicted by the Greeks, and ontological questioning.

From Oedipus to Antigone: Revisiting the Question of Feminine Desire

Establishing an Antigone Complex

One may, as George Steiner writes, ask what would have happened if psychoanalysis had chosen Antigone rather than Oedipus.[1] To some extent, we have already seen the results of such a shift. The Antigone figure is well on her way to replacing Oedipus as a paradigm of modern subjectivity. In contemporary thought, this figure has been made into a metaphor for individuation, ethical action, uncompromising desire, feminist revolt, and the collapse of heteronormativity. Lacan writes in *The Ethics of Psychoanalysis* that Antigone reveals "the line of sight that defines desire."[2] Oedipus has been replaced by an *Antigone complex* that either modifies Freud or puts his ideas into question. As is well known, the feminist critique of Freud has particularly targeted his writings on female sexuality. As early as the 1930s, he was criticized by female psychoanalysts for making female sexuality derivative in relation to Oedipus rather than attempting to define another kind of desire.[3] Rather than criticizing Freud's suppression of that relation, however, I propose to question the naturalization of desire and sexuality according to a given structural model. The philosophical usefulness of Antigone stretches beyond merely questioning the definition of the feminine as a reversal of an Oedipal subjectivity; Antigone does not demonstrate a feminine paradigm of desire comparable to that of Oedipus. She changes the premises from which the question of desire must be thought: rather than inverting the gendered bias of Oedipus as a symbolic structure, Antigone challenges the idea that desire can be reduced to a symbolic structure at all—be it social, linguistic, or something else. The argument of this book is that desire cannot be detached from the question of ethics, and the aim of this chapter is to demonstrate a path through which psychoanalysis and feminism can be said to open a philosophical elaboration of such an argument. My first move will be to show the inadequacy of understanding Antigone's desire in symbolic or structural terms. The key figures here are Simone de Beauvoir in her critique of Freud and Jacques Lacan in his theorizing of female sexuality.

The nature of sexuality is ambiguous in psychoanalytic discourse; it is considered both a product of cultural determinations and corporeal needs and as a force of culture itself. Freud, for instance, having famously suggested the thesis of an original bisexuality in *Three Essays on Sexuality*, implies that cultural norms force an otherwise untamed sexuality toward an acceptable set of objects.[4] Even more importantly in this context, however, sexuality or at least the sublimation of sexuality contributes to cultural structures, according to Freud. Never completely separating what one could perhaps call the sexual drives or the libido and issues of culture, the psychoanalytic movement tends to use the term "sexuality" when it refers to what Hegel would include in the domain of natural desire: sensuality, corporeal pleasure, satisfaction, and so forth. At the same time, the concept of sexuality refers to a lot more. In psychoanalysis, as Juliet Mitchell points out, sexuality not only refers to genital pleasure or libidinal drives: "It is always psychosexuality, a system of conscious and unconscious human fantasies involving a range of excitations and activities that produce pleasure *beyond the satisfaction of any basic physiological need*."[5] Given this element of excess in the conception of human sexuality, it can never be wholly reduced to a cultural or structural determination. This is particularly poignant in the theoretical treatment of feminine sexuality, which is badly adapted from and even threatening to the Oedipal structure. The Oedipus complex is articulated within a structural framework that makes male desire coherent with a patriarchal logic of prohibition and metonymic displacement. The law of prohibition is paternal, the object always feminine. The Oedipal function makes us into subjects in a negative space of prohibition, circumscribed by the law prohibiting incest. This law demands that the desire directed toward the mother be displaced. The Oedipus complex defines every female body as a potential object or substitute. Thus the function of the prohibitive law is not only to prohibit the maternal body as object but in fact to *construct* an object in its absence. The law therefore serves a twofold function: it creates an empty space where the maternal object used to be, an empty space that could be called the condition of possibility of desire. It also makes access to another object possible. Under patriarchal conditions, the object is provided by a certain order that is coherent with the aim of desire. The maternal body is prohibited and desire displaced onto an eligible woman. Beneath the Freudian argument lies the implicit presumption of structuralism—objects of desire can be exchanged and possessed. Freud's Oedipus therefore continues to live in the illusion that the lost maternal object can be continuously replaced by other women. But for women the case is different. There is no immediate coherence between the prohibiting law and the object of desire, and therefore no possibility of simply constructing a metonymic chain of displacements from the maternal body. Even more importantly, perhaps, there is no way a woman could imagine that she would be able to have or possess the object of desire. Her relation to the object must look different altogether.

Freud's Oedipal paradigm, at least as it has been presented in texts on feminine sexuality such as "The Dissolution of the Oedipus Complex" (1924) and "Female Sexuality" (1931), is concerned with father, mother, daughter, and son. In these texts, Freud's ordering of the family is intrinsically bound up with the theory of the Oedipus complex, which serves as the foundation of sexual identity and desire. Male heterosexual desire may be obsessive and fetishist, but in the many cases where feminine desire remains childlike and undeveloped, it does not even develop into a complex neurotic variety. By taking Oedipus as the paradigm of desire, Freud placed women outside of the founding structures of our culture. From a Freudian point of view, it is an enigma how women can desire at all. Lacking a phallus, a girl is castrated from the beginning. She takes up a passive position, hoping that another penis or a child will be given to her as a substitute for the paternal phallus.[6] At the same time, she takes up a defensive position in relation to her mother, who becomes both loved as an object and hated as a rival.[7] As many female psychoanalysts in the Freudian tradition, from Melanie Klein to Julia Kristeva, have pointed out, it is a far easier task for the boy than for the girl to undergo the process of separation, because of the girl's identification with the maternal body. Melancholy, a kind of "blank perversion," restrains and binds her, leaving her riveted to silence and self-hatred.[8] Her desire becomes self-destructive and incoherent.

For boys, the Oedipus complex is dissolved through submission to paternal law—castration. He gives up his mother. Identifying with the father, he wants to replace the prohibited maternal body with another woman. This transformation of infantile desire into a functioning model has significant cultural implications. But it should not be mistaken for a normative model, and it would be a mistake to read Freud as a normative thinker on the psychosexual models of gender, as the thesis of original bisexuality indicates. Sexuality is consistently regarded as an excess in relation to any possible social order, and the normative implications of the Freudian argument on Oedipus are problematized in an even deeper sense through a morality that is in itself perforated by the themes of pleasure and excess. Among the most significant cultural implications of the Oedipal model is the capacity to integrate a normative order and a moral judgment through the superego, a correlative of a definition of sexual identity that remains nebulous in Freud's writings. When the father institutes the law against incest, the nucleus of the superego is formed. The boy learns to sublimate and his desire becomes coherent with cultural and moral values.[9] Sublimation is a kind of desexualization of thought. It is not only necessary for the development of the individual and his or her capacity to think and reflect on the world. It is necessary to desexualize human behavior if society is to work at all and if culture is to develop. Desexualization and castration are two sides of the same process, making possible sublimation and the installation of moral judgment. This is the point at which the Enlightenment idea of feminine desire as intrinsically excessive and unproductive continues, it seems, to have an effect on twentieth-century psychoanalysis. Freud assumed the female superego to be less developed than its male counterpart. A woman is less capable of sublimating because she lacks the organ for it: the phallus. The status of that assumption—that the installation of law and the superego are less dominant in the development of her personality than in the boy—is quite ambiguous in his writings. It is easy to assume from that point of view that women are less morally capable, that they will never achieve the cultural and moral capacity that is acquired by boys with the dissolution of the Oedipus complex.[10] Since the superego is a prerequisite for social functioning, women become socially weaker. They lack ethical sensibility, are less developed, and are more prone to emotional responses in situations that are morally demanding.[11] Instead of transforming sexual energies and instincts into cultural and intellectual achievements, they remain bundles of sexual sensitivity. In *Three Essays on Sexuality*, Freud shows that infantile sexuality, as experienced and obliterated in memory in the so-called prehistory of the individual, is awakened not through the genitals but through other zones satisfying the auto-erotic impulses of the individual. To these zones belong the mouth and the pleasure of thumb-sucking, which in Freud's view is a continuation of the gratification gained in sucking the mother's breast: "No one who has seen a baby sinking back satiated from the breast and falling asleep with flushed cheeks and a blissful smile can escape the reflection that this picture persists as a prototype of the expression of sexual satisfaction in later life."[12] However, sexual gratification is later separated from the needs of nourishment, in the process where the child begins to discover his own auto-erogenous zones. Any region of the body, says Freud, can serve this function. The child has a polymorphously perverse disposition and can therefore be seduced into all kinds of transgression. Also, sexual difference is not yet explored in the pregenital phase, and so this form of sexuality has little to do with any cultural conception of identity. Later in life, however, women rather than men are left with the remainders of this phase as part of their erotic disposition. Freud famously suggested that women are polymorphously perverse, like children. Because their whole body is an erogenous zone, they are incapable of resisting sexual pleasure. They can, in principle, be lured into any kind of erotic excess, such as prostitution.[13] Failing Oedipus, the polymorphously perverted sexuality of the woman dominates her being and overshoots any attempt at Oedipal adaptation. Perhaps this is what Freud meant when he famously said that he did not know what women *wanted*: "Woman is the dark continent," the object of her desire is still "veiled in an impenetrable obscurity."[14] Rather than expressing a form of subjectivity different from the one structured by Oedipus, feminine desire is considered an Oedipal failure. At the same time, it is tempting to see Freud's hesitant conception of feminine sexuality as a symptom of the problematic theoretical status of sexuality, irreducible to cultural, social, biological, or "natural" factors. One must, again, be wary of reading Freud's remarks on the failings of Oedipal structuring in women as the result of a coherently gendered normative system. And if we look at the intrinsic relation between ethics and feminine desire that has been observed elsewhere in philosophy, then the real challenge of feminine desire lies not in the failure to identify with the phallus, but rather in a relation to the superego that remains either excessive or deficient.

Given the highly ambivalent status of the superego in Freud's writings, this could perhaps have been regarded as something positive. Ethical demands, for Freud, play an ambiguous role in the maintenance of the morality of the modern subject. Freud himself was the first to recognize the fact that ethics is always intertwined with desires and drives. Cultural and ethical values are supported by the superego, according to Freud, and the superego is as cruel as it is aggressive—situated in the domain of the drive rather than reason. In *Civilization and Its Discontents* (1930), Freud questions the value of ethical principles, equating their function with a punishing superego. Disclaiming their significance in the process of cultural and social change, he suggests replacing them with psychoanalysis.[15] A normative ethics, pressing the ego to respond to what it *ought* to do, does very little if man is permeated by an aggressive instinct that perpetually threatens society with disintegration. The only shield we have from aggression is the guilt produced by the superego, which watches over the aggressive instincts "like a garrison in a conquered city."[16] Freud identifies ethics as the kind of moral values that are passed on to us through religion, for instance, and therefore with "the command of the superego." Christian ethics is a therapy intended to keep aggression at bay.[17] However, through such injunctions the superego becomes hypertrophied and excessive, threatening to extinguish the self under a burden of impossible demands. Through the superego, we become reflecting, socialized beings. However, the superego also threatens to destroy us to the extent that it operates on the thin line between socialization and punishment under impossible demands. The more we sacrifice to the superego, the more punishing it becomes. For this reason, one could perhaps speculate that feminine perversity would bring productive aspects with it: if Oedipus is avoided, then the potential severity of the superego is undermined. If the installation of law and superego is weaker, then their aggressiveness, which causes so many problems in the Freudian notion of civilization, would be undermined. Feminine enjoyment—narcissistic, melancholic, hysteric, masochistic, or frivolous—may seem to point to serious gaps in the foundation of the so-called Oedipal structure, but Freud resists the idea that a failed or weakened Oedipus complex would be a fruitful challenge to a punishing superego. Feminine desire is considered anarchic in his writings, but not in a productive sense. In *Civilization and Its Discontents*, it is a disturbance and a threat to cultural values and ethical norms, but it does not alleviate the destructive tendencies of the superego, which feeds off these norms. Feminine desire is simply resisting the structures on which society builds. It is effectively detrimental to culture, a "retarding and restraining" influence.[18] Situating feminine desire at the margins of the culture, Freud, like Hegel, sees feminine desire as both a deficiency and an excess in relation to the ethical life of the community.

Beauvoir and the Situation of Sex

For Simone de Beauvoir, formulating a feminist critique of Freud in *The Second Sex* (1949), psychoanalysis is identical with patriarchy. Not only is desire viewed as male according to the Oedipal scheme, but it relies on a structural assumption of exchange that makes women into objects. It is therefore impossible to come up with a feminine model of subjectivity, which is the famous point of departure for Beauvoir's book: "One would have to ask whether women still exist, if they will always exist, and whether or not it is desirable that they should."[19] As Beauvoir shows, the categories used to explain sexual difference as natural or biological are mistaken or inadequate. But this does not mean that Beauvoir resorts solely to cultural forms of explanation—her critique of structuralism is very harsh, not least in the points that tie in with her critique of psychoanalysis. The problem with Freud, Beauvoir complains, is that he takes for granted the founding prohibition against incest. Psychoanalysis makes the analysis of femininity too dependent on a patriarchal structure of possession and exchange, whereas only an ontology that deals with notions such as finitude, natality, and projection could explain sexual difference *beyond* its social and cultural expressions. In a society where woman is made an object of desirability and given a certain mystique, expressions of femininity say little about the truth of her desire, or *projects*, if we may freely transpose Beauvoir's terminology into the topic of this book. In order to find a better theory of the nature of our projects or desire, we need to acquire a more adequate understanding of what it means to be a finite, embodied subject. Beauvoir's critique of the Freudian paradigm of feminine sexuality calls for an ontological analysis rather than a circular description of existing social structures. This means making sexual difference a question of ontology and no longer using existing social and cultural structures as means to explain things that are in fact pathologies resulting from these structures. Beauvoir rightly regards Freud as a kind of structuralist, with views comparable to Lévi-Strauss's theory of the incest taboo. What Lévi-Strauss calls "our elementary structure of kinship" is based on a certain pattern of exchange of goods and possessions, all dictated by one fundamental law: the prohibition against incest, which forces men to search for wives outside of the family.[20] The prohibition against incest makes man want to possess "that which he *is not*, he seeks union with what appears to be *Other* than himself."[21] But the real problem of psychoanalysis, says Beauvoir, is that it "fails to explain why woman is the *Other*."[22] Desire must be more than a simple consequence of the incest taboo. It has to do with the power of projection and the capacity of transcending oneself, a capacity that cannot simply be defined in terms of a social power structure. If we define desire only in terms of the incest taboo, feminine desire falls outside of this social economy altogether, although the model of possession and exchange may explain why women are alienated as objects. A woman sees herself mirrored in male eyes and tries to please. She alienates herself in choosing an object of identification through which she becomes Other also to herself.[23] Being her own imaginary object, she is unable to break the narcissistic game of the mirror. The only power women have is that they control the game of seduction. From this point of view, they are unable to authentically assume a subjective position.[24] Woman is split also in relation to herself. Psychoanalysis may show us the way this split functions, but it does little to elucidate the question of why women play the Other in our culture. And it does little to explain how femininity can be considered a form of subjectivity in itself and not simply be reduced to objectal status. It is not possible to presume that patriarchy lives off woman as an object of desire and then to define *her* desire starting from this fact. So long as psychoanalysis remains stuck in a structural model of possession and exchange, it does little to contribute to the ontological investigation of sexual difference.

How are we to construct an explanatory framework of sexuality that does not begin with patriarchal hierarchy? In other words, how are we to avoid the kind of circular reasoning that examines feminine desire from a given set of assumptions about the law, the body, and the status of femininity? Rather than relying on a structural explication of laws, Beauvoir makes *sexuality* into the point of departure of her analysis. Our view of the desiring subject has to be rethought from the perspective of the embodied, finite subject. Here, psychoanalysis helps us. It is a "tremendous advance" over biologism and its objectification of the body.[25] Psychoanalysis affirms the embodied subject as a *lived* body rather than as a head with detachable limbs or a mind detached from a thing-like body. In this way, Freud helps Beauvoir formulate a theory of sexuality that cannot be reduced to eroticism. Sexuality, for Beauvoir, is a "situation" or a "limiting factor for our projects."[26] It cannot be understood in the abstract sense as a life force either: "We could more fully encompass reality if instead of defining the libido in vague terms of 'energy' we brought the significance of sexuality into relation with that of other human attitudes—taking, capturing, eating, making, submitting, and so forth; for it is one of the various modes of apprehending an object."[27] From this point of view, femininity becomes a project rather than a simple biological fact. Sexuality determines the way we relate to the world, the way we project, and the way we perceive an object. Men and women project differently, not for physical reasons, but rather because they have a different relation to finitude. For men, the phallus and the capacity to transcend are the measure of their projects. For women, it is their bodies and their capacity to give birth.

The phallus is a tool of negation. With the phallus comes the power to desire what one is not, a means of transcendence projecting the little boy out of his corporeal prison into a world of culture and ideas. Phallic transcendence is not biologically determined, however. The idea that the phallus is an active organ, as opposed to a woman's passive one, is just a myth. The power of the phallus has to do with its value. The little boy mirrors himself in the penis as a source of power and pleasure. At the same time, he is not entirely at one with it. Through this split between corporeal pleasure and projective points, he acquires his identity.[28] Female penis envy has nothing to do with the organ itself, but comes from the presumed power of projection that derives from the split. Women, who are unable to transcend their corporeal situation, do not want to deprive a man of his penis: they want the access to transcendence that it brings. It would seem, then, that anatomy decides all, but Beauvoir dismisses the idea that the phallus is a given sign of distinction. A tool of negation and transcendence, the phallus signifyies a lack of being rather than being.[29] On the other hand, femininity is not simply determined by a lack of the phallus and thereby devalued. Men seek transcendence and find a way out of their corporal situation because they have a phallus. Women, in turn, are dedicated to the principle of natality.[30] They protect life, rather than risking it. The cost is a smaller capacity to transcend their corporeal situation. Femininity as natality is not simply biological determinism: "The perpetuation of the species does not necessitate sexual differentiation." In theory, we could all be hermaphrodites and still have children.[31] Moving from a biological description of sexual difference to sexuality, Beauvoir describes the relation between the sexes in terms of tension rather than complementarities. The sexes are a basic unit of *Mitsein* that complement each other as two halves, striving toward the continuation of mankind.[32] At the same time, they remain in conflict, dividing the community into the antagonistic entities of two sexes. Women, bearing children, draw the shortest straw. The duty of a woman is to protect life. She cannot risk anything in the ongoing conflict. If we look at Beauvoir's work as a whole, this idea is in line with her argument of the body as a situation. The fact that woman is Other in our society, that she is invoked as nature, unconsciousness, and flesh, has to do not only with the projections and fears that have been mapped onto her being. There is an element of woman's otherness that has to do with her corporeal situation, with the way she lives in her body. Determined by natality rather than phallic transcendence, femininity has a different relationship to the lack of being. But she is Other not only because she does not have a penis. Projecting as natality makes woman into too much body.[33] Beauvoir's ontological investigation into the question of sexual difference inspires a definition of desire based on sexuality, irreducible to social or cultural terms, rooted in a corporeal situation.

Lacan's Missing Phallus

There is a conspicuous absence of comments on Beauvoir in Lacan's work. They did get in touch with each other, however. Just before the publication of *The Second Sex*, the curious Beauvoir called Lacan to arrange for discussions on feminine sexuality. Lacan, however, asked for so much time that the meeting never took place.[34] Beauvoir includes a reference to Lacan's mirror stage in *The Second Sex*. Lacan, for his part, mentions Beauvoir only a couple of times in passing. Beauvoir scholars, such as Toril Moi, sometimes speculate on what might have happened if Lacan's influence on Beauvoir had stretched further.[35] The fact that Beauvoir could have had an influence on Lacan, however, has hardly been mentioned. The absence of Beauvoir is notable even in feminist introductions to Lacan, such as those by Jane Gallop and Elisabeth Grosz.[36] And yet it seems as if the very absence in Lacan of the name of the most important feminist of his day, working in the same Hegelian tradition as himself, ought to give pause. Even if Lacan insists on being a Freudian, and even if he lacks feminist inclinations altogether, he joins Beauvoir's search for an alternative to Freud's Oedipus, and makes feminine sexuality a central issue. Many years after the publication of *The Second Sex*, in *Encore* (the seminar from 1972–73), Lacan responds to Beauvoir's question of whether there are any women at all: "Woman does not exist."[37] This is not an existential argument, but rather relates to that other challenge from Beauvoir: the question of why woman is the Other. In Lacanian thought, this question must be analyzed in relation to the place of woman in the symbolic order—or rather in relation to her lack of place in it. Many feminist interpreters have found this aspect of Lacan's thought provocative, but in order to assess it, one must look closer at the status of the symbolic order as such. Close to the Oedipal structure, many have equated it with Lévi-Strauss's idea of the incest taboo as a founding civilizing order.[38] It is of course true that the paternal prohibition is the most poignant expression of the symbolic. The human order, says Lacan in the 1950s, "is characterized by the fact that the symbolic function intervenes at every moment and at every stage of its existence."[39] We are always inside of it, and we cannot get out of it.[40] At the same time, it is autonomous in relation to the experience of human beings. It is what is most elevated in man and what is not in man at all.[41] The symbolic order, therefore, is intrinsic to human subjectivity, the incorporation of the law being precisely that which makes subjectivity possible. But this does not mean that the symbolic order determines human subjectivity or sexual difference through a single castrating cut. In Lacan's work on feminine sexuality in *Encore*, which must be considered some of his most precise work on sexual identity and desire, the definition of the symbolic is an order of signifiers, which does not simply mean that it can be equated with a language operating autonomously in the subject. The symbolic intervenes in human life not through a simple discursive determination of experiences and phenomena, but rather through the effect of the signifier on the subject: although there is no possibility of a subject outside of symbolic sexuation, gendered subjectivity can never be unambiguously determined. Such lack of determination makes the symbolic order if not incompatible with structuralism and its ideas of the incest taboo, for instance, at least irreducible to it. Lacan seems to give the same crucial place to the incest taboo as Freud did, and the same prominence to the system of exchange of women. In patriarchy, woman is "what is indicated by the elementary structures of kinship, i.e., nothing more than a correlative of the functions of social exchange, the support of a certain number of goods and of symbols of power."[42] But at the same time, the structure of kinship transforms human beings into signs.[43] This means that subjects are never simply identical with the various family signifiers: mothers, fathers, daughters, sons, women and men, and so on. A subject is a signifier representing something for another signifier, and the subject is always *ex-static* in relation to the signifier: it is never completely at one with it.[44] There is no authentic form of subjectivity, neither for women nor for men. The moment we become signs for each other, marked by sexual difference, we also become signs to ourselves and alienated from our bodies. The subject never *inhabits* its signifier but is somehow always outside of it, foreign to himself—or herself. This aspect of foreignness belongs to the domain Lacan calls the real: it can perhaps be translated as corporeality, flesh, drives, and so on. Lacan never places the sexes in their bodies. His only interest in the factual body lies in its eluding qualities and its inaptitude to "fit" the signifiers. Sexuality causes a radical signifying ambiguity: "The function from which only life can define itself, namely the reproduction of a body, can itself neither be called life nor death, because it is sexuated as such, it carries both life and death."[45] Sexuated means marked by sexual difference, a mark that perforates all domains of our lives without being contained by signifiers.

Nowhere does the ex-static formation of the subject present itself more powerfully than in the relation between the sexes—or rather, nowhere does the component of the real present itself more powerfully. Sexual difference can only be referred to the symbolic, or perhaps rather the lack in the symbolic order, not to physiognomy or biological facts.[46] The inscription of sexual difference never results in a "safe" sexual identity. It leaves a kernel that resists positive definition. The desire of men and women never completes one another. What they want is missing in the first place—sexual difference is asymmetrical, not complementary.[47] The process of sexuation consists in taking up a position in relation to desire that is incompatible with that of the other sex. A male subject wants to *have* the phallus. A female subject wants to *be* the phallus. Thus she desires to be that which cannot possibly exist, a fulfillment and a totality in the symbolic function itself. There is no signifier for the sexual relation as such, only a cut between two asymmetrical positions. The lack does not refer to a missing object or thing. It implicates a void inscribed into the way the sexes are related to each other. In this way, Lacan challenges the traditional Oedipal theory of the castration complex, which reflects a phallic culture. For Freud, the missing penis is a significant lack.[48] The lack referred to in Lacanian theory is primarily the lack of a signifier that would cover, include, and explain sexual difference. The lack in the symbolic order represents a traumatic tearing out from the world, which presents us with a void: "Where there is no sexual relation, we find a 'traumatism.'"[49] There is always a component of the real in sexual identification. In short, one is never simply a man or a woman; some part of one's sexual identity always falls outside the possibility of signification. The asymmetrical relation assures that there is no moment when the mark of sexual difference could possibly affirm itself and the qualities of femininity and masculinity crystallize. Sexual differentiation means failure, not procreation and pleasure. Sexual difference is a traumatic lack inscribed into the symbolic system of signification as such. It is a common misconception that maternal night would precede the Law and motivate the need for symbolic castration.[50] There is no maternal precultural chaos, although Elisabeth Grosz has rightly pointed out that the phallus is an overdetermined symbol that can never be wholly disassociated from patriarchal ideology.[51] But Lacan's phallus is far removed from the paternal order described by Freud, or the jubilant transcendence described by Beauvoir. Traditionally, psychoanalysis asked about the female sex: why is there nothing instead of something? Changing the point of view, Lacan returns to the classical philosophical question: why is there something instead of nothing? Why has the phallus been made so culturally significant that it is possible to claim it as a primary signifier? The real question here, of course, does not really concern the significance of the phallus but rather the way in which a signifier functions. Lacan uses a famous metaphor to explain it: the "making" of the signifier could be compared to the making of a vase. The vase originates in the clay surrounding a hole, not in the hole itself. It actually manages to create a hole.[52] It is the same with the signifier: it refers to an absence rather than a presence, but at the same time it has the status of a something. The phallus has a similar function. We begin with the phallus, rather than the empty space of the female sex. The signifier of the phallus constructs a void and points to an absence. Lacan kept Courbet's scandalous painting *L'origine du monde* in his summerhouse. After having disappeared for years, it was found hidden behind his furniture. In the painting, which was considered so obscene that it could not be shown in Courbet's own lifetime, a woman opens her legs so that we see everything, from stomach to vulva. The title of the painting, *The Beginning of the World*, has a particular significance in this context. We may think of a creation ex nihilo: the creation of something out of nothing, the creation of the world out of the empty space of a vulva. In Gustave Courbet's painting, the cave-shaped sex of a woman symbolizes an origin depicted as an empty space. But the origin, in actual fact, is a construction *après-coup*, and not an origin literally speaking. The void of the female sexual organ is pointed to and depicted as an empty space only because the phallus has been made into a signifier.

The same logic applies to the famous proposal that woman does not exist. Woman can only "exist" as excluded from the symbolic chain that constructed her. She is not an object in the Lévi-Straussian sense, but rather a sign. The signifier "woman" covers a lack in the discursive order, and in this sense it is an "empty" signifier. "Woman" is that nonentity, that "signifying nothing" that threatens to disrupt the economy of desire. The contiguous relation between feminine desire and the signifier "man" reveals a constitutive failure in the symbolic itself, the open end of its construction. In the *Encore* seminar, woman is not simply the Other, but the not-one. Not a mirror of the male image, but a fantasmatic product of the patriarchal system. The lack in the Other, or the lack of sexual relation, is symbolically covered by, above all, "the woman," or rather the universal signifier "woman." The famous assertion by Lacan that "Il n'y a pas *la* femme . . . de son essence, elle n'est *pas toute*" (There is no such thing as woman, because in her essence . . . she is not-whole) refers to the fact that "woman" is a signifier, an arbitrary signifier like all others but a signifier that has been deeply mystified by culture.[53] There is not *the* woman in the universal sense, no feminine subjectivity that lends itself to the universalizability that language allows us to indicate. Femininity is not defined by the universal signifier of *the* woman, because there is no symbol that would supplement and define the signifier of woman with a plausible notion of her desire, for instance. Whereas masculine sexuality is founded on the phenomenon of castration and the installation of an object-replacement for the phallus, there is no such universal definition of feminine sexuality and, unlike the male position, there is no definition of a feminine coming into being that could univocally depend on a symbol like the phallus. The feminine subject incorporates an ambiguity that applies to all corporeal beings in language, an ambiguity that the symbol of the phallus may cover for the male subject—he may well live in the imaginary illusion of coherence between desire and being. Such coherence is necessarily illusory, since no object will ever return the phallus he has lost through castration—there is no complementary object that will affirm his having the phallus. The elevation of the phallus in Western culture, as well as the elevation of female objects, serves to cover a gap intrinsic to the system: there is no way of explaining or signifying sexual difference. Sexual difference is not some kind of split that can be remedied by a lucky reunion. When Lacan discusses the lack of a signifier for sexual difference, he wants to expose the fact that one cannot find neither a transcendental nor a natural cause for desire: it is not sustained by some metaphysical teleology aimed at a union between the sexes. For a feminine subject, the contiguous relation between desire and being is obvious—there is no symbol in the symbolic that would ever assert the aim or continuity of her desire, and in this sense, the relation between her being as an embodied, desiring subject and her being in the symbolic order of language reveals a deep split in her subjectivity. Since there is no such coherence, there is not *the* woman, no particular that would ever fully fit the idealization of the symbolic universal of *the* woman. Being both included and excluded in the symbolic order through the sign of woman, she is also split in herself. At the same time, it is her ambivalent relation to the phallic sign of woman that makes her into a sexuated being. The fact that *the* woman does not exist creates a gap or void in the symbolic order that assures that sexual difference can never be described as a complementary or perfect fit—in this sense, the linguistic signifiers of "man" and "woman" do not so much describe a heteronormative order defining sexual identities as they operate in the rift of a split between desire and being for all subjects. While castration institutes the lack in the male subject that the possession of a woman is supposed to fill, woman comes to incorporate the lack in the symbolic itself. Woman is a fantasmatic construction, substituting for the fact that the sexes never make up a totality, *une toute*. Woman is an empty signifier because she is both a nodal point tying the sexual positions together and a lacuna threatening to tear them apart. Lacan's intuition is similar to Hegel's on this point: woman is a threat or eternal irony to the same order that has created her, a void in the system that has created her.[54]

Given that the subject holds an ex-static relation to the signifier, Lacan's appropriation of Oedipus is not entirely compatible with the structuralist theory of exchange in which desire can be metonymically displaced from one object to another. A patriarchal society may well make women into objects of exchange and create their cultural fantasies according to the measure of their desirability—women are beautiful, mysterious, unpredictable, and so on. These fantasies, however, are signs of an impossibility inherent in the discursive foundation of woman's construction. Her beauty, her desirability, and her being something good is a fiction sustaining the system as such.[55] The idealization of the female object as enviable and beautiful—the poetic elevation of her in *courtly love*—is the result of a paradox internal to the function of desire as such. While the fiction of the beautiful woman is a sign of domination and control, she is also made inaccessible. What is beautiful is experienced as such because it can never be appropriated. It is beautiful because it *cannot* be had. The beautiful has the effect of "suspending, lowering, disarming desire. The appearance of beauty intimidates and stops desire."[56] The elevation of women into beautiful objects serves to hide the fact that desire does not concern possessions. Occupying an inverted relation to what psychoanalysis calls the object, our fascination with the beautiful touches an empty space. We may own the beautiful object in a symbolic sense, but we may never own or appropriate beauty in itself. This is the point where woman is transformed into an empty point of the system. Beauty becomes a screen, covering the lacuna in the symbolic system. She is the both the promise of fulfillment, which stands in for the failing or missing phallus, and the weak point of the system.

Thus feminine desire becomes the void of the symbolic system, the nihilistic disruption of its construction, opening an abyss of deficiencies in the symbolic system of signs and values. Incommensurable with the phallic discourse that is supposed to have created the desiring subject, feminine desire becomes enigmatic and seemingly uncontrollable. Determined neither by culture nor by biology, female sexuation is a construction of radical negativity in Lacan's theory, engendered around a void where the guarantee for desire is faulty or failing. The Lacanian notion of female sexuality has very little to do with eroticism, sensuality, affectivity, or corporeality. Instead, it is concerned with the void structuring a subject's being as such, the subject collapsing into that void through the phenomenon of *jouissance*. Both Beauvoir and Lacan use Bernini's statue of an ecstatic Saint Theresa to exemplify feminine enjoyment. She embraces an ideal man, says Beauvoir, seeking union with an idealized object, the man of her fantasies.[57] She embraces the void, says Lacan—the feminine enjoyment of a failing or missing phallus bears witness to the fact that it is nothing but an empty signifier—feminine desire is directed toward an impossibility.[58] Enveloping the void, she incarnates the lack in the symbolic system as such. The masculine subject is enjoying his organ, *la jouissance phallique*. Woman, for her part, does not need the phallus for her enjoyment. Woman has a supplementary *jouissance*, beyond the phallus.[59] The mythical status of the female orgasm is due to the fact that women may not need a phallus to enjoy. The capacity to enjoy without a phallus is both threatening and disconcerting, because it shows the empty status of the phallus. But at the same time, there is a strong attraction connected to this feminine position. Lacan has been widely criticized for focusing on the phallus, but in his late work the fixation is quite ambivalent. The feminine orgasm—which does not need a phallus—becomes more important. The logic behind this shift can be illustrated by the film *Boys Don't Cry* by Kimberley Peirce (1999), which is based on actual events. The main character is a transsexual woman (played by Hilary Swank), a girl who becomes a beautiful boy, extraordinarily seductive for the women who see him. He falls in love with one of the local girls, played by Chloë Sevigny, and hangs out with the local gang. Sevigny's role in this drama is crucial. She shows a superior indifference to the question of whether Swank is a "real" man or not, which turns out to be more than the other men can bear. Not only is Swank at least as good as one of the boys in giving pleasure, he is better. When the men in the gang begin to suspect that he is a transsexual, they go crazy. As they attempt to reveal him, the big issue for them is whether he has a penis or not—the film makes a lot of the violent scene where Swank is undressed by force. When they discover that he does not, the punishment is humiliation, rape, and finally death. According to the film, they kill him not because he has been pretending that he has a penis, but rather because he never had one all along. What enrages the gang most is not that s/he has been trying to act like a man, overstepping his/her boundaries; it is the fact that s/he has made the phallus superfluous, thus exposing the fantasy that female pleasure is dependent on the penis. Without it, feminine enjoyment becomes an extraordinary challenge to phallic culture.

Feminine desire, therefore, is not only a symptom of patriarchy but a deficiency with a challenging potential. This does not mean that it is emancipatory in itself. A woman may, as Beauvoir points out, mirror herself in male eyes and act to please. She may alienate herself by choosing an object of identification through which she becomes Other also to herself.[60] Being her own imaginary object, she is unable to break the narcissistic mirror game. Women's only power seems to lie in the fact that they control the game. Women are unable to authentically assume a subjective attitude of acting without the mirror.[61] Lacan pursues this line of thought. Feminine otherness may seem to guarantee the system, but in fact the contrary is true. The feminine is both an excess and an imminent threat. Woman is a fictive sign of plenitude and meaning that compensates for a lack of meaning and control. She incarnates the false promise that something will fill the lack on which the patriarchal economy is based. Femininity is, in this regard, a symptom of the symbolic order itself.[62]

This point of view is difficult to reconcile with a feminist viewpoint.

A woman's task is to maintain the mask. She is—and in this conclusion Lacan follows Beauvoir—in fact irrevocably split, a (false) guarantee also to herself.[63] She carries the possibility of the system breaking down with her. But she also carries it within her, and so becomes prey to the malfunction of the system. We have an excellent illustration in Laclos's *Liaisons dangereuses* and the serial game of seduction between Valmont, Madame de Tourvel, and the Marchioness de Merteuil. The latter initiates the game, initially seeming to hold both the erotic and the economic power that controls the game: a perfect illustration of an empowered phallic woman. But the weak and passive Madame de Tourvel deprives the Marchioness de Merteuil of her lover Valmont and turns her own games against her, thereby revealing the empty point of female erotic power around which the game revolves. Playing the marchioness in Neil Jordan's cinematic adaptation of the novel, Glenn Close gives evidence of the fact that she loses much more than her face when the game is revealed. She stares at her mirror-image in horror. When the stiff make-up breaks up and runs down her face, nothing remains of the masquerade she thought she has mastered. She dissolves in fury, not so much because she realizes that she has lost her erotic power, but because it was always a hollow shell, which dissipates in the moment the illusion is pierced in the eyes of others. In that moment, the mask falls also for herself. The only power of women seems to lie in the fact that they control the game. But when the illusion breaks and a woman's erotic power becomes hollow, she dissolves into nothingness. There is no woman left. A Lacanian rewriting of Beauvoir's well-known statement that one is not born a woman but becomes one would therefore sound something like: Some may be born as girls, but no one ever becomes a woman.

The Antigone Complex

Lacan's reinvention of Freud's theory of sexual difference and his symbolization of the phallus have significant consequences. Freud's Oedipus can continue to live in the illusion that the lost maternal object can be continuously replaced by other women. Freud's women, however, never achieve this capacity of metonymic displacement. They are incapable of sublimating the loss of the maternal object.[64] Therefore they are exposed as both deficient and excessive in relation to the mechanisms that regulate desire: polymorphously perverse, melancholic, hysterical, envious, incapable of sticking to moral rules (as has been argued). Desire is a problem in the Freudian construction of femininity. Lacan, however, does not consider feminine desire to be a failure. Not being able to deceive herself, rather, the feminine subject lives closer to the truth: there is, effectively, nothing to sustain desire. Desire has not an aim but a *cause*. A significant shift from the structuralist viewpoint has taken place. Desire no longer aims at possession. It is impossible to possess or retain an object. The implicit presumption of structuralism—that objects of desire can be exchanged and possessed—is undermined. The cause remains elusive. To the extent that a woman is more nakedly deprived of possessions than men are (one may think of the penis as the imaginary possession of a phallus), the elusive quality of that cause is laid bare. The male subject is more likely to cover the discrepancies of desire in creating objects, possessions, goals, and aims. The shift from object to cause changes the paradigm of desire from Oedipus to Antigone. In the Antigonean framework, Oedipus is already blinded, dead, and gone. Antigone, for her part, has a privileged relation to the void that the symbolic system is unable to cover. Desire is not a striving toward the possession of an object, but rather a movement of return toward an elusive origin, an unraveling of the structure of the subject. Desire is disinvested from the objects erected in a paternal hierarchy and referred instead to a traumatic origin. This kind of unraveling may provide us with a closer look at the point from which the subject develops fantasies and erotic investments. We hit upon the shadow of an object, the shape of a foreign body, placed at the intersection between nature and transcendence. This body has not yet been given specific qualities or symbolic significance. It is a Thing that has not yet taken on any of the qualities of an object, not yet been made into an object of beauty or desirability. It has no value in the symbolic order in the way that a phallus or a beautiful woman does.[65]

The *Antigone Complex* reveals something fundamental about the relation between objects and the law that provides them. Oedipus's desire is equivalent to the law, and the objects provided through that law. This makes it easier for him to live in the illusion that desire will be continuously sustained, uninterrupted, and provided for. Antigone is more disturbing. She demonstrates that desire is not guaranteed by any transcendental signifier or order. She does not have the capacity to invest and disinvest in replacement objects in the same way that Oedipus does. But that does not mean that feminine desire can be reduced to a failed Oedipus. The Antigone complex is a figure for desire in a symbolic order that *fails to provide the fictional objects that would sustain it.* Antigone, unlike Oedipus, struggles in a kind of void. Whereas the object appears in the Oedipal structure, it disappears in the Antigonean structure. She is closer to the eclipse and the fading away, sustained by a fragile shadow or thing. But the reason for her complicated relation to the object is not pathological—whether she is melancholic or hysterical is not the issue here. The reason is that the object was never really there in the first place. In this way, she unravels "pure" desire.

Lacan's engagement in what we have chosen to call the Antigone complex begins with a question as simple as it is intriguing: what is the beauty of Antigone? Occupying a central place in a seminar entitled *The Ethics of Psychoanalysis*, the question may seem odd. Sophocles does not describe Antigone in terms of beauty. What we find in her dialogue with Ismene is the wish for *kalos thanein*. To "die with honor" is the proper translation, but we could read: "die beautifully." Through her beauty, she incarnates a cathartic and purging effect.[66] Lacan's admiration for Antigone's beauty is in fact a fascination with her death. In this respect, he seems close to Heidegger's reverence for Antigone's poetic self-sacrifice. As we have noted, the idea that Antigone is both pure and excessive seems to be the source of her fascination. Lacan is no exception in the long line of interpreters who have admired her "pure" feminine heroism: Antigone's uncompromising desire is "the pure and simple desire of death as such."[67] But this statement is not to take *ad notam* as simply referring to the death drive.[68] Antigone brings us straight into the landscape that Lacan calls the zone between two deaths, which constitutes the Lacanian figure of finitude: the subject is situated either in a zone of desire or in a zone of enjoyment, and ethics cannot be thought without somehow taking account of this condition. The "beauty effect" reveals its function.[69] Why are we struck by *l'éclat d'Antigone*, the brilliance of Antigone, and why do we find it so unbearable? The reason is partly her uncompromising relentlessness and partly her uncanny resilience. But the main reason is that her act has a kind of moral dignity that has to do with her exposure and pathos. Although we can neither identify nor fully sympathize with Antigone's actions, we experience her figure as beautiful because she makes visible the finite existence in the zone between two deaths: "It is when passing through that zone that the beam of desire is both reflected and refracted till it ends up giving us that most strange and most profound of effects, which is the effect of beauty on desire."[70] Tragedy's play with absences and appearances, coverings and exposures, revolves around the startling function of beauty as a screen covering the zone between two deaths. The zone between two deaths refers to our exposure to the everlasting threat of *jouissance*, our incapacity to resist the fantasy that keeps us fettered as victims to what Lacan calls the enjoyment of the Other.[71] Antigone's pure desire allows us to explore that territory and to expose what Lacan calls an *ethics of the real*. Such an ethics is intrinsically interwoven with feminine desire.

Ate and the Inscription of Desire

An admirer and translator of Heidegger, Lacan may well have known his published 1935 reading of *Antigone* in the *Introduction to Metaphysics*. The one from 1942 was not yet published at the time Lacan's interest in *Antigone* was awakened, but he may have known about it from other sources. Since there is no documented evidence, there is no point in speculating on details, but there are important similarities. Most importantly, both presume, in contrast to Aristotle, that tragedy is not about action. In fact, there is very little action in Sophocles' tragedies on the whole; except for *Oedipus Rex*, "for all his heroes the race is run," as Lacan puts it.[72] Tragedy in this perspective has nothing to do with conflicts between characters, nor with dialectics; it is a poetic creation or re-creation of a negative space that is to be found at the origins of the community, touching the "non-foundational foundations" of the *polis*, as Philippe Lacoue-Labarthe puts it.[73] Both Heidegger and Lacan use tragedy to challenge the humanist idea of the subject as a moral focus or point of control. They also move beyond Hegel's notion of tragic modernity as a split between universality and particularity in the social order, making Hegel into their foremost target of criticism for his interpretation of Antigone's demand being distanced from the real metaphysical issues of tragedy. Tragedy cannot merely be described as a conflict between two orders of discourse. There is no tragic conflict between two equally justifiable orders—Creon's and Antigone's.[74] And tragedy is not an action in the proper sense of the word—instead it concerns the unraveling of a truth. The conflicting orders that clash in Sophocles' text are placed on a common source or ground, which for Lacan is the signifier that determines the desire of the hero. Antigone's actions do not concern the burial of the brother as a family task. The cause unleashing the events is Antigone's impossible desire for her dead brother Polynices. In Heidegger's reading, the tragic split is analyzed in terms of the ontological conflict incorporated by Antigone's chase after the impossible—invoking a Dasein whose projects are preceded by a temporality installed by death. Both Heidegger and Lacan refer the tragic split to an irreducible element, a kernel that cannot be sublated and that makes reconciliation impossible. And they both understand Antigone as being up against a limit that must be understood in ontological terms. Whereas, for Lacan, Antigone is beautiful or inhuman—in the sense of atrocious—because of her *ate* (the heritage of an incestuous crime), she is *unheimlich* for Heidegger. The most important dimension of Sophocles' text lies beyond Hegel's description of the ethical order; it is the point where the conflict begins, shaping the community's symbolic limits. Tragedy keeps the question of the *polis* open. The return to the prepolitical is a "poeticization" of the political, according to Heidegger, challenging the notion that the political is equivalent to the public sphere.[75] Lacan, for his part, places the tragic split between the desire of the subject and the symbolic system that determines that desire. Lacan, like Heidegger, places the political aspect of tragedy in the negative space of the community, the foreclosed space he calls the real.[76] The real is not presexual, in the same way that Heidegger assumes the neutral aspect of Dasein to be situated beyond sexual difference. In Lacan's understanding of Sophocles' text, the sexual undertone is clearly present. What he does, then, is to capture the sexual nature of feminine subjectivity without reducing it to nature or social identity.

The key word associated with Antigone in Lacan's reading is *ate*. His contribution to the long line of interpretations of *Antigone* derives from this observation. Like Heidegger, Lacan has his own reasons for bending the philological tradition with his interpretation. If Heidegger wants to unravel the question of being, Lacan wants to reveal the structure of desire and construct a pure version of Antigone's disposition. "Hymn to man," the second chorus, gives the key. Lacan makes a number of interpretative claims that may be outrageous for the classicist, but he captures aspects of the text that more prudent scholars fail to see. Why does Antigone kill herself? Why does she treat her brother's dead body like a stone more precious than her own life? Is the reason self-denial, denegation, or quite simply madness resulting from a family curse? We have to look for the origin of Antigone's actions in a domain that goes beyond her psychology. She is deprived of possessions, status, and family. But her persistence and defiance derive not just from personal or family concerns or feelings of love and affection for those she has lost. Nor is it a straightforward political demonstration. Antigone's desire is caused by something that is external both to

herself and to the community, a negative space or antibond that is foreclosed in symbolic terms. Lacan's reading of this negative space is, like Heidegger's, based on the final strophe of the "Hymn to Man." The chorus
celebrates the formidable ways of man; only in the face of death does he
find himself *aporos*, without solution. Death is the only phenomenon he
cannot conquer, "but he has devised escapes from baffling illnesses," as the
chorus says. Turning the meaning around "in the style of Prévert," the
negation inherent in the word "aporos" may be seen to allude to man's facing the future and not his resources: man never faces his future without being resourceless, he *always* lacks the means. That is why he is *aporos* to his
very nature, infinitely cunning in his capacity to get into trouble: "He always manages to cause things to come crashing down on his head."[77] He
has not just learned to escape strange illnesses, he has learned to escape
into them. Man's "clever constructions" are not just cures; they are the *mal-
adies* themselves. A parallel construction returns in the strophe where the
chorus expels the neighbor: "Never may he be a guest at my hearth or a
sharer of my thoughts, who does these things" (278). The chorus points to
both Creon and Antigone as "cityless" lawbreakers. But Lacan has another
interpretation. The passage, he says, is not about obeying laws; it is about
mixing them up.[78] Antigone therefore becomes the object of the passage.
Creon fails in his judgment. Antigone, however, is *deinon*: she confuses the
rights of the dead with the *desire of the dead*—contaminated by their desire,
going one step beyond the piety of sisterly duty because the signifier she
claims as the cause of her action, the rights of the dead, is the desire of her
dead brother operating in her. The dramatic cut produced by *ate* has a literal connotation of contamination in the play, which Lacan interprets in
terms of the signifying cut around which her subjectivity is structured: her
desire is *caused* by the dead. This does not mean, however, that the pure
desire she embodies would be reducible to the death drive.

Antigone's *ate* is often translated as "madness."[79] The *Ethics of Psychoanalysis*, on the other hand, opposes it to Creon's *hamartia*, his contingent mistakes and wrongful calculations. "Ate" designates "the limit that
human life can only briefly cross."[80] This is the limit Antigone seeks: not
just death, but the annihilation of desire, a return to the point of its inscription. *Ate* returns in the French word "atroce" (atrocious) in the sense
of inhuman. The play describes her thus in her uncanny transformation
into a wailing, birdlike creature at the side of her brother's body. She is
driven by something other than a belief in what is right, and she disregards

any kind of compensation or good resulting from her action, thus shedding the illusory layers of a final purpose.[81] Marked by *ate*, Antigone acts in conformity with her desire because she has, literally, nothing to lose. Rather than projecting her spookiness as death, Lacan makes her uncanny precisely because she is a woman, and this itself places her at the limit. In Greek tragedy, ate is part of the ethical vocabulary concerned with the relation between necessity and freedom.[82] Sophocles lets the word hint of both destruction and madness, while seeming to play with the Homeric sense of infatuation. He uses the word with particular sophistication in exploiting this indeterminacy. *Ate* is both a ruinous power descending from the gods, acting independently of the tragic characters, and a madness caused by the gods and internalized by the doomed hero or heroine as a god "leading his mind to disaster" (625).[83] It may be introjected as madness or associated with an outside that appears to turn against the subject: *tuche*. Man's capacity to exploit and master his world only manifests itself in the face of an ultimate defeat that derives from the dead contaminating the living. The text reveals this contamination throughout the play. The last root in the house of Oedipus is cut down by a bloody knife from the nether world (600). A first glance may tell us that these lines refer to Antigone. She will never have any children, she is promised to Hades. But these lines may also refer to Creon, who is left without descendants. In the text *ate* belongs *neither* to Antigone nor Creon. It is, the chorus tells us, the limit we should never pass, but at the same time nobody escapes *ate* (625). The uncanny nuances of the word derive from its indeterminacy: neither outside nor inside, neither object nor subject, because *ate* is the haunting from one generation to another. If human beings are *deinon* in their capacity to overpower the forces of nature, the overpowering force of *ate* is even more terrifying. The *ate* of tragedy can only be determined *après-coup*, through acts intended to oppose the destiny that they, in the course of events, turn out to fulfill. *Ate* is a form of contamination spreading from a transgression of the fundamental laws of the community. These laws, such as the law against incest in the story of Oedipus, are always founded upon the myth, or actuality, of an original crime. Put in another way, there is no law that does not carry the injunction of its own transgression within it. Creon's barring of the dead from the living may be intended to save the city from contamination, but instead it awakens the excessive forces proper to the dynamics of tragedy. The prohibition against touching the dead brother's body only reinforces the incestuous overtones of Antigone's desire. The limit of *ate* engenders the wish to embrace the forbidden things that lie beyond it. When Antigone goes beyond *ate* toward a reunion with her dead brother, she only pursues the path that was staked out for her to begin with. *Ate* is the original crime that has been inscribed by the law itself. From this perspective, the founding crime is not the incest of Oedipus but the desire of the mother, Iocaste. Lacan points to Iocaste's desire as the dark point of the unconscious: "The desire of the mother is the origin of everything."[84] Surprisingly, Lacan, like Heidegger, ignores the "Hymn to Eros," where the origin of *ate* is fixed. When Iocaste marries Oedipus, the crime is already committed: she has given birth to a son who is doomed to perpetuate *ate*. Her desire is inscribed in "the calamity of a mother's bed" (865), in a womb of disaster, which finds a metaphorical exponent in the cave where Antigone dies. The events are only manifestations of a strange logic of *creatio ex nihilo* applicable to the fundamental laws of desire—the crime is already committed when the prohibition is erected. The law inscribes the possibility of desire as such, as well as its destructive force: *ate*. Here we find an exemplarity reminiscent of Freud's idea of the Oedipus complex, where the law of desire is passed on from father to son. In Lacan's reading of the text, desire is passed on from mother to daughter, though a crime has always already taken place. *Ate* is both the inscription of desire and the fate of humankind in the face of that inscription, continuously evoking failure and dispersion. The poisonous embrace of Iocaste, pushing the house of the labkakids toward extinction, is mirrored in Antigone's extreme attachment to her brother. She could have another husband, another child, but her brother is irreplaceable. These "scandalous" words, considered of doubtful authorship, are nothing but a dialectical calculation, Goethe complained.[85] In other words, the incestuous overtones are only too obvious. Iocaste's children come from the "bloody root" of the labdacidean curse, according to Aeschylus's version of the story in *Seven against Thebes*.[86] Antigone's action can be interpreted as the expression of a particular bond with her mother. She reveres the genealogy of a maternal heritage.[87] But the reason she can never have a new brother is ultimately dependent upon the fact that she descends from a monstrous union. Blurring the lines of demarcation between death wish and love, she challenges the very structure of desire. Chasing the impossible, she remains transfixed at the limit of *ate*, immortalizing it—as Lacan puts it, the impossible moment of the second death, where we cannot remain for long. Nobody lives *ektos atas*, outside of *ate*, says the chorus, and they say so because *ate* coincides with the limits of desire, beyond which we touch upon the drive. Desire is a finite construction, the goal of which always disappears or fails, directed toward a space of fantasy originating in the impossibility of the object itself.[88] Unlike Creon, who aspires to know the good and do good for the community, Antigone understands the void beyond the inscription of desire.

Singularity and the Real

In Lacan's reading of Sophocles' tragedy, we encounter a familiar figure, the figure in which feminine desire is regarded as excessive or deficient in relation to moral norms and values. Here, however, the position of Antigone is considered extra-ethical rather than immoral: she is, according to Lacan, a part of our ethical sensibility. In *Antigone*, we find a symbol for the ethical subject that seems inapplicable to any moral faith other than that of the mystic. Her act could well be described as a kind of enjoyment that, according to Lacan, is inscribed in the structure of feminine desire as such: "The fantasm that guides feminine desire—from the reveries of pure young virgins to the couplings fantasized by middle-aged matrons—may be literally poisoned by the favored image of Christ on the cross."[89] Again, feminine desire is excessive—but this excess makes her enjoyment extra-ethical rather than unethical. This may seem strange, because the ethical subject is here set *against* the normative order of the community, not because her act is incompatible with its habits and customs (she does follow the divine law that says all human beings have a right to be buried) but because she acts with such absolute disdain for the values of life—her life, the life of the family, of possible future children. In some way, Antigone's act seems utterly self-defeating, as if she were crushed under the weight of a punishing superego demanding her death. But if Antigone forms part of our morality whether we like it or not, as Lacan puts it, it is because she is a feminine alternative to the oedipal structure of identification with the law in the sense that her death does not simply signify submission to the aggressive punishments of the superego.[90] This does not mean, however, that Antigone's order is a feminine alternative situated outside of culture, outside of universalizable norms and rules that we identify as the law. Antigone is part of our ethical sensibility not because she can do what she likes, without submitting her desire to norms and rules. She is part of our ethical sensibility because she touches the void inherent in any normative order, a void revealing the contingent character of its workings and the contingent character of any law that is universalizable, whether we call it the paternal law of the oedipal structure or something else. In this way, she reveals the subject's resistance to normalization, which is at the core of Lacan's ethics, a resistance to be found in that part of the subject that is foreclosed in any social and normative order.

The reference to Antigone doing the deed without reference to good or bad as "ethical" is really about her paying heed to a form of *singularity* that is unbound and undefined in terms of values in a social context. "Singularity," in this context, cannot simply be translated as uniqueness. What is singular is that Thing to which my ethical aspect is attached, that rugged and impossible object that has been delineated as the cause of desire, a form of being that Lacan simply speaks of in terms of *what is*: "What is, is, and it is to this, to this surface that the unshakeable, unyielding position of Antigone is fixed."[91] The brother is what he is, whatever qualities we ascribe to him, whatever the details of his biography may look like. The singularity of the brother is unequivocally attached to Antigone's being; he corresponds to "the break that the very presence of language inaugurates in the life of man."[92] Her unwillingness to compromise with the laws of Creon reveals "a pure and simple relationship" to "the signifying cut that confers on [her] the indomitable power of being what [she] is in the face of everything that may oppose [her]."[93] This signifying cut is Antigone's *ate*, her sisterhood: a *singular* and irreplaceable position. It is the *cause* of desire and it is her truth, the point at which she comes to be that which she is. And yet the phrases by which Antigone pays heed to the singularity of her brother are ambivalent. Oedipus is both brother and father, and she herself the fruit of a monstrous union. One may indeed argue, as Judith Butler has done, that the text enacts a confusion of sexual difference. In focusing wholly on Antigone's refusal of the feminine, however, one forgets that the contamination of the tragic process, the breaking down of distinctions, still manages to foreground the feminine in the end. Creon effectively succumbs to feminine grief and has to undergo the tragedy that was meant for Antigone. Therefore, one may still argue that Antigone's desire represents an excess that has to do with her feminine position and that is never closed or purified in the tragic ritual.[94] Antigone's desire presents itself at the limits of the symbolic community, where we find the singular point that refuses to give itself to or be symbolized by the symbolic. Lacan's reading is here circling around something we may call the truth of the subject, a moment in which she or he can no longer escape the determination of a founding signifier that he or she can never fully *become*. In this way, the ethics of psychoanalysis does involve questions of ontology. But as we will argue in the chapter on the Thing, there are elements in Lacan's understanding of tragedy that prevent him from making tragedy into ontology. The relation between language and world, in Heidegger's reading of tragedy, is the unraveling of *logos* or the function of truth itself as a violence inflicted through and upon Dasein. But there is no insistence on language as another order, existing independently or in another form of materiality than Dasein. In the case of Lacan, however, there is a material quality to language, which is where the truth-function is situated: a material quality that means language has the subject in its grip, not in the sense of meaning but in the sense of inscription. The effect of the signifier on the subject never ceases to elude it; the truth of the subject can only be articulated through a signifier that in itself remains nontransparent and opaque.[95] Something in it remains that refuses to open up a relation to the world— an opacity or material resistance that Lacan calls the Thing, and which remains the opaque cause of desire situated in the subject.[96]

The origins of Antigone's "cause" are also hidden to herself. It may well seem as if she were engulfed by melancholy, unable to escape the suffocating grasp of maternal desire. Her act has a cruel and unpleasant side to it. Certainly we find an echo of Iocaste's lawless and limitless desire in Antigone's attachment to her brother's body. We could well imagine the tragedy perpetuating itself in endless repetitions of deaths echoing a devouring mother's appetite. Rather than enforcing the maternal myth of a dark continent, however, Antigone performs an act that resists the masochist side of melancholy.[97] Paying reverence to Polynices' singularity, Antigone follows the appeals of his being *as such*. As a sister, she stands for a desire that cannot be reduced to melancholy and frigidity. The uncanniness of Antigone has nothing to do with the death drive as an urge to dissolve or disappear, but rather with the impossibility of her desire, the kernel of resistance that refuses to dissolve. When the object is eliminated, we are left with the "pure" formula of desire. Antigone's action is directed toward the singularity of *what is*: the numb, lifeless brother does not respond. The body of the dead brother presents the cause of desire as a dumb Thing. That cause never collapses; it is neither eaten nor engulfed into the blank perversion of melancholy. The dead body of Polynices remains a nonresponsive Thing, a limit that cannot be transcended. Her action may lack aim and goal, but that is precisely what gives it its ethical quality. Her desire is upheld *in spite* of its lack of response, beyond illusion, fantasy, and cultural fiction. The singular cause of desire that has been delineated by the signifier to which Antigone is fixed is figured by the dead body. The dumb, senseless body of the brother gives nothing back; his corpse is the hard, unresponsive kernel around which the tragedy turns, and therefore also the key to its ethical message. Its refusal to respond to her desire or be subsumed into it makes it the inhuman aspect of that signifier, the rugged kernel to which her desire is attached: the Thing. Every account of the relation between subject and object has to be constructed on a prohibition and a loss that is absolute, bound by a limit or law that contains an element of impossibility in it. Feminine desire, as shown by Antigone, has a particularly poignant relation to that impossibility.

Family Politics / Family Ethics: Butler, Lacan, and the Thing beyond the Object

Irigaray's Dionysian Hope

Changing the premises from which the question of desire must be thought, Antigone challenges the idea that desire can be reduced to a symbolic structure—be it social, linguistic, or other. Demonstrating the contingent foundations of any universalist claim invoking a symbolic structure, Judith Butler has shown the issues of the play to be bound up with pressing issues in family politics. While agreeing with Butler that the Oedipal model is contingent and therefore replaceable, I would like to suggest that Lacan's ethics of the real may in fact agree with her understanding of the implications of such a contingency. While Butler sees a naturalization of the social in the Lacanian symbolic, which finds its prolongation in a conservative family politics, I would argue for a Lacanian model of an ethics of the real as the basis on which all desiring relations must be thought, refusing any naturalization of the Thing in which desire takes hold. For this reason, I begin with a critique of Irigaray's ambiguous understanding of *Antigone* and her unwillingness to theorize the failure of Antigone in other terms than as the failure of the philosophical tradition, in order to prepare for a sustained discussion of Butler's family politics and a more thorough discussion of an ethics of the real, where I suggest that it is the irreducible character of the Thing that prevents an ethics of the real from becoming naturalized in any normative order. The final passages of this chapter demonstrate this fact: dedicated to two very different films on a woman's obsession with her piano, they demonstrate the resistance of the Thing that sustains desire.

Danish psychoanalyst and feminist Nina Lykke has discussed the girl's ambivalent relation to her mother, in which she attempts not to conquer the phallus but rather to retain the mother and save her from the alienating effects of patriarchy—which she calls the "Antigone phase." Replacing Oedipus with a symbolic Antigone, Lykke shows how phallocentrism mirrors the fetishistic values of a perverted symbolic economy, disrupting the bonds between mother and daughter. Antigone does something that patriarchy cannot tolerate: she transgresses paternal law and opposes the father's power to regulate the relation between women.[1] An investigation into the relation between mother and daughter therefore imposes itself in any reading of *Antigone*. In contemporary feminism, Luce Irigaray in particular has evoked Antigone as a symbol of feminine desire, replacing Oedipus not as a symmetrical alternative but as a figure representing another lineage. References to *Antigone* are spread throughout Irigaray's work. As we have seen in the chapter on Hegel, she is consistently critical of his definition of Antigone's place in the ethical order as being negatively determined. A symbol of Hegel's denial of feminine desire, she epitomizes the exclusion of women from the social model of recognition, in which feminine self-consciousness is prevented from developing.[2] In Hegelian dialectics, there is a difference between the for-itself, which is the mode of self-consciousness, and the in-itself, which is a mode of substance. Since women only exist in the function of wives and mothers, they are neither slaves nor masters, which means that there is no theory of feminine desire in Hegel: no access to singularity or the for-itself of self-consciousness.[3] This is also the case for Antigone, although she is neither wife nor mother but rather a sister whose only means of recognition lies in a nondesiring relation to her brother. Excluded from the laws of the city and therefore from the ethical order, Antigone's punishment in the cave is exemplary of her status as neither inside nor outside, neither citizen nor free person. Irigaray's primary critique of Hegel's definition of the ethical order, and the dialectics of identification and self-consciousness that it attempts to establish, is that it fails to theorize an *ethics of sexual difference*. Hegel's principle of universality is only a male imaginary, which means that it is isomorphic with masculinity—a universal reflection of the self.[4] An ethics of sexual difference must recognize the subjectivity of both sexes rather than resorting to an original myth of bisexuality, as Hegel does when he asserts that the brother-sister relation is asexual and devoid of conflict. In order for Antigone's fate not to be repeated, an alternative ethical order must be created, constructed around the principle of a love of the other that transcends the principle of the same, or the for-it-self. Hegel's ethical order is based on sameness in the world of appearance, which is the world in which the for-itself is constructed on the elimination of differences, the return as a form of identity. This means that life, the flesh of life and the meaning of life, is in danger of being forgotten. And this is why we have to return to the question of sexual difference. We must install a notion of femininity that escapes the dialectics of desire and the ethical order, and that escapes the dialectics of sexual difference. We must discuss an ethics of sexual difference, or the tragedy of Antigone will repeat itself. But for women's desire to find a form, for women's subjectivity to find an outlet in consciousness, women cannot simply be allowed access to the dialectics of recognition. Instead, the imaginary dimension of the transcendental must be transformed. The symbolic exclusion of woman as body and nature cannot be redeemed through universal ideals. Instead, femininity must be defined so as to show the feminine body as the threshold, the site of fecundity, openness. Thus, while Antigone incarnates the closure of the transcendental dialectic of modernity as it has been formulated by Hegel, she is also incarnating the possibility of another opening. Celebrating the heritage left by her mother and a matrilinear tradition, Antigone is the symbol not only of the closure of the ethical order as it is transposed into modernity, but also of the opening of an ethics of sexual difference. The fact that she and her brother come from the same womb emphasizes the genealogy of the mother and contrasts it with Creon's patriarchal order.[5] This has far-reaching consequences. Antigone's relation to her maternal heritage leads us toward a greater understanding not only of the mother-daughter relation—which is the darkest continent of our culture—but also of the necessity of replacing the existing transcendental structures of our culture with imaginary representatives, in order to allow for feminine subjectivity to come into being. The tragedy bears witness to the transformation from matriarchy to patriarchy, which Beauvoir assured us was depicted primarily in *Agamemnon*. Tragedy shows a maternal lineage doomed to succumb to a severing patriarchy that forbids an ethical order based on sexual difference. As in Hegel's depiction of the conflict, of one order threatening another, the kernel of the conflict is the symbolic value given to blood ties. The navel of a dark continent, the mother-daughter relation remains an explosive enigma in Western society, traditionally disrespected and denigrated by a patriarchal order that excludes mediation between women. The problem of femininity, then, is not that Western society is founded on an Oedipal structure that prohibits a functional relation, but rather that our culture lacks appropriate symbols of mediation. Above all, we must find a symbolic space for the maternal in order to allow feminine genealogies and processes of identification to assert themselves. Irigaray's writings are all dedicated to the creation of a feminine *logos* outside of the patriarchal symbolic. Antigone serves as a symbol of this function. Honoring the maternal origin through her love for her brother, who comes from the same womb, Antigone calls for an ethics outside of patriarchal hegemony, an ethics in which sexuality is affirmed rather than negated. Irigaray thus makes ethics intrinsic to human bonds, whether they are based on care, love, or sexuality. Irigaray attempts to establish an imaginary not based on appearance, but beginning from within, in between the fold, in which differentiation is thought not on the basis of identity and appearance, but out of a chiasmic unfolding of flesh and differentiation, a fecund form of differentiation: "The question being how to detach the other—woman—from the otherness of sameness."[6] Therefore, Irigaray refuses the Hegelian gesture through which the other—Antigone—is only allowed to be "representative of the other of the same."[7] An ethics of sexual difference would allow for love in a fecundity of differentiation, difference unfolding from within. In order for such an ethics to develop, the maternal heritage must be allowed to displace the patriarchal order. To same extent, Antigone performs such a displacement. At the same time, Irigaray's conception of Antigone is contradictory and ambiguous. While she is held up as a symbol of matrilineal bonds, she is also disclosed by her worship of death as someone who finds her enjoyment in the nether world rather than in life.[8] Rather than promoting the flow of life through blood ties, she resorts to the bloodless, to the abstraction of love that comes with the funeral, the giving up of life that comes with the love of the dead. Irigaray's Antigone is never fully detached from Hegel's; her call for a feminine imaginary stops short of the Antigone figure because it is bound up with the abstraction of a desire directed toward the universality of the guardianship of the dead.[9] In Irigaray's writings, Antigone never fully leaves the Hegelian role of being a "representative of the other of the same." While part of her may be opening for an ethics of fecundity and sexual difference, part of her short-circuits that flow in her love of the bloodless. Thus Irigaray's Antigone can be found at the crossroads between the flow of desire envisioned as femininity and the frightening relentlessness of a desire caught in its own impossibility, a relentlessness that Irigaray herself can only describe as an un-productive form of failure.

Butler's Antigone—Rethinking Kinship

In *Antigone's Claim* (2000), Judith Butler gives us her reading of Antigone, which stresses the confusion that surrounds not only the question of kinship or origin (Antigone's father being her own brother) but also the question of sexual identity (Antigone being more like a man than a woman). Antigone is confused in terms of origin and gender, but in this she shows us the arbitrariness of the determination of origin and kinship. Appropriating the figure of Antigone as a challenge to a conservative family politics, Butler shows the question of kinship to be not simply one of blood, but also of recognition; the family cannot simply be considered something given, isolated from the political sphere. The conditions of such a recognition, however, cannot be construed in Hegel's dialectical terms. Since the origins of kinship are shown to be arbitrary, the family cannot be detached from the state and situated in a separate sphere of the prepolitical. Everything that has to do with the family is bound up with the state, and vice versa. When Antigone claims to represent divine laws—the laws of the family, the bonds of love, the customs of heritage, and so on—she shows that these laws and bonds are as arbitrary as those formalized by the state. Moreover, they cannot be detached from the state. Readings of *Antigone*, such as Hegel's, that have insisted on the separation between family and state have effectively perverted the message of the play.[10] Hegel makes Antigone a representative of the "natural" sphere of love, family bonds, and blood ties, as opposed to the universal order of the state. Butler's suggestion is that we disassociate the question of origin from that of bonds. Rather than assuming that bonds are formed through blood ties and allowing for a dialectics between family and state in which the state's claim to universality becomes the measure of the status of the family, we have to find new means for recognizing bonds that have not been created in traditional ways.

In *Antigone's Claim*, Judith Butler continues the shift from Oedipus to Antigone that has been prepared in feminism and psychoanalysis. Questioning its norms of sexual identification and paternal authority, Butler adds her voice to a chorus critical of the Oedipal paradigm, confirming the impression that Oedipus may well be on his way to replacement by a kind of Antigone complex. Butler makes Antigone into a figure that challenges the heteronormative assumptions of thinkers such as Hegel and Lacan. Most importantly, however, she argues against the naturalization of family bonds and claims that the foundation of these bonds are as contingent as the norms of social relations. These two aspects, heteronormativity and naturalization of family bonds, both contribute to the way in which the family has been relegated to the domain of the prepolitical. In what way does psychoanalysis imply a family politics? Here Butler's standpoint is clear: it contributes to a reactionary ideology.

Both Lacan and Hegel, Butler argues, make the mistake of assuming that Antigone is precultural rather than an effect of culture itself. Hegel does not allow Antigone access to self-consciousness or an ethical order because she belongs to a sphere that is in opposition to the state. "Generalizing" her as womankind, he neutralizes the subversiveness of Antigone, because women are not given access to the mechanisms that would allow their appeals to be recognized by the state. His idea of woman as a perversion or irony of the ethical order is, in Butler's view, not really subversive, because it merely enforces their exclusion from the state.[11] Her critique of Lacan is based on similar grounds: the symbolic can only be thought in conjunction with its own outside, the real. But his conception of the symbolic for the most part mirrors his conception of the real: what is inside and outside is less important than how the limit of the symbolic is determined. Rather than relying on a conception of the symbolic that is assumed to be the foundation of our culture, Butler points to the contingency of its constitution, a contingency that the Lacanian theory of the symbolic cannot fathom: "It does not follow that the taboo itself [in the Lacanian symbolic] might appear as radically alterable or, indeed, eliminable; rather, to the extent that it does appear, it appears in a universal form. Thus this contingency, an ungroundedness that becomes the condition of a universalizable appearance, is radically distinct from a contingency that establishes the variability and limited cultural operation of any such rule or norm."[12] Antigone's claim "does not take place outside the symbolic or, indeed, outside the public sphere, but within its terms and as an unanticipated appropriation and perversion of its own mandate."[13] Given that the concepts of the symbolic and the real traverse culture, society, and subject in Lacanian theory, her critique must be noted not least for its resistance to the authority produced by the symbolic, which collapses symbolic and imaginary orders. Butler's criticism of Lacan is that no transcendental Law can be detached and formalized outside of a social order: "Norms do not unilaterally act upon the psyche; rather they become condensed as the figure of the law to which the psyche returns. The psychic relation to social norms can, under certain conditions, posit those norms as intractable, punitive, and eternal. . . . In other words, the very description of the symbolic as intractable law takes place within a fantasy of law as insurpassable authority. In my view, Lacan at once analyzes and symptomises this fantasy."[14] For Butler, Lacan's notion of the symbolic is another word for normative, but in a way that remains hidden. In Butler's reading of Lacan, nothing exists outside of the symbolic order of language or culture, and anything that challenges its limits suffers a real or symbolic death—such as Antigone. If we accept that all language is normative, we no longer have to struggle with the problematic separation between social and symbolic spheres and therefore get rid of hidden normative injunctions in theories that carry them, such as psychoanalysis. In Butler's reading, the tragedy has its origin not in the real but in confusion and contamination. Her theorizing of Antigone is focused on the performative act of claiming *other laws*, calling the limits of intelligibility. These limits are as contingent as the laws of the symbolic. The power of laws, then, stems not so much from principles as from language itself. Whereas the word or signifier is structured around an empty space for Lacan—the space of the real—it has a normative and performative power for Butler: there is no domain outside of language that could be considered prelinguistic or something like the real. When Antigone claims that she follows divine laws, the extraordinary power of these words lies not so much in their content as in the way they point to a crisis of intelligibility. Antigone does not so much go outside of the symbolic as show its limits. Within the symbolic, we can make sense neither of Antigone's heritage nor of her sex. Psychoanalysis, therefore, has a claim on culture itself. The nature of this claim is such that it will, naively, continue to assist the politics of conservative forces. In the process, the emancipatory claim of psychoanalysis is thwarted. Her critique on this point, in fact, echoes that of Beauvoir: the problem with psychoanalysis is that it takes the incest taboo and paternal power for granted, and confuses the social sphere with structural necessities. Lacanians would claim that the symbolic function can be separated from social content. The law of the father, which for Lacanians presents a fundamental structuring factor in intimate relations, does not necessarily have to be represented by a real father—it could be a brother, another woman, perhaps even a job. The main point is that the mother must have another object of desire than the child, or the child will be caught in a fantasmatic relation where it is simply the object of desire for another. Lacan liberated psychoanalysis from real mothers and fathers, and made these functions symbolic rather than personal, which means that the law of the father is not necessarily identified with a real, biological father. But for Butler, it is untenable to say that something else would fulfill the symbolic function of a father and consider this to be progressive, because one continues to enforce the father function as the final authority. The idea of the symbolic itself is, she says, nothing but a "sedimentation" of social practices.[15] The status of the father is only an idealization—the law is the father and the father is the law.[16] Lacan's formal concept of the family is stuck in a system according to which a subject's identity and desire is given according to a fixed maternal/paternal axis. Psychoanalysis enforces a cultural heritage of heteronormativity—either mother or father, either daughter or son, either man or woman.[17] It is reactionary, because it is blind to its normative grounds. In order to be productive, psychoanalysis would have to rethink these issues.

This is a pressing task, not least because the psychoanalytic conception of the family is derivative of the way it conceives of sexual difference, which for Lacanians is an extraordinarily important issue; the theory of sexual difference, for Lacanians, structures the desire of the subject unconditionally, although it may do so in fantasmatic and unexpected ways. The insistence on a normative order of sexual difference is particularly poignant in ideologies of parenting. Butler argues that there is a direct link between the psychoanalytic theory of sexual difference and, for instance, the French resistance to adoption by homosexual couples. In psychoanalysis, Butler argues, mothers and fathers are made into the foundation of culture: the two necessary poles, man and woman, of a child's upbringing. The consequence of this injunction is repressive.[18] Although this argument may seem rather extreme—not all French are Lacanians, and not all Lacanians are against the rights of homosexuals—Butler's challenge is important. Making Antigone into a political figure because she challenges our views on origins and kinship has a concrete background in a contemporary debate. One of the most pressing socio-political issues today is that of homosexual adoptions and the rights of homosexuals to parent. Although Butler does not discuss it explicitly, much of her argument revolves around this issue. But then it should perhaps be pointed out that it is not certain that homosexual adoption of children would seriously threaten the norms implicit in psychoanalytic thinking. Although they may be of the same sex, these parents are still couples. If we presume that parents should always be *two*, the shadow of a heteronormative system is still at work. A psychoanalyst could easily argue that a symbolic structure would be represented by such a couple; psychoanalysis does not assume that there must be a mother and a father, or even that maternal and paternal functions must be present in the symbolic sense. As long as there are two, the parent would still desire someone other than the child. This is what the incest taboo is about and what matters for the child's psychosexual upbringing from an analytic point of view. The idea of homosexual parenting in couples does not challenge heteronormativity. But the question of kinship has become complicated in a number of ways. There are an extraordinary number of parents, both homosexual and heterosexual, that may appear deficient in relation to the symbolic order. Should single people have the right to adopt, or knowingly give birth to children on their own, without a partner of either sex present? In most cases, there is a biological father somewhere. But in some cases, the father is not only missing, but altogether anonymous or perhaps even dead at the time of birth or even of conception. What kind of symbolic deficit—if there is one—are we encountering in cases where the mother has simply gone to the sperm bank? In other cases, where parents are more than two, there is a symbolic excess. There are gays and lesbians who decide to have children together as a threesome or foursome. New family formations keep spreading where children are living with stepparents. What function are they assuming? Facing these issues, we have to rethink our concept of family. The next question is then: how? Today, a number of feminist scholars have shown that kinship is not universally regulated according to the norms presented by Lévi-Strauss. Moreover, these norms have been shown to be a tool for Western, white domination, obliterating the rules and regulations of kinship for the slaves that were shipped to America, for instance.[19] We have already mentioned that families today do not look like the "kernel" presumed by Lévi-Straussian psychoanalysis. Butler speculates that the return to psychoanalysis from the very liberal sexual practices of the 1960s was to some extent motivated by the need for new constraints in a situation that had become too confusing. But the price was a move away from alternative family structures. Her suggestion is that we focus on the performative act of law-giving itself. We need to recognize the new kinds of family bonds that have started to form and renegotiate family laws and norms.

Thus Butler makes Antigone into a figure for whom gender and origin are called into question. Antigone figures "the limits of intelligibility exposed at the limits of kinship."[20] She acts upon a heritage that is not simply there, but part of a system that can be questioned and reconstructed. Moreover, sexual identity is not simply the result of identification with a mother or father. It is a consequence of the way in which such identification complies with a normative system. The system is then reiterated and reinforced through social practices, such as psychoanalysis. Antigone is an alternative to Oedipus because of her refusal to perform a "heterosexual closure" to the play. This does not mean that Antigone becomes a queer heroine, but she becomes a heroine with no easily recognizable gender. If one can speak of an Antigone complex in Butler's theory, it is situated at the point at which the Oedipal law (in Freud's terms, not Sophocles') is no longer intelligible: her father is her brother, and their maternal origin the same.[21] Unable to make sense of her origin, and placed precisely at the limits of cultural intelligibility, she becomes the victim of the vicissitudes of cultural norms and rules. The Antigone complex in a Butlerian version, then, does not make Antigone into a model of culture, like Oedipus, but precisely into the opposite: the limit of culture itself.

Family Politics or Family Ethics?

So is Butler right: is psychoanalysis working against emancipation? Or is it possible to use psychoanalysis for emancipatory purposes? The question is in fact as old as psychoanalysis itself. Ever since psychoanalytic practice started at the beginning of the last century, it has attracted feminists, with some of Freud's first pupils being politically and intellectually active women. Psychoanalysis has been married both to feminism and to the left for long periods over the last century, but it has been a complicated marriage, with new storms whipped up with the arrival of queer theory. Is psychoanalysis simply ignorant of the fact that it fits perfectly with a conservative and reactionary ideology? Or is it possible to build a progressive family politics on psychoanalytic grounds? The crucial issues here are the concepts of norms and normative. I take Butler's concept of normativity to imply certain codes and rules, so as to be regulative. A conception of kinship such as that of Lévi-Strauss is normative because it implies a certain "positive" law of what counts as kinship, but the symbolic structure does not necessarily have to be considered an authoritative system. Perhaps it is more interesting to consider Lacan's notion of the symbolic to be radically empty. The very *function* of the symbolic in its most minimalist version is to stand for a *prohibition tout court*, and the function of this prohibition is not to subjugate the subject. Rather, it constitutes a *remedy* for submission to authoritative systems. It is quite possible to suggest that the symbolic function can be detached from a normative content, and to situate it at the intersection between language and subject, between the universal and the singular; it cuts not only the limits of the subject, but the limits of a social and linguistic community as well. In this way, the symbolic does not prescribe norms, but rather limits the scope of any normative system.[22] Psychoanalysis does not know what femininity and masculinity are. If it tells us that *there must be sexual difference* then this does not necessarily imply that there must be men and women, mothers and fathers, daughters and sons of two well-defined sexes. What it does, however, is to delineate an aspect of the subject that is incapable of complying with demands such as "be a woman" or "be a man." The symbolic, in my understanding, is not the equivalent of a regulative order, but the enforcement of a gap between a normative order of values and codes, of practices and habits that we need to incorporate in our daily lives, and the function of desire. There is no healing symbol that would overcome this gap, but this protects us from the invasion, eradication, and submission to any kind of invisible symbolic authority that could be positivized as femininity, the father, the law, and so on. The subject originates in a necessary impossibility, both an obstacle to fullness and a shield from dissolution. It is the structure of this necessary impossibility that Antigone unravels, and in doing so, she points to something that in its most minimal version simply could be translated as the laws of finitude.

There is, in fact, a lot of common ground between Lacan's and Butler's readings of *Antigone*; the potency of the tragedy for contemporary thought lies in its call for a reexamination of the way our desire is determined—not simply from the point of view of authoritative systems and laws, but also from the point of view of the *failure* of these systems and laws to shape their subjects. Bringing us to the unintelligible limits of culture, to that point which is foreclosed—death, incest, *jouissance*, and so forth, in Lacan's reading, and the endpoint of the symbolic and of gendered structures in Butler's reading—Antigone opens up a space of questioning that compels us, draws us, and *calls for* an understanding. Call it the space of the real, the space of ethics, of contamination—what matters is not so much its actual nature. Rather than simply being an outside or margin to culture, it functions as a limit or an impossibility in the structure of a subject, which cannot be integrated into a symbolic structure. Since the real is always a limit-point determined by the symbolic, for Butler it is not useful in the determination of the incompleteness and complexity of the subject, which can never be covered by Lacan's notion of the symbolic.[23] Butler, like Lacan, posits that a part of the subject must always be foreclosed. She is right in criticizing Lacan for the ambiguous status he gives to the implementation of such a foreclosure: Lacan may be read as if he subscribed to the implementation of certain founding cultural laws, such as the prohibition against incest. She has pointed out that the function of foreclosure must be considered a function of arbitrary social prohibitions, and not, therefore, of what Lévi-Strauss would call founding cultural prohibitions. But the most potent aspect of the real is, I would argue, that it posits a part of the subject that would *not* be submitted to the normative order. Lacan's notion of the real allows for a consideration of the foreclosed space that may well open up dimensions that are counter to and even have potentially challenging effects on the symbolic. It refers to some kind of foreign body or alterity beyond the scope of the subject or agent: this other may be another person, nature, sexuality, or death. When Antigone evokes divine laws, she calls for the city to protect certain customs concerning these areas. These customs may be protected by the law, but they cannot be altogether formalized. Rather than enforcing certain practices and habits, the symbolic sets up restrictions and limits. Subjectivity must be structured around some kind of impossibility or limit. This impossibility would correspond to its status as finite and vulnerable. But it would also fulfill the function of defining us as desiring beings as such. The alternative could well be submission, invasion, and fatalism—the giving up of one's subjectivity in submission to an invisible authority. The reason psychoanalysis has claimed to work with a symbolic function that is separate from the state is that its theoretical grid can never be completely "positivized" and transposed into a system of norms and rules. From a Lacanian point of view, one may argue for the need for a radical break between the structure of subjectivity or agency and a normative order of values. Antigone is a figure whose desire is determined in an origin where the symbolic order fails and fades. This does not mean, of course, that the real is a subversive aspect of ourselves that is completely untouched by culture, discourse, or social contexts. What it means is rather that social and cultural norms do not simply form subjects, but are dependent also on the investments of those subjects. A cultural order is not to be understood merely on the basis of its values, but on the *desires* investing those values. These desires are structured around a founding impossibility, pointing to a limit that cannot be breached. It could be something with normative implications attached to the founding prohibition, like the incest taboo or the Ten Commandments. But it could be something completely different: death, the finite perspective of the principle of natality that stakes out the limits of our being as existants, the principle of sexuation that stakes out the limits of our desire and grounds it in a fundamental possibility inherent in our being. There are, in fact, gains in assuming the existence of a domain that is neither normative nor collapsed into the social order. If we remain strictly with the idea that everything that governs human behavior can be referred to a normative order in some way, the question of what lies beyond becomes uninteresting. It means that there would be no remainder, nothing left outside, no body, no flesh, no real to take into account. But most importantly, the space of the real implies that of *the ethical*. In this case, it means that one would also allow for a space that would disrupt or challenge the current norms of family politics, and thereby call for change: a space where such phenomena as desire, love, and the play with new identities find their nourishment.

On the other hand, Butler is certainly right in demanding a politicization of this domain, overcoming a distinction between state and family, universality and particularity, that no longer seems functional. The reason Antigone's demands and desire have been separated from the order of the state both by Hegel and Lacan is that she defends a domain they do not want to transpose into political discourse, a domain that touches on questions like love, desire, anxiety, and death. Certainly Butler is right in assuming that we can no longer merely rely on the state to recognize and legalize practices in these areas. But how are bonds of love and desire to be regulated if we do not assume that an order is in place that functions independently of the state, although it may be protected by it? Demanding a politicization of "apolitical" practices of love, desire, and family bonds, Butler is suspicious of the Lacanian tendency to depoliticize a structure that then becomes a naturalized form of normativity. I would argue, however, that Lacan's notion of an ethics of the real may indeed indicate a way out of this dilemma. The claim that normativity and ethics can be separated could also be made political—although this is a move that is not undertaken by Lacan himself. Ernesto Laclau, however, makes ethics an important category for the functioning of hegemony: the ethical is not the normative. As a matter of fact, it is precisely the tension between the domain of the ethical, which is a promise of fullness, and the "ought" of the normative that makes possible the renegotiation of the normative order: "There is an ethical *investment* in particular normative orders, but no normative order which is, in and for itself, ethical. . . . Hegemony is, in this sense, the name for this unstable relation between the *ethical* and the *normative*, our way of addressing this infinite process of investments which draws its dignity from its very failure."[24] If one translates this into the specific domain we have been discussing, namely the question of what is counted as and recognized as a family, then the ethical promise Laclau is talking about could perhaps be called love, and the normative could be what is recognized as love.

Butler's book focuses on the need to politicize the family. I would suggest that an ethics of the real, at least in the way I would like to read it, could reinforce her argument. Whereas a family politics on issues of homosexual adoptions, for instance, necessarily has to deal with questions of recognition, and therefore with the normative order, the question of ethics leaves that other space open, a space where the demand for recognition may arise in other contexts. This does not mean that the question of the family is apolitical. What it means is rather that what Hegel called the natural domain—the domain of desire, love, and care—cannot and should not be politically determined or controlled under a single regulative order, and to this I think Butler would agree. The problem with family politics is perhaps not that it has been naturalized, but an overly eager politicization under one regulative ideal. Under the banner of family values—not least in Britain and America—politicians have made more or less intrusive attempts to "normalize" the family. Because so-called family values and heteronormativity are pretty much the same thing, of course it is impossible to simply leave the question of the family out of the political sphere. Given this situation, perhaps the psychoanalytic demarcation line between the normative idea of what is to count as a family and an ethical sphere that withdraws from such norms could be used for a progressive family politics after all. Such a demarcation line takes into account that there is a gap between a normative order of values and codes, practices and habits, that we need to incorporate in our daily lives and the bonds that we form. There is no healing symbol that would overcome this gap. But this fact protects us from the invasion, eradication, and submission to an invisible symbolic authority that could be positivized as the good, the father, or the law. The subject originates in a necessary impossibility, both an obstacle to fullness and a shield from dissolution. This necessary impossibility is unraveled by Antigone.

Ethics, Desires, and Drives

If there is an ethical experience evoked by *Antigone*, it is not to be found at the level of the prepolitical, where the bonds between members of the family are inscribed in terms of love and care, but rather at a level of an ethical gesture motivated by the singular inscription that causes the desire of the subject. Rather than asserting the subject as responsive to and responsible for moral values, Lacanian ethics inquires into issues of alterity, transgression, and enjoyment. Lacan, who is interested in liminal experiences that cannot be subjected to the scrutiny of moral terms, asserts that a psychoanalytic notion of the ethical must be separated from moral normativity.[25] Desires and drives contribute to the creation of beliefs and value; every law carries in its very edifice the inherent possibility of a transgression, a crime or extreme action that simultaneously violates and affirms its foundations. Tragic transgression develops not in the face of external forces, but through inscriptions that are given in the very premises of the action. Ethics, in such a reading of Sophocles' tragedy, is not a moral code of behavior, nor an issue of right and wrong, but a definition of subjectivity itself. That feminine desire is an excess of the symbolic order does not mean that woman fails to incorporate or enact ethical norms, which was the Enlightenment view. It means rather that feminine desire indicates the possibility of an ethics situated in the rift between symbolic prohibition and normative injunction. Antigone allows us to formulate an ethics in which the subject is not only autonomous but also exposed, not only finite but also destructive, not only vulnerable but also monstrous. Her action is undertaken without concern for the good, where values are shown and proven through the experience of rewards such as happiness or pleasure, and it is Antigone's lack of concern for the good—or knowledge or possible experience of it—that makes her into a symbol of ethical action. The question of the good as a motive for ethical action is rethought from the point of view of desire: at "the limit of his own good, the subject reveals himself to the never entirely resolved mystery of the nature of his desire."[26] The "purity" of Antigone's desire refers to a void beyond the order of values where actions, like objects, are deemed to be good or bad. Instead of negotiating values, ethics becomes a question of negotiating that void. The *Ethics of Psychoanalysis* situates ethics beyond the moral "object" of the good. The task of psychoanalysis is to look beyond values and norms for an ethical foundation, since they are the product of a social construction which in itself is incapable of providing an answer to the question of what would constitute a real motive for ethical action. Lacan empties the moral "object" of social context. Pure desire means getting rid of objectives such as recognition.[27] This does not mean that the question of the good must be discarded or disregarded, but that it can be emptied of social, metaphysical, and perceptual content: we can neither know it nor experience it in a precise or decisive manner. It is the cause rather than the aim of those actions that can be considered within an ethical framework. The rugged Thing that confronts Lacan's Antigone serves as an image of such an empty object. There is a necessity in Antigone's pursuit of the Thing that points to the intersection between what Lacan calls desire and drive. At this intersection, the question of the symbolic is raised, which is where the issue of values is situated.

Lacan's symbolic order is, as we have seen, not an order of values or ethical norms. If it provides a construction of normativity, it does so in the form of a skeleton of limits rather than in the form of values. These limits are primarily constituted by prohibitions. Lacan uses the example of the Ten Commandments to prove his point: any moral law has to be given in the form of a prohibition if it is to support a symbolic order, because it is only in the form of a prohibition that the difference between desire and law is upheld.[28] Another such limit would be the prohibition of incest.[29] There is, therefore, a decisive rift between the social sphere and the symbolic order, a rift that cannot be closed because the symbolic cannot be represented by anything or anyone, whereas the social sphere is always represented, by the women, men, mothers, fathers, workers who make up the functioning community.[30] The question is at what level the Thing is situated, if we are referring to that cause of desire for the subject that the symbolic order has delineated. Some commentators have suggested that it is to be situated at a transcendental level, since it designates the condition of possibility of desire as such.[31] Other commentators have suggested that it belongs to a level where the category of transcendentalism does not apply, namely to the level of the signifier, which is analogous to but not the same as Kant's elaborations of the transcendental object.[32] What would speak against both these perspectives is the fact that the Thing, unlike the transcendental object, is described from the start as an ethical concept rather than as an epistemological one. It fulfills a function of alterity that is related to the corporeal encounter with the material world, an insistence that can never be fully negotiated in the symbolic order. It is singular, and can neither be represented in a social order nor as a knowable fact. It causes a splitting of the subject and is always unattainable. If it was to become accessible in the social order, or at a level where we might know it and recognize it, it would cause a collapse of the necessary rift between social and symbolic that Lacan's ethics is trying to negotiate. One could perhaps say that the Thing represents the split between the good as an object that gives us pleasure and the good as a moral value. If the rift between the two domains did not exist we would perhaps be able to construct an ethics on the notion of the good in which there was no opposition at all between what we know and what we desire, the good we strive for and the motivations behind the actions we undertake. As it is, however, the problem consists precisely of how we are to construct an ethics in which the value of the good as an ethical injunction and the knowledge of the good as an object that would give us pleasure are radically separated.

According to certain observations made by psychoanalysis, values are related both to desire and the domain of the drives, which for Lacan are situated in the real. The drives cannot be symbolized; they move in a circuit of endless repetition, lacking a proper goal.[33] The domain of the drive is the psychoanalytic equivalent of ethical nihilism. While psychoanalysis may question the idea that desire is aimed at an object—it is Lacan's claim that desire has a cause, and not an object—the equivalent in the domain of ethics would be to question the idea that an action can be motivated by the value it has in the normative order. The fact that the cause of desire is situated in the domain of the real indicates that a moral action has a cause and not an objective: if we reduce its motive to the calculation of its consequences, then we miss the domain where the motive is really situated, the domain where the subject is inscribed. The aim of psychoanalysis is not to do good but to turn us away from a fantasmatic position as victim or toy of an invisible Other, such as destiny, into a position where we recognize and assume our desire. This is Antigone's heroic gesture. It entails her death, but it also uncovers the true face of freedom, the fact that there is no Other of the Other, no Supreme Good, no relief or metaphysical justification to be found as the goal of our actions. The Law is contingent, and therefore cruel. There is no justice in its web.

Psychoanalysis lacks an explicit theory of ethics, and it has a dubious relation to moral values. Yet Freud's intuition when he founded psychoanalysis was ethical, Lacan claims, and psychoanalysis is essentially an ethical practice. This does not mean that it has a normative notion of what it should be doing.[34] Concerned with the question of the good, ethics theorizes how we should act and examines the values serving as guidelines for our actions. But psychoanalysis knows that we may well know what is good for us but keep doing what damages and perhaps even kills us. Moral laws, ethical prescriptions, and social expectations are continuously undermined or challenged by desires and drives, a fact that makes social and ethical norms into a problem for psychoanalytic thinking. This does not mean that psychoanalytic theory disclaims their function in everyday life—but it questions the usefulness of a moral theory that does not take into account the existence of desires and drives. For psychoanalysis, or at least for Lacan, the question of desire is intrinsically intertwined with ethics.[35] Good and bad are not just terms describing libidinal investments; they are also moral concepts. In this way, the analysis of the object is intertwined with ethical questioning, and the traversing of imaginary "good" and "bad" objects an ethical issue of pure desire.

Psychoanalysis has no ethics in the sense that it would subscribe to a certain code of behavior, and it says nothing about what norms we should conform to. It is, however, conceivable that psychoanalysis could have had or will have a profound effect on the ethical understanding of modern society and the way norms are erected and perceived. Modernity, as Habermas puts it, "can and will no longer borrow the criteria by which it takes its orientation from the models supplied by another epoch; *it has to create its normativity out of itself.* Modernity sees itself cast back upon itself without any possibility of escape."[36] It is clear, of course, that the religious vision of a future reconciliation where everything would be absolved will no longer do. Nor can the idealization of the Greek *polis* serve as a substitute. Incessantly trying to "pin itself down," modernity remains caught in a trap of self-reflection that for Habermas makes it necessary to focus on how a feasible theory of normativity is to be founded. Habermas would use psychoanalysis as a theory of interpretation, for the therapeutic aims of clarifying language. In other words, a normative foundation would be present already in the therapy, indicating how language should be used. The ethical function of psychoanalysis would then consist of clarification, serving a normative foundation laid without taking into account functions such as the unconscious or the drives. But if we read Freud, Lacan, and to some extent Melanie Klein on questions of ethics, it becomes clear that psychoanalysis conceives of itself as an intrinsic part of the process of self-reflection necessary for modernity. As we sketched in the last chapter, psychoanalysis would necessarily have a very dubious relation to any theory of normativity, and especially to a theory of normativity with a claim to a moral content. Concerned with subjective mechanisms investing or disinvesting moral values, and given that these mechanisms may seem contrary or subversive to morality, psychoanalysis has even pronounced doubts about grounding morality in demands that one *should* do something. The injunction to do what you know is the good thing tends to release unwanted effects, because such injunctions have a complicated effect on human desire. This does not mean that psychoanalysis disclaims or undermines the question of the good as a primary ethical concern, but rather that it is concerned with the effects that question has on us—as a demand, an object, and an ideal.

The originary psychoanalytic viewpoint held *pleasure* as the good. The body is inscribed in the psyche in the form of needs striving toward satisfaction, making the pleasure principle a primary factor in the development of the psyche. The sheer resistance of the material world, however, and the fact that any originary encounter with it is inscribed as a trauma for the subject, makes it impossible maintain such a principle. The idea that the human psyche is determined primarily by the quest for pleasure was later deconstructed by the theory of the death drive, or what Freud termed the realm beyond the pleasure principle. Our elevation of the good does not simply function in accordance with the pleasure principle. Neither does desire. While Aristotle considered pleasure as an experience intimately connected with knowledge of the good, Freud showed the opposite. If we are to take the Freudian lesson seriously, then any modern or post-Kantian ethics has to distance itself from an Aristotelian notion of the good as coherent with desire, and it will have to rethink the basic issues of ethical values from the point of view of desires and drives. The psychoanalytic framework shows that *we cannot rely on our desire to aim for the good.* Desire is intertwined with the pleasure principle, beyond which lies the death drive, which eradicates the authority of moral principles through a tendency to use them as much for the annihilation of our ego as for the improvement of our moral life.

In his seminar the *Ethics of Psychoanalysis*, Lacan attempts to throw light on these issues. During the seminar, he makes at least three claims that have a bearing on what we will call the problem of desire and ethics, a problem Lacan inherited from Freud. Firstly, Lacan claims psychoanalysis to be an *ethical* project. This does not mean that it aims to promote the good or even a good life: a job, a family, or meaningful relations. The definition of such goals may well be meaningful from a social point of view, but psychoanalysis must concern itself with the truth or foundation of the subject rather than the social construction of the good. The subject is not to be confused with the individual person. While an individual has personal integrity and a personality or character that must be considered separately from larger structures such as language, social environment, moral codes, and so on, the subject is marked by desires and drives that are inscribed in his unconscious. The ethical injunction of Lacanian psychoanalysis is well known: "Have you acted in conformity with the desire that is in you?"[37] This does not mean that it would be ethical to do what one wants or feels like—the desire in question is inscribed at the level of the unconscious, and psychoanalysis should be considered what Lacan calls an *ethics of the real*.[38] One way of understanding Lacan's ethics of the real is, to my mind, to contrast it with a normative position in general terms, or any notion of what one *ought* to do (the normative consideration) as opposed to what one *must* do (an ethics of the real). Although Lacan might well agree that the kind of moral values that are of use to us in everyday life belong to a normative sphere, it would appear that some actions carry a special weight for us, although they may seem contradictory to the demands of the community. Secondly, he questions the psychoanalytic notion of the good object, and shows the notion of the good to belong to an imaginary domain that psychoanalysis must traverse. The ethical experience of psychoanalysis is illuminated in the same light as the relation to the object.[39] The moral value of the good is questioned on the same ground as the good object. The object of the good can be understood both as an object of desire, a person we are attached and attracted to, and as an objective we aim for through our actions. The ethical experience of psychoanalysis is attached to a good that always eludes the subject, to a gap in what Lacan calls the symbolic order of norms and rules. Without formulating a theory of ethics, Lacan shows that psychoanalysis may well contribute to the understanding of how values are formed. Thirdly, Lacan shows that any notion of the good is a product of *sublimation*: we must raise the object to the dignity of the Thing. The object is constructed around *La Chose*, the

Thing, the remainder of a traumatic encounter with matter's resistance, symbolized in the signifier. Special attention is given to the aesthetic values of the Platonic tradition: notions such as the beautiful, the good, and the true. The Thing is the key to Lacan's ethics and his idea of how values are produced. Concepts such as good and beauty are often idealizations covering our lack of control.

Lacan, like Kant, Nietzsche, Heidegger, and others, is concerned with the slipping away of the object of the good and with the frailty of the subject investing in the good. The slipping away of the object is connected with what Lacan calls *jouissance*—a term with multiple meanings whose primary function is to point us toward the endpoint of desire, where no object is present. The slipping away of the good object opens the problem of ethics; it opens up a lack in the symbolic order of norms and values that only psychoanalysis is capable of negotiating properly. For Lacan, this lack is immediately attached to the problem of desire and the constitution of subjectivity. The subject's wavering between desire and *jouissance*, or enjoyment, exposes us to the fragility of ethical values. This wavering refers to the lack of symbolic support, as the subject is threatened with disappearing in the night of *jouissance*. In such a night, there is no "Other of the Other," no structure to support the values we have erected beyond our own capacity to invest in them.[40] As we have seen, such a condition does not refer to nihilism or relativism; rather it stands for a particular exposure: to the "ethical night" in which we are given to what Lacan calls the desire of the Other. There is no Other that would save the subject from himself—no benign symbolic order that would incarnate Justice or the Good. As we have seen in the case of Sade and Wollstonecraft, such an ethical night may produce a condition where the subject is able to prove his autonomy only through fantasies that lead to his own destruction. For Sade, this is a very good thing. For Wollstonecraft, it is a problem which means that the symbolic order that helps produce these fantasies must be renegotiated. For Lacan, psychoanalysis is the remedy: it allows for a negotiation of ethical values, resulting in a process of sublimation where the tendency toward destructiveness is turned around. The subject proves his autonomy through the traversal of his fantasies rather than his submission to them.[41] Limits and prohibitions are both upheld and challenged by our desires and drives, producing a wavering in which the subject—or, to speak in Lacanian language, the lack in the subject—constitutes an unreliable focus. We must negotiate the "end" of our desire in an ethical context because drives and desires cannot simply be seen as a *threat* to moral values, the way they were in the Enlightenment, for instance. Instead, they *contribute* to the construction of moral values. The subject is determined not by one death but by *two*. The projection of our own impending death is a rather abstract phenomenon for psychoanalysis. Death is rather something that has already taken place when the subject comes to be—through a cutting signifier, or castration. Through castration, we are thrown into the world as wounded, imperfect beings. Subjected to the symbolic order of desire, man's first "death" is a constitutive split between desire and drive. It consists in castration through the signifier, in which he submits to an impossible logic where he must either desire the impossible object or give it up, in which case it will disappear altogether and he will fall into the night of *jouissance*. The second death is the *transgression* of the original split, necessitated by the logic of desire itself. The two deaths implicate each other: "The path of the subject passes between the two walls of the impossible."[42] The impossible is the equivalent of the real, as in the reality principle—not just the obstacle to the satisfaction of pleasure, but also the motor behind the pleasure principle as such.

The aging Oedipus at Colonus, facing death, shows us this "inner limit" of desire. It is better never to have been born at all: *mae funai*.[43] "Rather not to be": never to encounter the impossibilities of desire. Heidegger's ontological question, the question of being, begins with a fundamental distinction between what is being and what is not. The logic of desire is constituted in a different way: all that is exists only "in the lack of being."[44] But the difference between Lacan's logic of desire and the questions of Heidegger's ontology is not as great as it might seem at first sight. To exist in the lack of being means, as Jean-Luc Nancy has formulated it, to lack nothing. There is nothing to be lacked, since being only manifests itself as lack—a logic reminiscent of Heidegger.[45] To lack nothing is certainly a condition of freedom that easily translates as nihilism. The idea of a second death, or *jouissance*, may seem to lead toward an eradication of all values beyond good or bad, an embracing of the ethical night in which Sade found his freedom. But as I have pointed out already, Lacan's situating man between two deaths—between lack, or desire, and its counterpart, the lack of nothing, the objectless night of the drive—does not merely lead to an eradication of values. If Lacan wants to construct an ethics around *jouissance*, it has to do with how we think a subject without any transcendental guarantees of the good. While an ethics of psychoanalysis releases man from the bonds of religion, it also forces him to face the destructive forces of his own subjectivity.

From a psychoanalytic point of view, values are intertwined with our instinctual apprehension of the world. Our desires and drives partake in the formation of cultural fictions: the symbolic order is constituted, according to Lacan, by "fictions" or signs we all agree to invest in. This does not mean that they function only at the level of fantasy, but there is no guarantee of their validity beyond the desire of the subject. The more powerful the fiction, the more exposed it is to the drive's tendency to destruction. One example is the deeply ambivalent figure of woman, a symbolic fiction constituted through a certain economy of exchange. Desires and drives partake in the formation of cultural fictions. From a psychoanalytic point of view, values are intertwined with an instinctual apprehension. Cultural fictions or signs become the object of our investments.[46] The fact that they are dependent on the subject does not mean that they function only at the level of fantasy. Subjective investments also contribute to maintaining the symbolic order. Norms, rules, and authorities may exist independently of subjective investments, but we have no guarantees that they will be sustained beyond the desires upholding them.[47] Lacan is uninterested in proposing any normative model for values, or any solution to the disbelief or discontentment that may be the consequence of a social and cultural crisis of values. His fictions are self-referential, reflecting the needs that have created them rather than any transcendental base. In a similar manner, the signifier is a structure that we work out as a fiction, filling it with something. The authorities represented by the father, the mother, the queen, and the king are abstract concepts of power, representing the symbolic order. The fiction contains, however, the seeds of its own disintegration. Authorities fall and fail, our investment in the signifier stumbles upon something that fails to concede to our demands. When we erect the signifier, we also erect the possibility of its own disintegration. The signifier is always there to fill a purpose. That purpose can never be wholly separated from the outline of the empty space that has been cut out. On the contrary, the more powerful the fiction, the more exposed it will be to the drive's tendency to destroy and undermine the authority it represents. But if the end of desire is an abyss, then what could possibly sustain it? There is no ultimate structure to sustain our values, no Other of the Other. In Lacan's later writings, the Other stands not so much for authority and paternal law as for what is always lacking and will continue to fail us. The lack

in the Other opens an absence of ground that means there is nothing to assert desire beyond the inscription of a signifier that never ceases to elude
us.[48] It asserts and sustains the movement of desire, but at the cost of continuous failure. Faulty and weak, the signifier is still a necessary support,
the nonmetaphysical or nonmaterial guarantee of desire. The fact that no
one can represent it opens a crack where the lack of foundation for our desire also opens the possibility of its collapse.

From a psychoanalytic viewpoint, the formation of ethical values is
intrinsically intertwined with the question of the object. Modernity, in the
form of Kantian moral philosophy above all, instigated a radical turn in
our understanding of the relation between desire and ethics. The focus is
on the subject and its relation to the law rather than the values and objectives of moral theory. Formulating a critique of Kant's "empty" formula for
ethics, Hegel replaces the formal conception of a universal morality with
Sittlichkeit. Ethics is no longer defined as an objective formula; it can only
be thought through a historically specific, functioning community. Kant's
moral law removes particular interests—the pathological domain of inclinations, idiosyncrasies, and personal desires—from ethical action. For
Hegel we can only sublate them, moving from the particular to the universal and continuously dispelling the disruptive moments threatening the
construction of an abstract legal order. We can, at least in theory, realize
freedom *in* and *as* the community.[49] It would seem that Hegel, who makes
ethical norms an integral part of a social structure, would be a more obvious model to choose for an ethics of psychoanalysis. But from a Lacanian
perspective, ethics can never be thought according to a social structure of
normativity: the ethical moment refers to an impossibility, the kernel of a
hard resistance that refuses to dissolve in *any* social or ethical order. The
moral object of the good slips away in pretty much the same way as the
good object, and is relegated to the same imaginary domain. The slipping
away dismantles the empty space that lies behind it and displays the "pure"
formula of the condition of possibility of desire. The moral law cuts away
the objectives of good and bad as the aim of morality. Instead, it points to
the law itself as the condition of possibility of moral values.[50] Lacan's ethics
of the real has a similar structure. Any notion of ethics has to go beyond
the fantasmatic relation to the object as good or bad and construct an alternative that does not rely on contents related to concepts or language.
Making the impersonal Thing an object of ethics means approaching the
empty space that those contents cover. The Thing, unlike the *objet petit a*,

is muted and resistant and brings us back to the traumatic inception of the signifier as an introduction to the phenomenal world. But the founding signifier is impossible to represent; it can only refer to an original loss, and its meaning will never cease to elude the subject.[51] From such a viewpoint, ethics is understood not as a normative foundation of values in a socially functioning community but as a dimension intrinsically bound up with (but not identical to) the *desires* investing those foundations, desires freed from aim or content: "A radical repudiation of a certain ideal of the good is necessary."[52] No goals of desire can be upheld in the form of recognition, belief in the good, or any kind of faith that would serve a modern, emancipatory project. Our values and beliefs have been erected in the rift between the unattainable object of desire and the void that threatens to engulf us in the guise of enjoyment. The drive is a circuit emptied of target. But whatever the terminology and the particularities separating desire and drive, the analysis of moral values coincides with the analysis of the subject. The question is not only how values are formed but also how subjects sustain or fail to sustain them. Values are based on contingent cultural motives that are continuously threatened by that realm beyond the pleasure principle, which ultimately forces us to pass from the normative order back to the unreliable subject. Philosophy reviews the values, norms, and beliefs that constitute the normative framework of the community. Psychoanalysis reviews the desires and drives that contribute or fail to contribute to those values. From the point of view of psychoanalysis, it is not only the *kind* of values that is put into question but their *function*. From such a perspective, ethical discourse is motivated by a web of desires and drives.

At this level, moral values can be compared with the function of objects. The psychoanalytic notion of the object is usually examined in all sorts of pathological ways: narcissistic, perverted, obsessive, melancholic, and so forth. Lacan's inquiry into the ethics of psychoanalysis is an attempt to distill a psychoanalytic theory that manages to traverse these pathological descriptions and come up with a "pure" theory of the object. At this level, we are also involved in a response to the psychoanalytic theory of thought, for which we can only relate to the object as good or bad: an idea Lacan vehemently challenges. Subjectivity originates in a moment when the object is just empty, when it is not yet integrated into a structure of desire that is socially determined. At this point, the object has not taken shape as a fictional and valued entity but remains a Thing, the shadow of an object, where qualities have not yet been formed. When values are ascribed to it, it has already been appropriated and integrated into an imaginary order of values. It has become a Kleinian object, situated in an imaginary domain.[53] The Thing lacks the determining properties of a social context. The Thing unravels the neurotic, possessive, obsessive, or melancholic relation to the object, the point where it is neither good nor bad. As such, the subject is referred back to the enigmatic origin of his being, which Lacan calls the inscription of the signifier as cause of desire, an inscription leaving the Thing as its trace. For this reason, Lacan's inquiry into the ethics of psychoanalysis is focused on the Thing.

The Threat of the Neighbor

In psychoanalytic terminology, "object" is another word for our relation to the other. The Thing, in turn, is a preformation of that other, taking shape before the fantasmatic and neurotic screens that will hide it in a social and cultural context. Lacan separates what he calls a brother, a *semblable*, somebody who is similar, from a *prochain*. While we are able to identify with *le semblable*, our *prochain*, or neighbor, is foreign and therefore threatening.[54] The brother, *le semblable*, remains within an economy of mirroring and narcissism, while the neighbor bursts those limits. *Le prochain* opens the gap to what Lacan calls the real, which threatens the image and cover of the self. To love *le prochain*, one's neighbor, as oneself, as the Christian injunction tells us to, is an impossible principle. As we saw in Chapter 4, Freud was the first to recognize the fact that ethics is always intertwined with desires and drives.[55] In *Civilization and Its Discontents*, Freud questions the value of ethical principles, equating their function with a punishing superego. Operating on a thin line between socialization and punishment under impossible demands, however, the superego also threatens to destroy us. What introduced us to civilization to begin with— the repression of the drive—later *becomes* the drive. The more we sacrifice to the superego, the more punishing it becomes. This claim widens the scope of the psychoanalytical task in a significant way. Freud lets us understand that the kind of values we submit to are of less importance than the mechanisms instituting them. It is therefore necessary to observe how ethics functions, not just in its cultural articulations, but also in subjective processes. The problem of a modern ethics, as it is presented to us by psychoanalysis, could then be formulated as such: how are we to bridge the gap between the normative order where moral values are erected and the domain of desires and drives, where these values are erased, undermined, or made useless? The injunction to "love thy neighbor as thyself" is a particularly ambiguous case. Although it seems to be supported by the inclination to narcissism as a function of love, if we look at the actual function of narcissism, the message is more dubious. To love one's neighbor or *prochain* as oneself, as the New Testament tells us, is an impossible principle because every relation to a neighbor is colored by instincts. The instincts of men are neither loving nor caring, but aim to preserve a self threatened by the other, as the history of Christianity clearly shows: "Their neighbor is for them [human beings] not only a potential helper or sexual object, but also someone who tempts them to satisfy their aggressiveness on him, to exploit his capacity for work without compensation, to use him sexually without his consent, to seize his possessions, to humiliate him, to cause him pain, to torture and to kill him."[56] While the idealization of your loved one may seem to protect you from destroying him, any relation may turn into its opposite and the destructive forces be released. As Freud pointed out, religion is bad therapy for aggression. It only serves to amplify the neurosis of civilization and widen the guilt inherent in the modern condition, spurred by the drives of aggression. Psychoanalysis is a much more useful tool than further reinforcement of the superego through education or religious injunctions. Only the struggle to lessen guilt and ease the burden of moral punishment will serve to improve ethical consciousness. Although Freud does not formulate an ethics, one could draw the conclusion that whatever we subscribe to, it can only do the work if we minimize the burden of the superego.

Facing up to the challenge, Lacan makes psychoanalysis into an ethics and does so through the structural elaboration of the law. An ethics can never be founded in positive terms, in the normative form of the *ought*; it must be grounded in prohibition and loss. A maxim such as "love thy neighbor" will only serve to release the principle of excess and vanishing called *jouissance*. To love one's neighbor as oneself is impossible, because no prohibition breaks the mirror between self and other. We must differentiate a neighbor from a brother, a *prochain* from a *semblable*, someone foreign to me from someone similar to me.[57] The brother is a principle of self-sameness and identification. The narcissistic phenomenon of identification, however, only covers the foreign trace through which the other really becomes the other, a trace that threatens to dissolve the shield of protection that constitutes the ego. The relation to the outside world is colored by a continuous conflict in which the neighbor, the foreign, is associated with fear of extinction. Whereas the relation to the brother of similarity, *le semblable*, appears to confirm the self and conform to the limits of narcissistic mirroring, the neighbor is a threat.[58] Love of the other is only stimulation of the excess that ethics must prevent rather than encourage. The message of love of the neighbor only encourages the logic of idealization that governs the punishing superego. Instead, we must take a step back, to the prohibiting God of the Old Testament who has nothing to do with love, or we must go on to Kant, who shows us that morality is precisely about puncturing the logic that makes us believe that we know the good. This is the problem of nihilism for Lacan: if God is dead, then the problem is not so much that moral values are eradicated, but rather that we are left with an impossible object at the heart of the question of how moral values are erected.[59] While this may seem to open numerous possibilities for us, it also presents a danger of eradication of the limit set up by the absolute prohibition. We are left with a void, where the absence of limit or prohibition produces the impulse toward submission to an invisible authority or symbolic system. The consequences of this are discussed in, for instance, Žižek's essay "Love Thy Neighbor? No Thanks!" Žižek diagnoses the problem of modernity as a pointless and ceaseless enjoyment in which the subject submits to the Other not because he has to, but because submission is an enjoyment he cannot resist. This is how all the big systems, from Marxism to Nazism to capitalism, uphold their authority: through a space of fantasy in which desire collapses into *jouissance*, where the production of servitude becomes the primary principle of the system itself. The problem of modernity is, then, that ideological systems are produced in order to serve the production of enjoyment itself, not just as a secondary form of payoff or giving up or nihilism, but rather as a culture of servitude.[60]

The Thing beyond the Object

For Lacan, the question of a modern, or rather psychoanalytic, ethics turns not on submission to a big Other, but on the impossible object we encounter in any system of values we erect. This does not mean, of course, that it would be pointless to erect notions of the good, but this is not the business of psychoanalysis. *Le prochain* is introduced as a primary principle for the ethical in the *Ethics of Psychoanalysis*: the *prochain* is neither good nor bad, but the foreign object against which all moral principles must be measured. When Lacan talks about *le prochain*, our neighbor, he is referring also to Freud's concept of *das Nebenmensch*. The word is present in Freud's first model of the psychic apparatus, *Entwurf einer wissenschaflichen Psychologie* (*Project of a Scientific Psychology*), from 1895. In *Entwurf*, Freud investigates the human individual as an example of organic life, comparable to all other life forms, whose reactions and defense mechanisms can be understood in terms of excitement and relief. The organism is driven by *die Not des Lebens* (the exigencies of life), or *ananke*, the demands and needs of survival.[61] The organism must negotiate both outer and inner excitement, both hunger and the search for satisfaction. Between these poles, the self develops, not as a kernel but as a protecting shield.[62] The organism avoids displeasure, and in an analogous way, the child learns how to avoid or cope with threatening situations by screaming for "help from the outside." Man's original helplessness, says Freud, constitutes "the origin of all *moral motive*."[63] In other words: our relation to good and evil is colored by an original absolute helplessness. Our *Nebenmensch*, our neighbor, is both a medium of satisfaction and a threat. On the one hand, we mimic the gestures and learn to communicate with that parallel universe, a *Nebenmensch*. On the other hand, our neighbor is external and foreign. The part of the neighbor we cannot assimilate Freud calls the Thing, *das Ding*.[64] The difference between self and other is mediated through a judgment, a capacity of the organism to negate and set up limits. Lacan, who takes up the concept of the Thing from Freud, underlines its ambivalent character. Whether it is situated in the self or the other can never be fully determined. The Thing is produced by a split: one part is attached to the organism, the other to its outside. By isolating the trace of something foreign, the Thing breaks the narcissistic game of mirrors. Freud, in his first attempt to ground a psychology in the natural sciences, gives a particular place to pain in this process. The organism learns gradually to avoid pain as displeasure, but the initial experience of pain makes an imprint on the organism as if it was "struck by lightning," opening gates between psychic levels that normally are kept closed.[65] The penetrating power of pain, original trauma, opens up gates to the world and forces the organism to create the protecting shield of the ego, negotiating relations with the outside world, which initially presents itself as hard and impenetrable.[66] The split may be painful, but it creates an ethical relation. The trauma of the signifying cut creates the relation to an alterity that will always compel the subject.[67]

But the ethical relation to our neighbor has not been determined.

The object, as Freud puts it, is never found, it is always re-found.[68] We may interpret this as if our desire were always directed toward a trace or shadow of an object. The Thing has a material quality in its link to the traumatic cut by the signifier, where the relation to the body is situated. Because its genealogy is to be found in the resistance breaking the narcissistic shield of the human organism, shattering its autonomy or self-enclosed economy, it must be considered neither inside nor outside, neither self nor other.[69] The Thing turns us toward the outside world. Or rather, it tears us out, opening the gap between sign and subject. It is "that which in the real suffers from the signifier," which means that language is always tainted by the real.[70] This does not mean that the real belongs to an archaic universe beyond language and culture, and it does not mean that the real can be considered "maternal." It may seem easy to qualify the Thing as maternal in its very nature, where the mother plays the role of an engulfing, threatening Other. The function of the Thing, however, does not reinvoke any pre-Oedipal experience of the maternal body, and is not to be confused with the maternal object. Cut out by the law against incest, which forces the traumatic inception of the signifier, the Thing can only be maternal absence, and so can never be identified with the mother per se:

The desire for the mother cannot be satisfied because it is the end, the terminal point, the abolition of the whole world of demand, which is the one that at its deepest level structures man's unconscious. It is to the extent that the function of the pleasure principle is to make man always search for what he has to find again, but which he will never attain, that one reaches the essence, namely, that sphere or relationship which is known as the law of the prohibition of incest.[71]

The Thing is the remainder of that necessary cut between need and desire, maternal body and self, other and self. We must literally desire nothing if the structure of desire is to be upheld. Our relation to the *Nebenmensch*, the experience of the other, is connected to an infantile need for satisfaction, as Freud has described. The child is introduced to the desiring structure of subjectivity by a maternal lack. We cannot *represent* that lack or transcribe it in visual terms. Rather it is the dynamic presence-absence itself that installs it, regulated by the signifier.

Lacan defines the subject as a signifier representing a subject for another signifier.[72] One may take this to refer to a rather simple idea of representation, through names, symbolic functions, social roles, and so on, that makes subjects representable to each other in discourse. But at the same time, the discussion of the Thing shows us that the signifier—and thereby the subject—always contains a part that is unrepresentable and therefore impossible to appropriate. Some part of the subject eludes, through the cutting effects of the signifier, the fictional aspects of the symbolic. It is precisely that eluding and evasive part of the subject that calls for an ethics of the real. Such an ethics is founded neither on the compelling foreign face of the other nor on concern for our neighbor, but on that part cut out through the signifier, which is erected in the symbolic but always eludes its *fictional* aspects. It is dumb, fearsome, and lacks qualities. And yet it forces our curiosity and hunger. The Thing is the resistance of a phenomenal world that refuses to dissolve as language, values, discourse, poetry, love, or any signifying activity in which we may engage. Not responding but withdrawing, not presencing but absencing, the Thing maintains a structure of desire and a limit of alterity where the relation to the other is situated. In its inhumanity, therefore, the Thing is what makes us human.[73] Given that the Thing is both a function of alterity and radically ambiguous in its status, the ethics of psychoanalysis cannot escape its insistence. Our field of vision, our relation to being, is always circumscribed by the relation to an alterity we cannot subsume. It never equals pure hard matter, but is mediated through the Other. The question of the Thing, therefore, leads us not into an ontological inquiry about the status of the subject, but to the ethical implications of the fact that the subject has its origin in the inscription of alterity. But we cannot, like Levinas, think alterity as the face of Other, forcing infinite responsibility.[74] We have to insert at least a fragment of mediation. That fragment is the Thing. If we remove it, we lose that rugged element that in fact *saves us* from invasion of the Other, the *jouissance* of the Other that Lacan talks about in terms of too much submission, too much obeisance, the obliteration of the self to an invisible authority. The subject originates in a necessary impossibility, both an obstacle to fullness and a shield from dissolution. An ethics of the real denies unity, simplicity, harmony, and totality. Instead it introduces failures, faults, mistakes, and the impossible as the categories from which ethics must be thought.[75]

The Beauty of the Thing

The Thing is a foreign element lacking determined qualities, and as such it is not just an ethical but also an aesthetic concept, although it is impossible to represent. Artistic creations touch upon the Thing because they are driven toward that original loss, which could be described as some kind of mythical origin, but which in reality is nothing but the cut between representation and phenomenon.[76] Art touches the discursive limits of our being. It makes us see things in a new way, engage in the world in a new way. That engagement takes place not just on a sensual level or at the level of shapes. The artistic object contains in it a Thing—a gap, an empty space—that always threatens to break the illusion through a gap or empty space. And yet that Thing constitutes the compelling aspect of the object. In Heidegger's *Origin of a Work of Art*, the Thing is an invisible insertion among the phenomena of everyday life, challenging our understanding and creating an impetus for our thought. Its compelling force insists that we search for its meaning, directing us toward an evasive origin. The meaning is never given. The Thing is a unique but "empty" phenomenon that remains when we consider it beyond its usefulness as equipment. In itself, the Thing has no qualities.[77] The fact that equipment plays a significant role in its determination in Heidegger's analysis is important—the equipment is a mediating term between the "empty" Thing and the finished work of art. The Thing never appears on its own; rather it serves as a tool for Dasein. Heidegger famously chooses an empty pair of shoes from a painting of van Gogh as his example, a pair of shoes that in his interpretation belong to a peasant woman. There are no determining qualities to the peasant woman's shoes, but they nevertheless bring us back to the earth she was working in and on, they give witness to the human struggle on that earth, the daily effort to use it, win bread, and survive through it.[78] In Heidegger's version, the Thing appears through an engagement in which Dasein's being is uncovered. Such a notion of the Thing can also be compared to Heidegger's first reading of the "Hymn to Man," where man is defined as plowing the earth, conquering—failing only in death. Existence is a tragic predicament, one violent turn following upon the other. We heroically struggle both against and toward our destiny, constructing the tools of our own failure. But we are not ultimately *suffering*. For Lacan, however, we are. We do not construct tools, we construct signifiers. Also for Lacan, the Thing is possessed by an "empty" quality that provokes and challenges our thought. It is not related to our being in the world, however, but to a foreign and threatening part of our subjectivity. Situated between desire and *jouissance*, the subject is not essentially *equipped* to live in the way Heidegger proposes. A fundamental inability or impossibility is inherent in every relation to the object: the resistance of the Thing. Art moves us at a level where we intensely experience our relation to the Thing; artistic creations allow us to see the point or moment in the object when it questions our perception and understanding. We can use a vase as a metaphor for the act of creation, a metaphor that Lacan uses after Heidegger. What makes up the thingness of the container is not the material out of which it is made, but the emptiness around which it is constructed.[79] Heidegger's thing is the unity toward which logos is attracted. Lacan, however, also uses it as an analogue for the signifier. The signifier and the vase are material constructions. But they seem to be formed around an empty space. The vase is there to be filled with something, as is the signifier. We can of course fill it with poetic meaning, and Lacan himself talks about Cezanne's apples. But if we are to follow Lacan's philosophy of art, today we would come closer to filling it with crap and making it a challenge to society's norms, existing at the limits of discourse, which is Lacan's claim.[80] We make the vase into our Thing. We fill it with crap, because that is the way we are, us humans. Then we make it beautiful in order to hide the crap.

The important term to introduce in this context is sublimation. Sublimation is a word derived from the concept of the sublime. The definitions of the sublime, as they were given in the school of German Idealism, all signify the overwhelming and incommensurable, that which cannot be symbolized or merely contained in artistic expression.[81] Sublimation, for Lacan, is this *overvaluation* of the object, a form of overvaluation that naturally negotiates the shadows in the background. We sublimate when we *raise the object to the dignity of the Thing.*[82] This means: the artistic object must be made so beautiful that it corresponds to the horror it displaces; it must be so good that the evil that glares openly behind stays hidden, and it must be so true that the empty space it touches is filled. Desire is always directed toward the empty space of the Thing, glaring through the signifier. If sublimation creates a bond between us, that bond is a negative one rather than an affirmative one. I am touched, not *through* social codes, as Freud holds, but through the negative space they open up through their challenge, in the display of what cannot be contained in symbolic discourse.[83] Freud gives two definitions of sublimation, which both refer to the notion of subjective creativity. The first means displacing the cathexis or libidinal investment in an object. In order to avoid repression, we invest in something else; thus we are able to satisfy the drive.[84] Art and intellectual work constitute, for Freud, socially accepted forms of sublimation. In *Civilization and Its Discontents*, suppression of the drives is the unconditional price civilization has to pay to uphold its legacy. The sublimation of the drives is one of the most important features of cultural development: "It is that which makes it possible for higher psychical activities, scientific, artistic or ideological, to play such an important part in civilized life."[85] The polymorphously perverted body of infantile sexuality, governed by pleasure or displeasure, is prevented from showing its limbs. Aggression, hatred, and lust are replaced or displaced in an acceptable way. Art is a social medium of sublimation. The artist, like the scientist, uses art or science as a socially acceptable form of deviation for the drives to work through complexes developed through the unsatisfied drives of infantile sexuality.[86] For Julia Kristeva, the Thing is the shadow of an object created by love or transference toward another. As such, it has a creative function in the painful process of separation: although we may be forced to lose the object, we may always guard and protect the love for that object. It can be introjected and projected, kept as the beloved part of a melancholic self, but also projected and used as a creative tool.[87]

Aesthetic sublimation creates another space, a space of fantasy. But it often seems as if the fantasies circle around a fixed point. This point is the experience of beauty. Lacan displaces the ground for an ethics from the good to the experience of the beautiful, or the "beauty effect." The beauty effect is the split between ourselves and our objects of desire. The effect of beauty, which of course is analogous to the effect of the fantasm, points to something we desire that we cannot interiorize or integrate. By analogy, we cannot interiorize the human objects of our desire.[88] The limit and gap that separate us are also the limit of desire. Thus the beauty effect unravels the void behind it. This entails traversing the screens of narcissistic gratification. When Lacan discusses the beautiful, he carries out a genealogical investigation. The question is not how we experience beauty. The question is how we come to regard something as beautiful. Beauty then no longer follows the good in a simple manner. Art is beautiful per se, for Lacan, because it hides what is frightening and unbearable—for example, the hidden skull in Holbein's *Ambassadors*, which becomes visible only if you see the work from a certain angle. Beauty covers the distorted face of death.[89] The famous example of courtly love is another case in point: the beautiful woman is elevated above the reach of her loving admirers, only to be degraded in another context. The ambiguity of the Thing cuts both ways.

"The beautiful, the good, the true" is the formula of Neoplatonism. The aesthetics of Neoplatonism related these concepts to one another in the idea that the beautiful would lead to the good, and finally also to the true. Psychoanalysis necessarily formulates this differently. If we were to follow Lacan, it would be crap, evil, death. Beauty does not convey knowledge. It is, above all, something that we simply elevate. The beautiful touches or moves us, without our being able to touch it or grasp it. The beautiful object affects us, without having to do with harmony or pleasure. Our respect for it gives witness to something else, which is bound up with the process of sublimation.[90] The experience of the beautiful is a screen, a protection, from a tendency toward disintegration that is integral to every Thing.[91] The Thing is both beautiful and fearsome, a fantasy construction originating in a fundamental exposure of the subject between transcendental and material domains. The Thing keeps us riveted to the deformities of our own needs and desires, not knowing where they originate, where they may be heading, or what their purpose might be. The Thing is situated between the site of the nether world and the sphere of possible transcendence. It is the body we can never fully sublimate or transcend. But, at the same time, it is detached and foreign through the signifier, transcending the corporeal registers through language.

Of course, the notion of the Thing is a kind of fiction or fantasy that does very little to answer questions of what would constitute a feasible ground for an ethics. But that fiction does take into account the fact that we have to construe an ethics that is based on some kind of fundamental prohibition, some kind of symbolic or contingent structure that relieves us from claiming knowledge of the good. Such a prohibition has the power to create an object of desire beyond our capacity of appropriation. It is not in spite of, but because *we do not know* the true essence or nature of the good that we become ethical subjects, acting according to drives and impulses that may seemingly go against any conceptual or intellectual knowledge of moral values. An ethics of the real is not based on the kind of ethical life we have to lead in the community as social and morally educated beings. It is based, instead, on the part that is foreclosed and excluded from such education, a part that nevertheless takes its toll in the life of the subject.

The Purification of Desire

The most scandalous fiction of psychoanalysis is, naturally, the drive, the idea that a life force would perpetuate itself eternally in the life of the organism and make that into the psychic goal of that organism as well. Unwilling to leave the domain of the symbolic in favor of a somatic or corporeal realm, Lacan makes the drive into a form of "pure" desire. In order to get to purity, we need a theory of purification or catharsis. The concept is interpreted according to three roots: Aristotle, early Freud, and the Cathars. The Aristotelian definition, which Lacan defines as "moral catharsis," carries the sense of both pleasure and purification.[92] It can only occur after we have traversed pity and fear—that is, the domain of fantasy. The Freud who wrote *Entwurf* makes psychoanalysis to a cathartic theory. Lacan aligns himself with this theory, which dates back to the childhood of psychoanalysis: therapy helps bring forth an "Abreaktion," a kind of relief. It is, however, a form of relief that, in relation to the trauma that releases it, always leaves something unsolved.

The medieval religious sect, the Cathars, finally interests Lacan the most. They saw their own death coming with stoic calm. The goal for their faith was to escape evil matter, and life was considered to be only a preparation for death, which in itself stood for a form of purification. Like Sade, they held nature to be evil and evoked suffering as the element into which humans are born. Catharsis is not just relief from the tension induced by an original trauma, a purification of desire in the sense that it reveals the imaginary character of the object. Pity and fear, the emotions that bring us through the cathartic experience of tragedy in Aristotelian theory, belong to the sphere of the imaginary that surrounds the object.[93] These emotions are raised in relation to an object, but they have no function outside of the imaginary. One may therefore conclude that ethics has nothing to do with emotions. Feelings may guide us toward an ethical domain, but they do not constitute moral guidelines in themselves.

Can we discuss the ethical dimension of tragedy without considering emotions? Can we really, like Lacan, reduce the importance Aristotle gives to fear and pity as imaginary effects lacking implications for the ethical kernel we are looking for?[94] Most contemporary interpreters of Aristotle avoid mistaking catharsis for purification in the sense of relief.[95] Catharsis, says Martha Nussbaum, transgresses the Platonic division between emotions and intellect. It refers to a "clarification" of feelings rather than relief, and therefore has a moral function.[96] Emotion is an integral part of ethical knowledge, not a hindrance to be surpassed in search of a higher goal. The capacity to integrate intellect and emotion is a measure of ethical maturity. The concept of *pathei mathos*—learning through suffering—gives witness to the emotional complexity of ethical experience.[97] For Nussbaum, Kant's description of a universal, formal, and irreproachable law of morality is a step back in relation to tragedy's unity between feeling and intellect. Conflict calls for particular insights and solutions, not formulas, and an Aristotelian notion of Greek tragedy goes against universalizing concepts. The Kantian discovery of the moral law makes the ethical subject autonomous, detached from the encounter with actual events, disregarding our engagement in the empirical world. In contrast, the Greek conception of ethical values includes a large measure of chance. Tragic heroes and heroines fall into misfortune in spite of themselves, making themselves guilty of criminal actions against their own better knowledge, showing that moral values are created as responses to events in a world that cannot be controlled, to concrete happenings where the moral conclusion can never be given in advance. The gap between our intentions and the pressure of the outside world is demonstrated by the relation between the character and the actions in the outside world: *tuche*. How much chance can we encounter, how can we learn to stand that which we cannot control? The test of our dignity arises in the tension between outer and inner world, forcing us to question the Kantian thesis of an absolute moral law, which is valid independently of the events we encounter.[98]

Such an interpretation of the ethical message of tragedy is contrary to Lacan's, where it is not man's ability to encounter the unexpected, but on the contrary his ability to get into trouble, that demonstrates his moral capacity. It is this unavoidability that is manifested by *tuche*. Those things *will* fall into our heads—freedom is not the measure of subjectivity. The ethical message of tragedy does not concern the gap between an objective world that we are unable to control and our ability to encounter chance. The ethical message lies in the fact that *tuche* is a moment produced by our own actions, a resistance created by and through our own agency, confirming us as autonomous, moral agents.[99] *Tuche* is an encounter initiated by ourselves rather than an arbitrary effect. It is not chance, but what *seems* to be chance: *tuche* is an encounter happening *as if by chance*.[100] Tragedy always encircles the moment of *tuche* and makes it visible in that very form; it leaves little space for the unforeseen and makes us aware of the necessary conditioning of what would otherwise appear arbitrary. The ethics of psychoanalysis follows the same logic. Rather than negotiating freedom of choice, such an ethics makes visible the necessary conditions of seemingly arbitrary actions and events. Lacan never really discusses the term "freedom" in his writings, and when he does, it is only in order to point to its illusory character.[101] The ethics of psychoanalysis becomes instead to act according to your desire. The only thing we can be guilty of is the failure of that action, because "there is no other good than that which may serve the price for access to desire—given that desire is understood here, as we have defined it elsewhere, as the metonymy of our being."[102]

In such a perspective, emotions have only an instrumental worth. They are as unreliable as our opinion of good and evil, and as deluded as our reliance on the acquisition of an object for our happiness. They constitute a necessary passage toward the elevation of the Thing as cause of our actions, but lack particular value in themselves.[103] Such a conception may appear both limited and technocratic in comparison with Aristotle's rich evaluation of the role of emotions in moral actions, which Nussbaum recapitulates. However, the causality of fate is not necessarily divine: what befalls us comes from a necessity related to our place within a larger context, and to a failing link between the singular and the social and legal community.

The cathartic point can only show itself with the recognition of the signifier as cause.[104] In Antigone's case, it is *ate* creating her impossible desire to redeem herself through the unresponsive dead brother. The cause of our desire, therefore, also threatens to destroy us. It may sound surprising, therefore, when Lacan states that the analyst's desire is the most beautiful thing that he can give.[105] This statement, however, should be taken *ad notam*: unless the analyst presents his or her desire to know rather than a pretense to understand, we find ourselves in a short-circuit where the analyst becomes the engulfing mother rather than the midwife delivering the truth. Certainly these words are spoken to the analyst, as an ethics of the psychoanalytical clinic. The end of analysis can only consist in the recognition that there is no phallus, and therefore no resolution or reconciliation.[106] Getting back to the *Hilflosigkeit*, or helplessness, the original status that initiates the relation to the neighbor and the trauma that tears us out in the world, we have come full circle.[107]

Psychoanalytic judgment transgresses the rational reflection of reason. Being touched by the other has much more to do with the experience of beauty, of pity and fear, than with actual understanding. An ethics of the real must necessarily entail that we go through the imaginary, through pity and fear: "Analysis is a judgment. . . . It is because, from a certain point of view, the analyst is fully aware that he cannot know what he is doing in psychoanalysis. Part of this action remains hidden even to him."[108] That is the paradox of analysis: it can only create meaning against a background where we have no guarantee that our lives will become better.

An Ethics of the Real—Playing the Piano

So does Lacan's ethics possibly constitute anything like a modern-day paradigm? Could an ethics based on the truth of the subject rather than the good, on singularity rather than universality, on signifiers rather than values, on desire rather than responsibility, possibly apply outside of the psychoanalytic practice? Follow your desire is the message—but the question remains what an ethics of the real would actually consist in.[109] Two powerful representations of feminine desire allow us to speculate: *The Piano*, by Jane Campion, and Elfriede Jelinek's *The Piano Teacher*. Jelinek, one of the defining authors of postwar Europe, has explored the darker sides of desire without compromise. Obsession, possessiveness, and perversion are all part of a literary milieu that could be likened to that of Sade and Bataille. However, there is, as has been shown in the second chapter of this book, a big difference between the exploration of feminine desire in its perverted forms, as we found in Wollstonecraft for instance, and its male version. Jelinek does not immerse her characters in perversity in order to uncover forbidden pleasures or to uncover the end of desire in an atheist explosion of *jouissance*. As in Sade's work, perverse sexuality challenges the constraining and confining norms of society, but the stakes for Sade and Jelinek are not the same. While Sade's heroines have learned to use submission for pleasure, Jelinek's heroines are representatives of her sustained revolt against repressive social and cultural structures, which make submission a possible source of *jouissance*. Perversion does not offer a way past these structures; it enforces the severing restraint of the superego.

The piano teacher is Erika Kohut, a middle-aged woman working at the Conservatory of Music in Vienna. Erika, who lives with her mother, spends her days confined to a narrowly defined routine that has her hurry home after each piano lesson. In his adaptation of the novel, Michael Hanneke shocks viewers with an early scene that reveals the excessively tight bonds between mother and daughter: they sleep in the same bed. Rather than guaranteeing the daughter's submission to the life of an asexual "old maid," however, the mother's attempt to control her causes Erika's life to revolve around the secret outlets of her sexuality. Regularly escaping the surveillance of her mother to visit the same pornography stalls as men do, she hides in the bathroom and cuts up her vagina. When she falls in love with a young man, the obsession quickly transforms into masochistic games. The story then pursues the increasingly violent love story, only to end with a desperate pledge and Erika stabbing herself, though not fatally. Having lived for many years with her aging mother in a flat from the heyday of the Viennese bourgeoisie, Jelinek in some respects makes Erika into her alter ego. At first glance, the novel might appear to be a revelation of the secret life of the bourgeoisie, of the perverted fate of a woman suffocated by her mother, but the real story is that of a desire thwarted by the punishing constructions of the superego, which is enacted by a real controlling mother but is the incarnation of a "culture of death" itself. Throughout her work, Jelinek has persistently explored a violence and nihilism echoing that of older, more violent times. Shades of the past linger in the desires of the new generation, who are all children of a "culture of death": not just a culture of monumental dead figures but also of the death it has produced.[110] Inspiring a feeling of sunkenness, the bourgeois circles in which Erika the piano teacher moves are above all marked by *weakness*. The place of the führer is markedly absent, and the domination of the superego seems to be induced by his very failure to rematerialize. In that environment, the heroines find themselves dominated by what Jelinek calls the petite bourgeoisie, but which could perhaps be called a weakened normative order incapable of restructuring itself. In Jelinek's work, this becomes shockingly blatant in the configurations of desire. The mother is both internalized and a real, embodied führer supplementing the lack of a strong leader with a demonized and sexualized superego. Erika's enjoyment is really the mother's; the daughter is the fetishized object of her fixation and her phallic supplement. This becomes clear in a scene where Jelinek attempts to insert something that in her own mind was never represented in world literature: driven to despair over her inability to pursue her passion for Walter, the young man, the daughter attempts to rape the mother. The rape fails, Jelinek explains, because the daughter is castrated and powerless: the phallus belongs to the mother. The daughter is her object, still attached to the maternal body. The mother being the living superego in the psychic life of the daughter, there is no way out of the *jouissance* of the daughter's submission. Enjoyment never becomes an emancipatory possibility, as in Sade-Wollstonecraft. It remains caught in the superego because there is no primal repression of the *jouissance* of the Other and no way past that Other's *jouissance*.

The place of the piano is interesting in this context. One would perhaps like to see the piano as a means of sublimation, as the artistic outlet beyond perverted obsessions and behaviors. When Erika falls in love with the young man, their mutual adoration of music inspires their passion and allows it to grow. But in the traditionally bound conservatory of Vienna, music is an obvious part of the "culture of death." Even the expressions of music are dominated by the superego, music being part of a culture of domestication to which children are introduced by their piano teachers. In a scene that is as ambiguous as it is illuminating, Erika puts glass in the pocket of a nervous piano pupil about to make her first appearance in a prestigious recital. The scene might be interpreted as if Erika, already in love with Walter, was jealous of the girl, but in fact the severing of the girl's hand will not only prevent her from becoming a pianist but also liberate her from the domestication forced on her by her own mother, and from the punishing superego introduced through that domestication, prevalent in a culture obsessed with music. Rather than assuming that Erika's crime is one of jealousy, one may perhaps interpret the severing of the girl's hand as the displacement of a castration or cut that has never been performed in the relation between Erika and her mother, and therefore as the displacement of an emancipatory gesture. With a severed hand, the girl escapes from the punishing demands placed on her both by her mother and her teacher. Erika herself, however, continues to play with the same excruciating discipline and the same punishing self-criticism. The girl's hand is severed, but perhaps she has attained her desire. Erika's fingers continue to perform, but her sex is repeatedly cut up in frigid desperation. The *Piano Teacher*, therefore, is not so much a story of Viennese life as of the failings of feminine desire. Erika's passionate love story with Walter leads only to imposed rejection, displaying a denial of desire that is as inevitable as it is painful to watch.

So let us finally offer another suggestion of why feminine desire could be an example of an ethics of the real. Jane Campion's film *The Piano* provides us with a fable that may give us some indication. As we noted before, a Lacanian notion of ethics seems applicable to a situation of exposure: it refers to a "pure" desire that has no objects, no objectives, and no rewards in sight. *The Piano* suggests that such an exposure seems to be bound up with a feminine situation. Campion's film is situated in mid-nineteenth-century New Zealand, where Ada has been brought with her daughter from Scotland. Although it is not made explicit, it is quite clear that her daughter was born outside of marriage and that Ada is a woman with a sexual curiosity deemed unacceptable by her community. Her father has sent her away to get married, so she is now being shipped from one man to another, lacking any possessions other than her piano. Because Ada is mute, the piano is one of her two means of communication; the other is her daughter. Having lost as a child her capacity to speak, she relies on mediators. Her music is the expression of her desire, a "song of the sirens" seducing the men around her. They love hearing her play; her music is as strange and new as it is enticing. Ada is experimenting with erotic pleasures, as we can see in her involvement with her husband's friend as well as her own husband. When her jealous husband chops her finger off, it is an act of castration: she can no longer play the piano. The muteness becomes even more symbolically charged than it was, representing the castration of women as such. In the highly controlled economy of exchange of women between fathers and husbands, the desire of a daughter or wife represents a threat to the bonds between men. Ada incarnates such a threat, and her lack of speech is a metaphor for the fact that her own desire is never voiced outside of clandestine and forbidden circumstances. Her finger chopped off, she is no longer able to play the piano and lacks voice altogether. The most interesting role in the film, however, is played by the piano itself. It is, of course, a mediator of a certain language, replacing the speech Ada has lost. As such, it is part of herself. Without it, she is deprived not only of expression, but of passion and emotions. Her husband takes it away from her, incapable of seeing that the piano is not only a symbol for Ada's desire—it *is* the desire of Ada. Without it, she is lost to depression, the ground for her projects giving way. In itself, the piano is a clumsy box of wood, a dead weight that travels only with great difficulty. In the first images of the film, when it is being carried to the shores of New Zealand and later over the mountains, it seems a metaphor for Ada's stubbornness and unwillingness to submit. But later on, the weight of the piano becomes something else: dead matter rather than a mediator of language, a function of resistance rather than sound. It plays, in all its ambiguity, the conspicuous role of what Lacan calls the Thing, irrevocably attached to Ada's subjectivity. It is her speech and her expression, and literally an inalienable part of her own body. But at the same time, the piano is foreign and nonhuman, a mediator between matter and transcendence, as can be seen toward the end of the film, when Ada's husband releases her. Castrated, her freedom seems meaningless to her. Stepping onto the little boat that will take her to a ship bound for England, Ada asks the men to throw the piano overboard. It has become, as the rowers say, nothing but a coffin. Placing her foot in the rope attached to it at the crucial moment, Ada is dragged down with it; she floats for several seconds toward the bottom and an extraordinarily beautiful death, but then something pushes her back to the surface, something that is both attached to and separated from the piano. It is both the most unexpected and most important moment of the film, turning Ada's desire into an affirmative rather than destructive force: "What a chance. What a surprise. Has my will chosen life?" The Thing has become too deadly to carry, it is transformed from a living organ into sheer weight. Ada later learns to speak, and from the perspective of Lacanian ethics, the transformation from muteness to language makes perfect sense. Following that Thing that is part of herself until the very moment when it is no longer possible, she is detached from its physical insistence, although it continues to have effects in a sublimated form. The transformation means that she is no longer subjected to the material and physical weight of the Thing, which has been serving a double cause. It may have given her a voice, but it has also sustained her linguistic muteness throughout the film: her symptom, as Lacan would call it. Moreover, the piano has been serving as an agent for the forbidden dimensions of Ada's desire, as an object of displacement. When the piano is reduced to a mere musical instrument, Ada's transgressions stand out on their own. When she drops the piano, it becomes clear that Ada's attachment to it has been ambivalent, both restraining and liberating. There is no guarantee that getting rid of it will serve the purpose of making her life more fulfilling. In the end, it is an action undertaken through a necessity the essence of which is hidden even to herself. The choice is not conscious. The events happen by a will working through her, not in her. And although her choice is an affirmative one, it does not simply produce emancipation or freedom.

So what happens when the unreliable subject is made the focus of ethical questioning? What Lacan shows us, reinventing Antigone as pure and beautiful in her state of deadly contamination, is that ethics is not just a function of values, but a field beyond the projections, creations, and fantasmatic viewpoints that normally determine not just our relation to the other in a literal sense, but the space in which desire originates. This is why Antigone's beautiful death touches a chord of ethical consciousness deep within us all: it is driven by a necessity over which Antigone has no control and of which she has no awareness, by other kinds of laws than those we formalize and elevate into injunctions. In Lacan, we find a new take on what it means to say that feminine desire is an excess or a deficiency of the normative order: that part of the subject that is foreclosed in the symbolic order is also where ethical actions have their origin. It can neither be discursively motivated nor symbolized; it is not experienced or lived as a good, but it nevertheless has a claim on us. Feminine desire surpasses the phallic function, where the value of the good would be erected as a healing symbol. And if feminine desire combines with an ethics of the real, it is perhaps most of all because we would not be responsible for sustaining such an ethics; it is rather the other way around: all we need to do is affirm something that is sustaining us, between those two walls of impossibility that we are up against. What a chance, and what a surprise!

Notes

INTRODUCTION

1. Steiner (1984, 18).

2. Lacan (1992, 247).

3. I first came across the concept of an Antigone complex through implications in the writing of Danish feminist Nina Lykke, who talks about an Antigone phase in order to illuminate the enigmatic relation between mother and daughter. See Chapter 4.

4. In *The Gender of Modernity*, Rita Felski draws on texts by Marie Corelli and Rachilde in order to construct a more complex web of gendered texts than we normally see in accounts of modernity. But I do not agree with the assumption that "abstract philosophical theories of the modern are of little *use* to feminist analysis, insofar as they tend either to subsume women within a single unilinear logic of history or else to position them outside of modern discourses and institutions in a zone of ahistorical, asymbolic otherness" (Felski 1995, 8). I would rather assume that the marginality of femininity in these theories provides another kind of key to the conflicts of modernity that are being considered.

5. This is also true in novels by woman philosophers. In literature we can begin by referring to the novel analyzed in the first chapter, Mary Wollstonecraft's *Maria or the Wrongs of Woman*. But the tendency is quite clear also in Beauvoir's work, including *The Mandarins*, and *Detruire dit-elle*. The former has been taken as the model of Julia Kristeva's *Samouraïs*, which ends with the decapitation of the protagonist. Female pain and enjoyment is thoroughly explored also in films, plays, and novels by Marguerite Duras, not least *The Pain* and *The Lover*. We may also refer to recent French films, such as Coralie Trinh Thi and Virginie Despente's *Baise-moi* (2000), in which women have sex and then kill for revenge, or Claire Denis's *Trouble Every Day* (2001), about the erotic delights of eating men, which is also the theme of *The Taste of a Man* (1997) by Croatian author Slavenka Draculic, just to mention a few examples.

CHAPTER I

1. Kant (1960, 81).

2. See the discussion and references to Freud in Chapter 4.

3. The latter has been much less commented upon than the first few, and was left out of Habermas's study on the discourses of modernity, for instance (1987). As Alice Jardine has shown (1985), however, twentieth-century French theories of modernity are intrinsically dependent on speculations about the feminine as a figure of dispersion and difference. Critical of the fact that all feminine experience has been excluded from such constructions, she calls for a selective use of such theories for feminist purposes.

4. See, for instance, J.G. Fichte and Bettina von Arnim, who both advocated women's rights. J.G. Fichte, *Grundlage des Naturrechts*, 1796–97. See also Seyla Benhabib's discussion of Hegel and the romantics (1992).

5. Carter (1979, 36).

6. "A free woman in an unfree society will be a monster." Carter (1979, 27).

7. "We can see a priori that the moral law as ground of determination of the will, by thwarting all our inclinations, must produce a feeling which can be called pain. Here we have the first and perhaps the only case wherein we can determine from a priori concepts the relation of a cognition (here a cognition of pure, practical reason) to the feeling of pleasure of displeasure." Kant (1993, 76 [73]).

8. Kant shows this in the third chapter of the Analytic in the *Critique of Practical Reason*, "Of the Drives of Pure Practical Reason" (1993, 75–92 [72–89]).

9. Kant (1993, 30 [31]).

10. "Prenons comme maxime universelle de notre action le droit de jouir quel qu'il soit, comme instrument de notre plaisir." Lacan (1986, 96).

11. Blanchot (1963, 28).

12. Carter (1979, 146).

13. Sade (1987b, 98; my translation). "O Juliette! tu vas me trouver bien tranchante, bien ennemie à toutes les chaînes; mais je vais jusqu'à repousser sévèrement cette obligation aussi enfantine qu'absurde, qui nous enjoint de *ne pas faire aux autres ce que nous ne voudrions pas qu'il nous fût fait*. C'est précisément tout le contraire que la nature nous conseille, puisque son seul précepte est de *nous délecter, n'importe aux dépens de qui*. Sans doute, il peut arriver, d'après ces maximes, que nos plaisirs troubleront la félicité des autres; en seront-ils moins vifs pour cela? Cette prétendue loi de la nature, à laquelle les sots veulent nous astreindre, est donc aussi chimérique que celles des hommes, et nous savons, en foulant aux pieds les unes et les autres, qu'il n'est de mal à rien."

14. Adorno and Horkheimer (1997, 72).

15. Adorno and Horkheimer (1997, 105).

16. Adorno and Horkheimer (1997, 105).

17. Adorno and Horkheimer (1997, 111).

18. As Renata Salecl has pointed out, the sirens represent the promise of a limitless *jouissance* through their song. They are pure voice, lacking any other representation or language (1998, 59–75).

19. Beauvoir (1955, 82): "Le prochain ne m'est rien: il n'y a pas le plus petit rapport entre lui et moi."

20. Beauvoir (1955, 36–43).

21. Beauvoir (1955, 36–37).

22. Beauvoir (1955, 55).

23. "S'il refuse à autrui une reconnaissance éthique fondée sur les fausses notions de réciprocité et d'universalité, c'est pour s'autoriser à briser concrètement les barrières charnelles, qui isolent les consciences." Beauvoir (1955, 76; my translation).

24. See her critique of Kant's disembodied ethics in the *Ethics of Ambiguity* (1994, 14, 17, 19). Desires and inclinations cannot be disassociated from the ethical sphere; they are integral to the way we form our values. Beauvoir's reading of Sade is relevant to her own ethics, which regards the subject as embodied, sexual, and singular rather than a universal product of reason.

25. "Prêtez-moi la partie de votre corps qui peut me satisfaire un instant, et jouissez, si cela vous plaît, de celle du mien qui peut être agréable." Sade (1987b, 109); Lacan (1992, 202).

26. Lacan (1989, 68).

27. Lacan (1989, 60).

28. Monique David-Ménard has clarified the different steps of Lacan's comparison with regard to the vicinity of Kant's "Highest Good" and Sade's "Highest Evil." Although Kant postulates the existence of a "Highest Good," where duty becomes happiness, there is not necessarily a function of happiness involved in the fulfilling of the moral law. In Kant's erection of the moral law, the place of the Highest Good is absent. The absence creates a split between the "pathological" demand for pleasure or happiness and the function of the moral law. Working through the modalities of a similar split, Sade has shown that the place of the Highest Good might as well be occupied by the Highest Evil in its inaccessibility. As David-Ménard points out, however, the *Antigone* reading shows that Lacan does distinguish the unconditionality of an ethical action from the black nihilism of Sade (1994, 23–28).

29. See, for instance, Count Noircoeil in *Juliette*. Sade (1987b, 529).

30. Sade (1987b, 421).

31. Sade (1987b, 424).

32. Sade refers to the *molécules malfaisantes* in *Juliette*, where the sadist Saint-Fond fantasizes that life after death is as painful as the death he himself causes his victims. Sade (1987b, 425). The evil molecules, therefore, represent a death beyond death, a second death that has nothing to do with putrefaction or disappearance, but with "pure pain." The crime committed by the sadist would then equal a break in "the horrific routine of nature," where "the fainting of the subject would be doubled." Lacan (1989, 64).

33. Lacan (1992, 261).

34. "Let us retain the paradox that it should be at the moment when the subject no longer is faced with any object that he encounters a law" Lacan (1989, 56). "In the experience of the moral law, no intuition offers a phenomenal object" (1989, 57).

35. In seminar II, Lacan defines the *objet petit a* as the junction between desire and demand: it stands for the lack in the Other with which the subject comes to identify, and ultimately for a signifier that will define the subject beyond its own knowledge. Lacan (1998b, 168, 270–71).

36. Lacan (1992, 62–63).

37. "Ein Grenzbegriff zwischen Seelischen und Somatischen, als Psychisher Repräsentant der aus dem Körperinnern stammenden, in die Seele gelangenden Reize, als ein Mass der Arbeitsanforderung, die dem Seelischen infolge seines Zusammenhanges mit dem Körperlichen auferlegt ist." Freud (1957, 122; *Gesammelte Werke*, p. 214).

38. Lacan (1998b, 167–68).

39. There is no guarantee that the edifice of norms and rules will save us from violence and humiliation. On the contrary, they may release another kind of violence, which, according to Slavoj Žižek's analysis, dominates the modern condition. The fact that any kind of symbolic order represents a master increases the pathological effects of servitude or enjoyment. See, for instance, the analysis of Nazism, which is historically doubtful but makes a theoretical point (1997, 56).

40. In the Christian tradition, women's political and intellectual power has been intrinsically interwoven with mysticism. Female saints such as Catherine of Sienna, Bridget of Sweden, Jeanne d'Arc, and Thérèse d'Avila—the list could go on—all gave themselves up to the service of the church. At the same time, they used mystical visions in order to achieve significant religious, political, and cultural power. While open claims produced disbelief and ridicule, an exaggerated servitude under an often sadistic figure or voice representing God achieved the wanted results. In the case of Catherine of Sienna, for instance, who was dedicated to the political project of transferring the site of the pope from Avignon to Rome, the hideous and humiliating expressions of her religiosity intensified the glory of her visions and made her sainthood more credible in the eyes of the religious establishment. These expressions included starving herself, licking the wounds of the sick patients she was nursing, and drinking their body fluids—a piousness that seems to have been credible at least up to a certain point, when her superiors began to react to the exaggerations. These excessive expressions of humility have often been compared to anorexia in contemporary society—a suffering induced by denegation of the self. It must be remembered, however, that such a suffering must be considered more than a symptom. It carried a great deal of reward with it. The expressions it took were determined by a power structure. The fact that feminine desire took on the excessive character of painful, limitless enjoyment was determined not just by ahistorical determinations of the feminine, but by social, political, *and* religious factors.

41. Carter (1979, 49).

42. My translation. "La continence dans une femme est une vertu impraticable, mon enfant; ne vous flattez jamais de l'atteindre. Lorsque les passions s'allumeront dans votre âme, vous verrez que cette manière d'être nous est impossible. . . . Ne vous y trompez pas, Justine; ce n'est pas la vertu que l'on exige de

nous, ce n'est que son masque; et, pourvu que nous sachions feindre, on ne nous demande rien de plus. . . . Ce qui conduit au vrai bonheur n'est donc que l'apparence de cette vertu où les préjugés ridicules de l'homme ont condamné notre sexe." Sade (1987a, 45–6).

43. Sade (1987a, 46).

44. Sade (1987a, 44).

45. Rousseau writes about this in the famous fifth chapter of *Émile*, where it is determined that women are supposed to please men: men are strong and active, while women are weak and passive (1933, 322–23).

46. Wollstonecraft (1989, vol. 5, 73–74).

47. The ambivalent use of the term "feminine" has been noted by many of Wollstonecraft's commentators. See, for instance, Sapiro (1992, 221); Gubar (1994).

48. Wollstonecraft (1989, vol. 1, 104).

49. Wollstonecraft (1989, vol. 5, 57–59).

50. Moira Gatens, for instance, argues that Wollstonecraft does not go far enough in her criticism of Rousseau's philosophy of sexual difference. Gatens examines problems in Wollstonecraft's thought from a metaphysical and ontological perspective. She notes that Wollstonecraft remains within a Cartesian framework, where the mind-body problem prevails, as well as the distinction between nature and reason. From her perspective, Wollstonecraft ends in an impasse where she is forced to operate with binary oppositions, denigrating passion in order to prove the neutrality of reason. See Moira Gatens (1991, 21–26). I would claim that while Wollstonecraft remains within a Cartesian conception of divine reason, she detaches a notion of the passions from such a framework, elaborating a concept of freedom in which the passions cooperate with reason.

51. See, for instance, Geneviève Fraisse (1995).

52. Wollstonecraft (1989, vol. 5, 25–28).

53. "Sure it is madness to make the fate of thousands depend on the caprice of a-fellow-creature, whose very station sinks him *necessarily* below the meanest of his subjects!" (1989, vol. 5, 23).

54. Wollstonecraft (1989, vol. 5, 40–43).

55. Mary Poovey has shown the overly sensitive eighteenth-century woman to be an ideological construction that was partly received, partly opposed by Wollstonecraft, a conflict that can be traced in her writing (1984, 48–81). Syndy McMillen Conger has shown that *Maria* can be read as catalogue of the lexicon of sensibility. McMillen Conger reads *Maria* as a novel of emancipation, freeing the "imprisoned" sensibility of women. I am sympathetic to her argument, which goes against the idea of Wollstonecraft as misogynist, and I agree that Wollstonecraft distinguishes between a "true" sensibility, which is an auxiliary to reason, and a deluded sensibility, which imprisons women. At the same time, sensibility can never be anything but free, which makes it into a feminist weapon, potentially an "active and 'heroic' virtue," as Conger puts it (1994, 177).

56. Wollstonecraft (1989, vol. 5, 73–74, 161–64).

57. Wollstonecraft (1989, vol. 5, 27–30). Or, as she puts it in *Maria*: "True sensibility is the auxiliary to reason" (1994, 110). Virginia Sapiro has convincingly argued that one of Wollstonecraft's original contributions to political theory is her attempt to reconcile "passion" and "reason." Reason is not a transcendental faculty of cognition, but a form of conscience that can be taught. It is a process and not an end. Sapiro (1992, 48–62). Virtue is the aim of the relationship between reason and the passions. It cannot develop in a society based on dominance, tyranny, and servility, in regard not only to gender but to all structures of dominance. Sapiro's point is that Wollstonecraft's notion of virtue is part of a political theory that includes a critique of hierarchical structures. Sapiro (1992, 78–82). Without arguing with Sapiro on this point, it could be noted that her political theory elaborates the relation between ethics and desire as a subtheme. It may also be noted that one of the most interesting aspects of Wollstonecraft's moral philosophy is her ambition to distinguish different aspects of desires and inclinations, only some of which are compatible with moral reason, while others must be excluded from the ethical domain. Whether or not a systematic differentiation is performed in her work and what the categories used actually mean are questions that remain to be examined. Perhaps one of the most interesting aspects of *Maria*, for instance, is the rich tapestry of feelings and sensual experiences pointing to a transparency in the relation between subject and object, which is a significant point in Wollstonecraft's ethics.

58. Wollstonecraft (1989, vol. 5, 127–29).

59. Wollstonecraft (1989, vol. 5, 129–32).

60. Wollstonecraft (1989, vol. 5, 71–73).

61. Gubar (1994, 454).

62. Wollstonecraft (1989, vol. 1, 83).

63. Wollstonecraft (1989, vol. 5, 284–87).

64. Carter (1979, 51).

65. Wollstonecraft (1989, vol. 1, 96–100).

66. Wollstonecraft (1989, vol. 5, 284–87).

67. Introduction by Anne K. Mellor, Wollstonecraft (1994, xi).

68. Wollstonecraft (1989, vol. 1, 34–38).

69. Mellor makes this comment. Wollstonecraft (1994, xiv).

70. Wollstonecraft (1989, vol. 1, 49–53).

71. Wollstonecraft (1989, vol. 1, 33–37).

CHAPTER 2

1. An odd mixture of dreamy *Schwärmerei* and political engagement, European romanticism created an ideal woman who could be regarded both as a friend and as an idol of worship. The most telling example is perhaps the mythical twin soul of Friedrich Schlegel's *Lucinde*, a novel derided by G. W. F. Hegel because he thought that only marriage could give moral dignity to sexual relationships (*Philosophy of Right*, §164).

2. "On Love," Hegel (1998, 33).

3. The readings referred to are mainly undertaken in *On the Scientific Ways of Treating Natural law* (1802–1803), *The Phenomenology of Spirit* (1807), and *Lectures on Aesthetics* (1835).

4. The idea that Hegel's subject begins as a deficiency in *polis* has been pointed out also by Christoph Menke (1995, 93), who makes it into a starting point for showing that Hegel's discussion of tragedy in fact encircles a central problem of modernity: the subject of freedom or autonomy on which the normative is construed is not reconcilable with the modern ideal of authenticity, where the individual is assumed to be able to live a good life and fulfill his needs and ideals. Modernity could be regarded as the split between two kinds of freedom: authenticity or the right to happiness on the one hand, and on the other hand, autonomy or the capacity of the community to create a normative system in and out of itself. This conflict, which has to do with the fact that the normative order is constructed in forbidding and prohibitive terms, is precisely what constitutes the "Tragödie der Sittlichkeit." The rise of autonomy itself leads to an unsolvable dilemma, since it is incommensurable with authenticity, or the striving toward the good life, according to Menke (1996, 251).

5. Hegel uses the notion of *Sittlichkeit*, or ethical life, differently from *Moralität*, or morality; the former is concerned with the customs and practices of a functioning community and the latter with the moral consciousness of a reflecting individual. While the ancient community represents a form of *Sittlichkeit* that works, it does so only to a degree, since it is intrinsically divided between the conscious elements realised in and by the state and the unconscious elements of the family. Hegel divides the ethical community into a substance or a whole that is divided between consciousness, or a substance of laws and conscious ethical actions, and a substance that simply is: "This moment which expresses the ethical sphere in this element of immediacy or [simple] being, or which is an *immediate* consciousness of itself, both as essence and as this particular self, in an 'other,' i. e. as a *natural* ethical community—this is the Family. The Family, as the *unconscious*, still inner Notion [of the ethical order], stands opposed to its actual self-conscious existence; as the *element* of the nation's actual existence, it stands opposed to the nation itself; as the *immediate* being of the ethical order, it stands over against that order which shapes and maintains itself by working for the universal; the Penates stand opposed to the universal Spirit" (*Phenomenology of Spirit*, 450). In other words, the problem for the state will be how to integrate the ethical bonds between family members into its self-conscious discourse of laws and rights.

6. The analysis of the tragedy as an escalating excess of violence is based on the observations by Richard Seaford. He has shown that tragedy emerges through a lack of balance in rituals of reciprocity. The acts of violence, in turn, are significant because they are perversions of rituals that otherwise would be used to consolidate balance and reciprocity. Seaford's excellent analysis gives an account of the various rituals perverted in the *Oresteia* (1994, 370–82).

7. Vernant and Vidal-Naquet (1990, 76–84). Justice is a legal construction, but it also carries an element of irrationality and brutal force in it. Vernant and Vidal-

Naquet (1990, 26). Set at the limit between the human and the divine, tragedy's double symbolic spaces make the notion of justice oscillate between the intentional action of human agents and the accidents produced by the gods. Human agents never dominate the action; they only create discrepancies, breakdowns that the gods have to adjust (1990, 47–48). See also Zak on the undecidability of justice in the *Oresteia* (1995, 35).

8. See, for example, Beauvoir (1989); Cavarero (1995); Zeitlin (1996); and Bouvrie (1990), who all comment on Bachofen in some way without reducing their claims to a historical issue. Bouvrie argues for a symbolic understanding of tragedy, pointing to an evaluation of woman's status as wife and childbearer, but denies woman's freedom and social status. Rabinowitz's (1993) interpretations are constructed around similar conclusions. Cavarero argues for alternative strategies of interpretation for ancient philosophical texts, in which we study the female figures in the margin, allowing us to discern the female subject buried in philosophical texts through the traces of an original act of erasure. Cavarero (1995, 5).

9. Dettenhofer (1994, 15–40). Tragedy emerged around 400 B.C., in a state that had instituted democratic rule, where free men participated in the decisions of the city. The performance of tragedy was intimately linked to democracy, and all free men were expected to participate in the celebrations when the tragedies were played. The members of the chorus, representing the *polis*, were elected. The system excluded slaves and women, however. The fact that no concept in the Greek language refers to a female citizen bears witness to this fact. Women were viewed as a foreigner with an unclear social status, not quite belonging to the *polis*. The male dream of giving birth without women shows their low status. Songe Møller discusses this in her chapter on the ancient dream of autochtony in Greek philosophy, the dream of men being able to give birth without women (1999, 30). See also Loraux (1981, 119–53).

10. Cavarero (1995, 5).

11. Beauvoir (1989, 79).

12. Klein (1988, 287). Inspired by Klein, interpreters of tragedy have suggested that the transformation of the Furies into benevolent Eumenides at the end of the play not only signifies a development from chaos to justice in the *polis*; it is also a symbolic reparation for a persecutory maternal image. See, for instance, Alford (1992, 163–64); Wohl (1998, 121–23).

13. Zeitlin (1996, 91).

14. There are, as Nicole Loraux has shown, a disconcerting number of women who die in ancient plays. The city of Athens seems to have treated them in its tragedies in a way that to some extent corresponds to the way it treated them in the *polis*, as secondary citizens. Death, in tragedy, is always bound up with marriage, which was the status through which women came to exist. The death of women in tragedy is always depicted in the most demeaning way possible. Loraux (1991, 7–26). Nancy Sorkin Rabinowitz's study of Euripides' tragedies aims to show that tragedy circles around a patriarchal system of exchange in which women are victims. In *Hippolytos*, for example, Phaedra is a sacrificed victim of exchange

in an economy of desire of which father and son are the actual agents. Rabinowitz and Richlin (1993, 173–88). Zeitlin, in turn, has argued that the feminine threat is the very motive of tragedy. The mimetic relation between reality and event, in Froma Zeitlin's understanding of tragedy, entails a tension between inside and outside that is gendered in itself. The scenes often take place outside of a house or palace, in a male public space. The horrors, such as Clytaemnestra's slaying of her husband or Medea's slaying of her children, take place inside. Tragedy's Dionysian side is to be seen in the way it calls into question what we know and how we think we know it. Its lures, disguises, and appearances concern what was regarded as feminine deceitfulness: the Other inside the house. Zeitlin has shown that women are not only the object but also the motive behind the mimesis of tragedy: a male actor plays the Other for a male audience trying to control her alterity in this way. The Greek image of women is a distortion designed to control an inner enemy. Women constitute the Other in a male Athenian community. Because they form the limits of that society, they are simultaneously kept outside of it and regarded as a threat: "The vigorous denial of power to the female overtly asserts her inferiority while at the same time expressing anxiety toward her persistent but normally dormant power that may always erupt into open violence." Zeitlin (1996, 90). The same problem, that of conjuring an inner enemy, is found in Aristophanes' comedies, by the way, where the sexual conflict is politicized. In making one of the most eager female revolutionaries in *Lysistrate* a Spartan woman, for example, and in depicting her as physically strong and unafraid and therefore frightening, Aristophanes mocks the Spartan enemy: they are unable to control their women. In response to the ambiguous representation of women in tragedy, Sue Ellen Case has argued that tragedy's women have very little to do with historical women: "As a result of the suppression of real women, the culture invented its own representation of the gender, and it was this fictional 'Woman' who appeared on stage, in the myths and in the plastic arts, representing the patriarchal values attached to the gender while suppressing the experiences, stories, feelings and fantasies of actual women" (1988, 7).

15. Tragedy is, Jean-Pierre Vernant and Pierre Vidal-Naquet argue, a symbolic space where divine, social, and legal spheres collide in a human individual, showing that individual to be as contradictory as the tragic universe itself: an incomprehensible and failing monster, both culpable and innocent, both master over his environment and lacking control over himself, both an acting agent and an object being acted upon. Vernant and Vidal-Naquet (1990, 29–32). The heterogeneous construction of that symbolic space creates a universe of ambiguity, set between the political and the religious sphere. The political context depicts a human being striving for autonomy. The religious subtext, however, which provides the real meaning of tragedy according to Vernant, will always contain something exceeding that autonomy, setting its limits and barriers. Vernant and Vidal-Naquet (1990, 45–48).

16. Hegel (1999, 151).

17. Menke (1996, 10, 12, 33–35).

18. The basic principle guiding ethical life is, according to Hegel, life itself. This means, of course, that it is opposed to death, and that the objects of pleasures and possession constitute its focus and the relations of dependence at the core of ethical life (1999, 141–42).

19. Hegel (1999, 106).

20. This is Hegel's comment in his lectures on aesthetics. Hegel (1970, 544).

21. This argument is developed both in the essay on natural law and in the lectures on aesthetics, where the *Oresteia* is used as an example. Hegel (1970, 550).

22. It is clear that Hegel is thinking of the *Oresteia* throughout his essay, although it is given only a page of explicit reflection: ethical life can only come to being in the recognition of what is foreign to it, through the death of its "second nature" or the inorganic or destructive aspects of "the divine" or ancient customs. Hegel (1999, 152).

23. "Tragedy arises when ethical nature cuts its inorganic nature off from itself as a fate—in order not to become embroiled in it—and treats it as an opposite; by acknowledging this fate in the [ensuing] struggle, it is reconciled with the divine being as the unity of both." Hegel (1999, 152).

24. Honneth (1995, 15).

25. Hegel (1999, 162).

26. Honneth (1995, 173).

27. As is well known, Hegel considers *Antigone* to be the most perfect of all tragedies, according to his lectures on aesthetics (1970, 550). Steiner (1984) considers *Antigone* to be the most important text of the Western tradition.

28. Again, we are moving in the ambivalent space of tragedy, where religious supersedure and political conflict become inseparable, resulting in a kind of ambivalence that Vernant and Vidal-Naquet tell us must be made into the object of tragic catharsis (1995, 21).

29. Arguing for a nondialectical conception of justice, Martha Nussbaum has suggested that the problem with Creon is in fact that he is Hegelian in his concept of justice. The most important conflict in the play, according to Nussbaum, is that between Creon's ambition to create a pure and simple scheme of justice, a scheme that is in conflict with the rich and complex notion of justice that prevailed in tragedy, where justice can only be approximate. The conflict in tragedy is between the value of consistency (freedom from conflict) and the value of richness (1986, 81).

30. The question of who is to be considered the tragic hero in *Antigone* is therefore not that interesting. Many interpreters have identified Creon as a tragic hero according to the poetics of Aristotle (for instance Kitto [1961]). He is the one who falls from fortune to misfortune. But another theory suggests a diptych: a tragedy of *two* characters mirroring each other—Creon *and* Antigone. Kirkwood (1957, 42–46); and Bowra (1944, 63–116).

31. Loraux (1991, 48).

32. As Segal notes, Creon's problem is Antigone's femininity. He does not understand her womanhood, and must reduce her actions to echoes of his own in order to make sense of them (1986, 151).

33. Loraux discusses at length the gendered nature of the beautiful death, showing that it constitutes a figure of masculinity both in the case of the Spartan honorable warrior and in the depiction of Socrates' death. The honor of death had nothing to do with beauty in the modern sense. According to Loraux, the aesthetic ideal of beauty did not apply to women but was associated with the male body (1995, 63–75, 153–58).

34. She challenges the conception of femininity and masculinity. See Chapter 4.

35. Segal has shown that the complaint of the female mourner has a double function: it is a ritual guiding the body of the dead to the underworld, and it plays the role of purifying the community in this sense. But the mourning is also a sign of chaos and destruction, which is the form of tragedy and which the closure of tragedy serves to control. At the end of *Antigone*, however, Creon's grief creates a remainder that cannot be contained within the tragic form. Segal (1986, 132–33).

36. Nicole Loraux (1995, 88–101) has shown that the symbolic representation of sexual difference is an idea of exchange rather than a fixed category in ancient texts: man becoming feminine, woman becoming masculine, an ongoing process rather than a fixed construction. The fluidity and mobility of gender makes it a temporal rather than a fixed state, as soft and penetrable as the body itself. A brave man is manly, but he has to pass through the test of vulnerability—get wounded, bleed, and suffer like a woman.

37. Hegel (*Phenomenology of Spirit*, 450–62).

38. The low regard for Euripides and the high esteem for Sophocles highlight such a perspective. Euripides is considered to be a woman-hater because he makes women weak and inferior to men, in the words of A. W. Schlegel. Here, Schlegel could be thought to be a defender of women's cause. But the accusations of weakness and inferiority stem from the fact that female love is depicted as sensual and corporeal. It is therefore considered a less dignified feeling than masculine love, from Schlegel's point of view. Certainly Schlegel's point could be regarded as no more than a comment on what actually goes on in Euripides' plays. Women represent forces like aggression and sexual appetite, tearing apart the organic order of the community. In Euripides' *Bacchae*, a mythical representation of the birth of tragedy, Dionysos is a deceitful androgynous figure with the capacity to bring forth immeasurable destructive forces from his female followers. The excessive appetites or needs of women shape the doomed universe also in, for instance, *Medea* and *Hippolytos*. The scorned *Medea* murders her children. In *Hippolytos*, the *aidos* or shame of Phaedra, who has fallen in love with her stepson, pushes her to commit suicide and blame Hippolytos, an act that causes the tragic deaths. But Schlegel's perception of Euripides is already colored by a certain view of what dignified feminine desire should look like. While Euripides is discarded for his depiction of feminine desire, Sophocles is idolized. The figure of Antigone is a fe-

male ideal of great strength, says A. W. Schlegel, because her love for her brother comes before any sexual or sensual involvement (1966, 95–107).

39. Hegel (*Phenomenology of Spirit*, 450). The table of antinomies in this reading would look something like this:

Singularity	Universality
Divine law	Human law
Family	State
Woman	Man
The unconscious	Consciousness
The nether world	The public world
The naturally ethical	The universally ethical
Death	Desire

In *Philosophy of Right*, §166. Hegel continues to distinguish the sexes in a similar manner, arguing that Antigone presents us with a sublime example of piety, which is her ethical disposition, and which stands for the emotive and subjective substantiality to be realized in the family. Such a form of subjectivity is contrasted with the capacity of universal reasoning of the statesman.

40. "In her vocation as an individual and in her pleasure, her interest is centred on the universal and remains alien to the particularity of desire; whereas in the husband these two sides are separated; and since he possesses as a citizen the self-conscious power of universality, he thereby acquires the right of desire and, at the same time, preserves his freedom with regard to it" Hegel (*Phenomenology of Spirit*, 457).

41. Hegel (*Phenomenology of Spirit*, 457) argues that the sister is a particular kind of woman since her function is not contingent, as is that of the wife: she has an important function to fulfill in that she is irreplaceable, unlike the wife. In *Glas*, Derrida published letters between Hegel and his sister that make their relation look less than pure (1974, 171–83).

42. Derrida (1974, 187–93).

43. "Nature, not the accident of circumstances or choice, assigns one sex to one law, the other to the other law; or conversely, the two ethical powers themselves give themselves an individual existence and actualise themselves in the two sexes." Hegel (*Phenomenology of Spirit*, 465).

44. Gearhart has commented on this: "Despite the distinctions Hegel lays down between the woman and the man, his discussion of *Antigone* reveals that the various elements of the family are all equally ethical and thus equally rational. The feminine form or embodiment of the ethical cannot be any less ethical, any more natural than the masculine, because the ethical resides in the *negation* of nature and is not a question of degree of proximity to nature. From this perspective, the conflict between Antigone and Creon appears to be rooted not in the difference between (her) nature and (his) reason but rather in their shared ethicity and rationality, and in this sense it cannot be resolved in terms of the underlying har-

mony or unity of the ethical substance." Gearhart (1992, 68). Whereas I agree with Gearhart that the sexes are not symmetrical in Hegel, I see the problem as having to do with the question of universalization rather than rationality: they cannot both claim to have their concepts of the law elevated into a universal one, and so their conflict is already from the beginning the mark of a deficiency in the ethical order.

45. Hegel (*Phenomenology of Spirit*, 452). In this passage, Hegel makes death part of the antagonism that marks ethical life, the end of individual endeavours that makes clear that the symbolic and universal level of ethical life can never completely coincide with the individual, who is finite and mortal.

46. This tragic remainder can be identified as, for instance, feminine individualism and irony, which will be discussed further below: "The community . . . can only maintain itself by suppressing this spirit of individualism, and, because it is an essential moment, all the same creates it and, moreover, creates it by its repressive attitude toward it as a hostile principle." Hegel (*Phenomenology of Spirit* 475).

47. Again we see the logic where Hegel claims that it is not the universal that is exerting violence over the individual, but rather the other way around: here he argues that the individual "changes by intrigue the universal end of the government into a private end, transforms its universal activity into a work of some particular individual, and perverts the universal property of the state into a possession and ornament for the Family." Hegel (*Phenomenology of Spirit*, 475). The link to the tragic argument lies in this violence of particularity exerted on the body of the community.

48. See for instance Luce Irigaray (1985a, 214–26); Tina Chanter (1995, 88–102); Kelly Oliver (1996, 67–90); Judith Butler (2000, 13–14, 34–35).

49. Hegel (*Phenomenology of Spirit*, 178).

50. Hegel (*Phenomenology of Spirit*, 184).

51. See Beauvoir's account of sexual difference and Hegel's master-slave conflict (1989, 64–65).

52. Irigaray (1985a, 219).

53. Oliver (1996, 81).

54. See the discussion of the lack of interiority in tragic characters in his lectures on aesthetics (1970a, 110–12).

55. This is the reading of Christoph Menke, who shows how the failure of *Sittlichkeit* or the unity of ethical life revolves around the necessity to recognize not just the individual but the singularity of the individual—*this* specific person, a gesture that is forced by Antigone (1996, 142).

56. Kierkegaard (1959, 141).

57. Kierkegaard (1959, 147).

58. Hegel's denunciation in *Philosophy of Right* of Schlegel's eroticism is a case in point. It is quoted and commented on by Benhabib, who considers it to mark the end of a revolutionary, utopian vision on gender relations (1992, 250–56).

59. Benhabib (1992, 257).

60. Benhabib (1992, 257).

61. Menke (1996, 142–49). The feminist criticism overlooks the fact that the idea of a feminine irony is an ethical revolution in contrast with the romantic ideal of femininity: "Es ist nach Hegel zuerst in der 'Weiblichkeit' und ihrer Ironie, in der sich das *Individuum* konstituiert" (1996, 142). See the quote from Hegel in note 46 above, which supports Menke's argument.

62. This is true, as Charles Segal has shown, not only of ethical codes in the moral sense but also of the codes governing rituals, the organization of the family, linguistic patterns, sexual difference, and so forth: "The original orders are suspended, forcing the mind to reach beyond those structures in the painful search for other principles of order or in the more painful admission that there are no principles of order. Here men must face the chaos their mental structures—social, linguistic, political, sexual, spatial—deliberately shut out." Charles Segal, "Greek Tragedy and Society: A Structuralist Perspective," in Euben (1986, 48). The totality of these codes makes up the ethical order in Hegel's sense.

63. This is Irigaray's critique of Hegel's phenomenology, repeated numerous times in her writings. See for instance 1985a, 214–26.

CHAPTER 3

1. Aristotle, *Metaphysics*, 1/986a.

2. Heidegger (2000, §38): "Being, as the basic theme of philosophy, is no class or genus of entities; yet it pertains to every entity. Its 'universality' is to be sought higher up. Being and the structure of Being lie beyond every entity and every possible character which an entity may possess. *Being is the transcendens pure and simple.*"

3. Of course, this proposition has been debated by feminist philosophers. For Irigaray, in *The Forgetting of Air in Martin Heidegger*, Heidegger's disjunction between being and beings is a product of sexual difference rather than a response to it. Language as the habitation of the essence of man becomes, in this perspective, essentially male, a morphology of ejaculation and erection and a tool to construct a notion of being that is strictly separate from the body as nature. Dasein, then, is caught in what Irigaray calls a logic of the same, where alterity is always the other of the same: "At the point where he is thrown-projected out of himself, he will again recover himself. He will once more set himself this project as his very source. He will make of his ek-stasis the way to return to himself: the permanence of his Being" (1999, 65). Being is a rejection of the maternal realm of *phuein*: "The elementality of *physis*—air, water, earth, fire—is always already reduced to nothingness in and by his own element: his language. An ecstasis relative to his own homeland that keeps him exiled from his first homeland" (1999, 74). One could regard Luce Irigaray's reading of Heidegger as an attempt to tackle this problem, as Tina Chanter has shown. Irigaray's forgotten question of sexual difference corresponds to Heidegger's forgotten question of being (1995, 127–46).

4. Categories such as will, wish, addiction, and urge are considered to be

founded on care, but they are not identical with it. Heidegger (2000, §39). Being as care is described in *Being and Time* §41 as the way in which Dasein understands and projects its potentialities for being, for which Being is an issue. It is perhaps possible to derive from this position Beauvoir's idea that sexual identity is a "project."

5. In other words, the question of neutrality has a bearing on what the task of philosophy must be if the finite conditions are considered, but it does not mean that philosophy has the capacity to transcend the factual forms of human existence: "The approach that begins with neutrality does imply a peculiar isolation of the human being, but not in the factical existential sense, as if the one philosophizing were the center of the world. Rather, it is the *metaphysical isolation* of the human being." (Der Ansatz in der Neutralität bedeutet zwar eine eigentümliche Isolierung des Menschen, aber nicht in faktisch existentziellem Sinne, als wäre der Philosophierende das Zentrum der Welt, sondern sie ist die *metaphysische Isolierung* des Menschen.) Heidegger (1992, 137; *Gesamtausgabe* 26, 172).

6. Jacques Derrida remarks, in a famous essay on the neutral character of Heidegger's Dasein, that the discussion of sexual difference puts in question the distinction between being and beings, which is the only difference Heidegger wishes to elaborate. Derrida discusses Heidegger's notion of sexual difference with certain passages in *Being and Time*, referring sexual difference to an ontology of life, which is as impure a category as sexual difference in Heidegger's thinking: it is neither an appearance nor a form of being (1987, 411–13).

7. Heidegger links it also to facticity: "Neutrality is not the voidness of an abstraction but precisely the potency of the *origin*, which bears in itself the intrinsic possibility of every concrete factual humanity." Heidegger (1992, 137; *Gesamtausgabe* 26, 172). The fact that Heidegger attaches Dasein to a neutral origin is a way of emphasizing its historical character, avoiding systematization of its definition.

8. "The species-like unification [of Dasein as sexually differentiated human beings] metaphysically presupposes the dissemination of Dasein as such, that is, being-with as such." Heidegger (1992, 139; *Gesamtausgabe* 26, 174).

9. "Here we are dealing with . . . a description of the multiplication . . . which is present in every factically individuated Dasein as such. We are not dealing with the notion of a large primal being in its simplicity becoming ontically split into many individuals, but with the clarification of the intrinsic possibility of multiplication which, as we shall see more precisely, is present in every Dasein and for which embodiment presents an organizing factor." Heidegger (1992, 137–38; *Gesamtausgabe* 26, 173).

10. "Zum Wesen des Daseins überhaupt gehört seinem metaphysisch neutralen Begriff nach schon eine ursprüngliche *Streuung*, die in einer ganz bestimmten Hinsicht *Zerstreuung* ist" (Dasein's essence already contains a primordial *bestrewal* which is in a quite definite respect a *dissemination*). Heidegger (1992, 138: *Gesamtausgabe* 26, 173).

11. This is why this rather obscure point in Heidegger has been remarked by the deconstructive movement. See Derrida's demonstration of Heidegger's notion

of sexual difference as a category that is undecidable within his own temporal ontology, because Dasein is neither not sexual nor determined by the dual difference
of gender. In "Différence sexuelle, différence ontologique" (1987, 395–414).

    12. Heidegger (1982, 195; *Gesamtausgabe* 12, 74).

    13. Heidegger (1986, 167; *Gesamtausgabe* 12, 46).

    14. The idea that a dead woman is the most poetic subject of all comes from
American author E. A. Poe, and has been made the theme of a study by Elisabeth
Bronfen (*Over Her Dead Body* [Manchester: Manchester University Press, 1993]).

    15. Still begegnet am Saum des Waldes
    Ein dunkles Wild;
    Am Hügel endet leise der Abendwind,
    Verstummt die Klage der Amsel,
    Und die sanften Flöten des Herbstes
    Schweigen im Rohr.
    Auf schwarzer Wolke
    Befährst du trunken von Mohn
    Den nächtigen Weiher,
    Den Sternenhimmel.
    Immer tönt der Schwester mondene Stimme
    Immer tönt der Schwester mondene Stimme
    Durch die geistliche Nacht.

Sebastian im Traum (1915), *Dichtungen und Briefe*, Band 1 (Salzburg: Otto Müller
Verlag, 1987), p. 118.

    16. As Irigaray points out, Heidegger presents us with a hope-giver for future
generations in the form of a young boy, keeping the *Geschlecht* together, bridging
over the disturbing discord manifested by the gap between boy and girl. Irigaray
(1999, 119–20).

    17. Freud (*Standard Edition*, vol. 17, p. 231).

    18. Irigaray (1985a, 55).

    19. Heidegger (2000, 186–89). Michael Düe (1986, 83–86, 105–6) has com-
pared the Freudian concept of *Unheimlichkeit* and the two forms of the concept in
Heidegger. In the first case, *Unheimlichkeit* is close to the drives in the sense that
it has to be kept covered; in the second, it is uncovered, like the unconscious. *Das
Unheimliche*, for Freud, gives rise to anxiety. For Heidegger, it is to be found in the
Stimmung of anxiety, which means that it opens up the originary negation of nothingness, Dasein's original relation to being. This is, interestingly enough, compared to the development of the subject and its relation to the primary object described by Freud in *Entwurf einer wissenschaftlicher Psychologie*—a primary object
Freud calls the Thing. As we will see, the Thing plays a crucial role in the Lacanian analysis of the origin of desire.

    20. Heidegger (1996, 74; *Gesamtausgabe* 53, 91).

    21. Heidegger (1996, 119; *Gesamtausgabe* 53, 147).

    22. Martha Nussbaum is a good representative of this tradition, pointing to

ways of reading tragedy through Aristotle's ethics in *The Fragility of Goodness*, 1986.

23. Heidegger (1996, 103; *Gesamtausgabe* 53, 128).

24. "For us moderns . . . the beautiful is what reposes and relaxes; it is intended for enjoyment and art is a matter for pastry cooks. It makes no essential difference whether the enjoyment of art serves to satisfy the sensibilities of the connoisseur or esthete or to provide moral edification. For the Greeks *on* and *kalon* meant the same thing (presence was pure radiance): The esthetic view is very different; it is as old as logic. For esthetics art is representation of the beautiful in the sense of the pleasing, the pleasant. But art is disclosure of the being of the essent [beings]. On the strength of a recaptured, pristine, relation to being we must provide the word 'art' with a new content." Heidegger (1959, 131–32; *Gesamtausgabe* 40, 101–2).

25. Unconcealment is *Aletheia* in Greek; Heidegger takes pains to point out that we have to be careful in translating it as truth. The term "unconcealment" is used in order to indicate that truth is coming into being in a mutual movement between appearing and nonappearing, showing and nonshowing. Unconcealment therefore has to do with the way being manifests itself—it is not something which lies beyond being or which is hidden from view. Heidegger (1959, 102; *Gesamtausgabe* 40, 78).

26. Heidegger (1959, 107; *Gesamtausgabe* 40, 81).

27. Lacoue-Labarthe (1990, 57, 66–68). Lacoue-Labarthe lists several dimensions to this idea: that art is a *techne* achieving the revelation of *polis* as a "beautiful formation," that the Greeks are the people of art par excellence and therefore the political people par excellence, and that the political state is organic and therefore natural.

28. Taminiaux bases an interesting and wide-ranging critique of Heidegger's reading of tragedy on precisely this point. He shows that Heidegger's readings in fact turn around issues of authenticity that are connected to Germanic being. Heidegger uses tragedy in order to ascend above the issues that are engaged in the play, distilling a theoretical view of being above and beyond the praxis, and substituting authenticity for issues of the good life. In this way, his tragic philosophy constitutes a perversion of the Greek philosophical heritage, which has been explored more faithfully in the philosophy of Hanna Arendt, for instance. Taminiaux (1995, 192–99).

29. In *Being and Time* §44, Heidegger undermines the idea that truth is a matter of correspondence between a knowing subject and an object of knowledge; it is rather an uncovering or making seen of the phenomenon that is wholly dependent on Dasein's specific conditions.

30. Conflict is essential to the knowledge produced by poets, thinkers, and statesmen. The relation between beings and being shows itself through splits, jointures, and intervals. The idea that being shows itself through conflict leads Heidegger to Sophocles' tragedy (1959, 62; *Gesamtausgabe* 40, 48).

31. Heidegger (1959, 159; *Gesamtausgabe* 40, 122). In Heideggerian terms, such

knowledge would reveal being and the essent of being: "It is through the work of art as essent being that everything else that appears and is to be found is first confirmed and made accessible, explicable, and understandable as being or not being." I will not go into the details of the terminology, since it would require a more developed argument on Heidegger's philosophy.

32. See in particular Lacoue-Labarthe (1990, 53–59, 69), who has shown that the romantic tradition of thinking the work of art as an organic entity is transmuted into the political domain, a fact that makes *techne* into Heidegger's most doubtful ideological concept, according to Lacoue-Labarthe.

33. Heidegger (1996, 81; *Gesamtausgabe* 53, 100). "*Polis* is usually translated as city or city-state. This does not capture the full meaning. *Polis* means, rather, the place, the there, wherein and as which historical being-there is. The *polis* is the historical place, the there *in* which, *out of* which, and *for* which history happens." Heidegger (1959, 152; *Gesamtausgabe* 40, 117).

34. Heidegger (1996, 94; *Gesamtausgabe* 53, 118). If the political is determined through the modern state, it is grasped according to consciousness in a "technical" manner. In this way the "political" comes to rest on a notion of certainty and fails to question itself: "The failure to question 'the political' belongs together with its totality." This totality has nothing to do, according to Heidegger, with modern forms of totalitarianism, only with the way the concept of the political is based on the modern state.

35. As noted by H. G. Liddell and R. Scott in the *Greek-English Lexicon* (Oxford: Oxford University Press, 1968).

36. Heidegger (1959, 149–51; *Gesamtausgabe* 40, 114–16).

37. Heidegger (1959, 163; *Gesamtausgabe* 40, 124).

38. Heidegger (1959, 163; *Gesamtausgabe* 40, 124): "Gesetzt-sein als die Bresche, in die die Übergewalt des Seins erscheinend hereinbricht, damit diese Bresche selbst am Sein zerbricht."

39. Heidegger (1959, 151; *Gesamtausgabe* 40, 116). "Man is the strangest of all, not only because he passes his life amid the strange understood in this sense but because he departs from his customary, familiar limits, because he is the violent one, who, tending toward the strange in the sense of the overpowering, surpasses the limit of the familiar."

40. Heidegger (1959, 152; *Gesamtausgabe* 40, 117).

41. Heidegger (1959, 158; *Gesamtausgabe* 40, 121).

42. This is described by Seaford as a perversion of rituals like weddings and funerals. Seaford (1994, 381–82).

43. This is the reading of Doyle (1984, 107).

44. *Poetics* 1449 b. I have not seen this observation in any previous literature on *Antigone*, and do not claim that it has anything to do with Aristotle's poetics.

45. Heidegger reads Hölderlin in order to find a "Heimischwerden" of the Germans through contrast with the unfamiliar Greeks at the origins of the German historical position. Many scholars who stress the political impact of the Greeks, he says, endeavor to liken the German state to the glory of the Greeks: but

"Nationalsozialismus" does not *need* to be regarded as the same as the Greeks (1996, 80; *Gesamtausgabe* 53, 98). There are other implicit compliances with Nazi rhetoric. Hugo Ott uses the "Ister" reading to indicate the immobility of Heidegger's position between the Rektoratsrede 1934 and 1942 (1988, 278, 287). Otto Pöggeler claims that the rejection of a contemporary notion of the political is a reaction against National Socialism (1990, 224). Philippe Lacoue-Labarthe points out that Heidegger's position strays from a bleak repetition of Romantic National Socialism in the sense that the Greek "roots" he seeks are an origin that was never there (1990, 57–58). Instead, he sees the relation of Heidegger to politics in the aestheticization of the political through the concept of *techne*. As Taminiaux has remarked, Heidegger avoids commenting on the interaction that for Aristotle signifies the ethical nature of tragedy as *praxis*, in order to read *dike* or justice as the ontological necessity that corresponds to *techne*. Jacques Taminiaux sees the ontologization of *techne*, the necessity of violence incorporated in the act of creation, whether it be poetical or political, as an excuse for the violent aestheticization of the ruling Nazi party (1995, 213–21).

46. Again the discussion leads us to the concepts of finitude and *techne* that were presented in the *Introduction to Metaphysics*, but in the second reading Heidegger makes more of the German poeticizing of Sophocles' ambiguous language. One might infer, then, that the superior poeticizing of the German language lies in this capacity to relate the essence of the human being to his need for origins, a home, whether we consider that home a nation, a language, or a historical destiny—*Heimlichkeit*. Heidegger (1996, 66–73; *Gesamtausgabe* 53, 82–90).

47. As Taminiaux has remarked, one might refer this whole discussion to the question of authenticity. Heidegger distinguishes unreflected everyday life from philosophy, art, and politics, which are forms of *techne* that would open an authentic relation to being. While this may not be an ideological move in itself, the problem is that authenticity belongs to a people rather than the individual (1995, 180–86).

48. Heidegger (1996, 52; *Gesamtausgabe* 53, 64).

49. *Deinon* can mean "extraordinary," which is Hölderlin's choice: "Ungeheuer ist viel. Doch nichts/Ungeheuerer, als der Mensch." Heidegger, in his own version of Hölderlin's translation, changes it into "unheimlich"—uncanny—and points out that it can also mean powerful or awesome, the fearful or the inhabitual (1996, 64; *Gesamtausgabe* 53, 78). Cf. Hölderlin's translation (1988, 299). Heidegger explains the principles for his reworking of Hölderlin's text as a way of bringing out something that is in fact already present in it: a question of belonging (1996, 68–69; *Gesamtausgabe* 53, 83–86).

50. Heidegger (1996, 74; *Gesamtausgabe* 53, 91).

51. Heidegger (1996, 74; *Gesamtausgabe* 53, 91). "Das Unheimisch-sein ist kein blosses Entweichen aus dem Heimischen, sondern eher umgekehrt das zuweilen such selbst nich kennende Suchen und Aufsuchen des Heimischen. Dieses Suchen scheut keine Gefahr und kein Wagnis. Überall fährt es und überallhinaus ist es unterwegs".

52. Heidegger (1996, 84–85; *Gesamtausgabe* 53, 97–100). Heidegger interprets Aristotle's description of man as a *zoon politicon*, or political animal, in terms of belonging: man is what belongs to the site of *polis*, while being foreign to it at the same time (1996, 82; *Gesamtausgabe* 101–2).

53. Heidegger (1996, 76–77; *Gesamtausgabe* 53, 94–95). "Whatever human beings undertake turns in itself . . . counter to what humans are fundamentally seeking from it, namely, becoming homely in the midst of beings." (1996, 84; *Gesamtausgabe* 53, 104).

54. Heidegger (1996, 119; *Gesamtausgabe* 53, 147).

55. Heidegger (1996, 103; *Gesamtausgabe* 53, 128).

56. Heidegger (1996, 87–89; *Gesamtausgabe* 53, 109–10).

57. "Des Unheimlichsten das höchste Unheimliche." Heidegger (1996, 104; *Gesamtausgabe* 53, 129).

58. "What determines Antigone is that which first bestows ground and necessity upon the distinction of the dead and the priority of blood. What that is, Antigone, and that also means the poet, leaves without name. Death and human being, human being and embodied life (blood) in each case belong together. 'Death' and 'blood' in each case name different and extreme realms of human being, and such being is neither fulfilled in one nor exhausted in the other. That belonging to death and to blood that is proper to human beings and to them alone is itself first determined by the relation of human beings to being itself." (Was Antigone bestimmt, ist jenes, das erst der Auszeichnung der Toten un dem Vorrang des Blutes den grund und die Notwendigkeit gibt. Was das ist, lässt Antigone, und d. h. zugleich der Dichter, ohne Namen. Tod und Menschsein, Menschsein und leibhaftes Leben (Blut) gehören sowohl zusammen. . . . Die dem Menschen und nur ihm eigene Zugehörigkeit zum Tod und zum Blut ist selbst erst bestimmt durch den Bezug des Menschen zum Sein selbst.) Heidegger (1996, 118; *Gesamtausgabe* 53, 147).

59. Miguel de Beistegui has shown that the Ister course makes the prepolitical into a major concern. According to Beistegui, Heidegger opposes the prepolitical to "the overwhelming and totalitarian presence of the political," and so the discussion of tragedy constitutes a critique of modernity that is aimed at the modern state as a function rather than as a site of continuous questioning about its own nature. Beistegui (1997, 115, 137–38).

60. Heidegger (1996, 118; *Gesamtausgabe* 53, 147).

CHAPTER 4

1. Steiner (1984, 18).

2. Lacan (1992, 247).

3. In the 1920s and 1930s, a debate on feminine sexuality was conducted by Ernest Jones, Helen Deutsch, Karen Horney, Jeanne Lampl-de Groot, Caroline

Müller-Braunschweig, and Joan Rivière. For bibliographical references and accounts of these debates, consult Brennan (1992, 39–83).

4. See Freud (*Standard Edition*, vol. 7, 141–49). "It seems probable," argues Freud, "that the sexual instinct is in the first instance independent of its object; nor is its origin likely to be due to its object's attractions" (*Standard Edition*, vol. 7, 148). The object in the sexual drive is contingent and tends to disavow all social norms for its satisfaction. At the same time, however, Freud sees a link between abnormal sexual behavior and lack of morality in other domains, showing to the difficulty of shaping sexual instincts according to social norms.

5. Mitchell and Rose (1982, 2; my italics).

6. See, for instance, "The Dissolution of the Oedipus Complex," where Freud establishes that the girl tries to compensate for her lack of a phallus by taking up a feminine position in relation to the father, desiring to have his child (*Standard Edition*, vol. 19, 176–79).

7. The maternal object is both given up and retained. See, for instance, "Female Sexuality," where Freud has recourse to a pre-Oedipal domain dominated by the maternal sphere in order to explain the ambivalent relation to the mother as the key to the problems of feminine sexual identity (*Standard Edition*, vol. 21, 230).

8. Kristeva describes feminine castration as an irrecuparable loss that makes its way into the feminine psyche as the eruption of an inner rather than an outer loss: "Even though a woman has no penis to lose, it is her entire being—body and especially soul—that she feels is threatened by castration. *As if her phallus were her psyche,* the loss of the erotic object breaks up and threatens to empty her whole psychic life. The outer loss is immediately and depressively experienced as an inner void." Kristeva (1989, 82). See also Kristeva's account of the melancholy in Marguerite Duras's work, which she describes as texts written in the midst of that inner void, exploring it without alleviating the weight of it through catharsis, which is otherwise part of the poetic experience (1989, 221–59).

9. Freud (*Standard Edition*, vol. 19, 176).

10. Freud (*Standard Edition*, vol. 21, 130).

11. In "Some Psychical Consequences of the Anatomical Distinction between the Sexes" (1925), Freud writes: "I cannot evade the notion (though I hesitate to give it expression) that for women the level of what is ethically normal is different from what it is in men. Their super-ego is never so inexorable, so impersonal, so independent of its emotional origins as we require it to be in men. Character-traits which critics of every epoch have brought up against women—that they show less sense of justice than men, that they are less ready to submit to the great exigencies of life, that they are more often influenced in their judgments by feelings of affection or hostility—all these would be amply accounted for by the modification in the formation of the super-ego which we have inferred above" (*Standard Edition*, vol. 19, 257).

12. Freud (*Standard Edition*, vol. 7, 182).

13. "Children behave in the same kind of way as an average uncultivated woman in whom the same polymorphously perverse disposition persists. Under ordinary conditions she may remain normal sexually, but if she is led on by a clever seducer she will find every sort of perversion to her taste, and will retain them as part of her own sexuality. Prostitutes exploit the same polymorphous, that is, infantile, disposition for the purposes of their profession; and, considering the immense number of women who are prostitutes or who must be supposed to have an aptitude for prostitution without becoming engaged in it, it becomes impossible not to recognize that this same disposition to perversions of every kind is a general and fundamental human characteristic." Freud (*Standard Edition*, vol. 7, 191).

14. Freud (*Standard Edition*, vol. 7, 151). The quote "What does a woman want?" is taken from a conversation (*Standard Edition*, vol. 19, 244), but there are many similar expressions in print, such as: "the sexual life of adult women is a 'dark continent for psychology'" (*Standard Edition*, vol. 20, 212).

15. It is precisely the superego that is the target of psychoanalysis. Although Freud distinguishes between the superego as "cultural" values and the aggression inherent in the individual superego, he makes clear that analysis must attempt to lower the demands of the superego regardless of whether those demands conform with moral norms (*Standard Edition*, vol. 21, 142).

16. Freud (*Standard Edition*, vol. 21, 124).

17. Freud (*Standard Edition*, vol. 21, 142).

18. In *Civilization and Its Discontents*, Freud argues that cultural norms and values reinforce the superego, which is a major destructive factor in Western cultural pathology. It should be pointed out that women are not necessarily more pathological than men, but they do not identify with the normative system in the same way (*Standard Edition*, vol. 21, 130).

19. Beauvoir (1989, 45–46).

20. See chapters 3 and 4 in Lévi-Strauss (1969).

21. Beauvoir (1989, 74).

22. Beauvoir (1989, 49).

23. Beauvoir (1989, 54). Beauvoir identifies a homosocial structure as the basis of male desire: men trading women with each other (1989, 78).

24. Beauvoir (1989, xliii, 672).

25. Beauvoir (1989, 38).

26. Beauvoir (1989, 34). The situation of the body cannot, however, be reduced to biology or descriptions such as weakness, since technology has made corporeal weakness secondary.

27. Beauvoir (1989, 50).

28. Beauvoir (1989, 48).

29. Beauvoir (1989, 752). Beauvoir's ethics are also constructed around a notion of negativity, or a "lack of being." Our projects, engagements, and desires are all related to such a lack of being. Moral values, Beauvoir argues, can never be detached from projects and desires that have to do with our immediate engagement in our life world. The capacity to negate and thereby transcend ourselves through

moral values stems from such a foundational lack of being (1994, 12–13). In her book on ethics, Beauvoir does not relate the sexes to such a lack of being; *The Second Sex*, however, argues that the capacity to negate and to relate to the fundamental lack is based on the relation to the phallus.

30. As Eva Lundgren-Gothlin has shown, we are here touching a moment that could be considered both at a social and a biological level, a moment out of which Beauvoir's theory of sexual difference is constructed (1991, 104–23).

31. Beauvoir (1989, 7).

32. Beauvoir (1989, 35).

33. Not by her being-toward-death, then. This is the reason Beauvoir points to the shortcomings of the Hegelian master-slave model of the desire for recognition and consciousness. See Beauvoir's account of sexual difference and Hegel's master-slave conflict (1989, 64–5). It should be added, however, that the capacity for childbirth is individual, and a woman's relation to it is colored by her economic and social situation (1989, 35).

34. Roudinesco (1997, 169).

35. See, for instance, Toril Moi's discussion of alienation (1994, 156–64).

36. See Gallop (1982) and Grosz (1990). Jürgen Reeder's *Begär och etik* contains a chapter that constitutes an exception to this rule, in which he discusses the relation between Beauvoir and Lacan (1990, 50–189). David Macey points out that Lacan discusses Betty Friedan's *Feminine Mystique* rather than Beauvoir (1988, 196).

37. Cf. Beauvoir (1989, xix) and Lacan's seminar *Encore*: "Il n'y a pas *La* femme, article défini pour désigner l'universel. Il n'y a pas *La* femme puisquede son essence, elle n'est pas toute" (1975, 68). "There's no such thing as Woman, woman with a capital *W* indicating the universal. There's no such thing as Woman because . . . in her essence, she is not whole." Lacan (1998a, 68–69). In other words, woman is a phantasmatic construction substituting for the fact that the sexes make up a totality, "une toute."

38. Butler (2000, 41–44).

39. Lacan (1988b, 29).

40. Lacan (1988b, 31).

41. Lacan (1988b, 116).

42. Lacan (1992, 146).

43. Lacan (1992, 75).

44. Lacan (1966, 835). See further discussion of this proposal in Chapter 5.

45. "Life is always 'contaminated' by death since 'reproduction' as such, insofar as it is sexual [*sexuée*], involves both life and death." Lacan (1998, 30).

46. This is shown more specifically in the *Encore* seminar (1998a), which suggests that the question of being must always refer to "sexed being" and the fracture and break that erupts with jouissance. Lacan (1998, 11). Lacan, elaborating further on this issue, insists that sexual difference is in fact what creates an ek-static relation to truth. Sexual difference is a product of the symbolic, not physionomy: the

external and deranging ex-istence is what marks the speaking being as opposed to the merely sexual being. *Les non dupes errent*, 21 May 1974, 21 (manuscript at the Bibliothèque de l'Ecole de la Cause Freudienne). The same script repeats the famous formula: there is no sexual relation, which is where the fantasy about the other sex originates. *Les non dupes errent*, 19 Feb. 1974. In her volume *Sexuation*, Renata Salecl has put together a series of Lacanian interpretations and definitions of what the term "sexuation" means. In Colette Soler's words, the term "sexuation" refers to the fact that all subjects are determined by castration on the one hand and *jouissance* on the other, a fact that singularizes women as the Other because they have access to a supplementary *jouissance* beyond the phallus: "As soon as we speak of sexual bodies, the order imposed by discourse proves incapable of correcting the 'denaturing' of the speaking being and has nothing more to offer but the phallic semblance." Salecl (2000, 41).

47. See, for instance, "La signification du phallus." Here Lacan explains that the phallus must be considered the model for a signifier rather than a symbolic organ of power or domination (1966, 692).

48. As in Freud (*Standard Edition*, vol. 19, 248–58).

49. "Là où il n'y a pas de rapport sexuel, ça fait 'troumatisme.'" *Les non dupes errent*, 19 Feb. 1974. The trauma is the encounter with a kind of *trou* or hole, the absolute negativity that for Lacan is the very being of sexual difference, a negativity that allows difference to emerge without ever asserting the quality, kind, or teleological goal of that difference: "Ce qui est de l'être, d'un être qui se poserait comme absolu, n'est jamais que la fracture, la cassure, l'interruption de la formule *être sexué* en tant que l'être sexué est intéressé dans la jouissance." *Les non dupes errent*, 19 Feb. 1974.

50. We can, for reasons of pedagogy, polemicize against Swedish psychoanalyst Jürgen Reeder's account of the symbolic order: "Women give birth and feed the human offspring, through her maternal function woman becomes associated with the nonsubjective, which must be deserted and replaced by the representability of the symbolic order. . . . At its most profound level, the phallus could perhaps be regarded as the symbolic entity that establishes the difference between subjectivity and the nonsubjective; as an image of jubilant transcendence, it designates the transfer from nature to culture, from the imaginary to the symbolic" (1990, 148, my translation).

51. Grosz (1990, 140–46).

52. Lacan (1998a, 121).

53. "There's no such thing as Woman, Woman with a capital *W* indicating the universal. There's no such thing as Woman because, in her essence . . . she is not-whole.) Lacan (1975, 68; 1998, 73). This famous quote has been submitted to a number of interpretations, the most interesting one perhaps by Jacqueline Rose, who illuminated its emancipatory dimension: the idea that woman is a linguistic construction rather than an object of exchange relieves feminine sexuality and

identity from a specific content, and makes them subject to cultural and political change. Mitchell and Rose (1982, 47).

54. Woman is the Other but there is, Lacan says, no Other of the Other: this means that there is no metalanguage beyond the phallic function that would fill or designate the feminine position (1998, 81). In this sense, Woman is what Ernesto Laclau would define as an empty signifier, excluded from any discursive chain informed by the ideological promise of a totality or an ideal: the "emptying of a particular signifier of its particular, differentiated signified is . . . what makes possible the emergence of 'empty' signifiers as the signifiers of a lack, of an absent totality" (1996, 42).

55. Cf. Lacan's discussion of Bentham (1992, 229).

56. Lacan (1992, 238).

57. Beauvoir (1989, 673–74).

58. Monique David-Ménard provides an interesting critique of Lacan's enigmatic notion of femininity as the not-all: for her, Lacan has not gone far enough in his commentary on women's problematic position as the "lack in the symbolic." He considers women's sexuality to be caused by a lack they themselves know nothing about, since this lack is as enigmatic and nondiscursive as their own sexuality. David-Ménard objects to the mystification of feminine desire through tautological reasoning, and she objects to the claim that "woman does not exist": there is a feminine experience that is particular and that can be illuminated by Lacan's formula of sexuation. Her interpretation of the nonuniversality of the woman has to do with the relation to the object. The male, castrated subject is split from its object as cause of desire. For a woman, however, it is the object that causes the split. A woman knows that a penis is not the phallus, that the eroticized object is split from the symbolic object of a sexual liaison that makes her enjoy. The pleasure she may take in the sexual act and the love she may feel for a man are not the cause of her enjoyment. That cause is, as she knows, a part of herself, although hidden from her knowledge. Regarding the notion that women lack a place in the symbolic, Menard contends that it is rather that the relation to the symbolic, and to the object, is more distinct for a woman than for a man. From a Lacanian perspective, the object of the drive, *l'objet petit a*, is that which divides the subject and causes his desire, and it is precisely this object that a woman is bound to encounter through the split between phallus and enjoyment: "Dans la sexualité féminine également, l'objet divise le sujet; ce qui fait jouir une femme apparaît comme étant rencontré en un autre mais correspondant à ce qui est le plus inassimilable et pourtant constituant d'elle-même." David-Ménard (1994, 117).

59. Her enjoyment is supplementary rather than complementary: a *jouissance* to the woman who does not exist, that is, who is undetermined by the phallic function of the signifier. Lacan (1998, 73–74).

60. Beauvoir (1989, 54).

61. Beauvoir (1989, xliii, 672).

62. Woman is a symptom of man, Lacan says in the seminar *Le sinthôme*.

Here, Lacan changes the concept of symptom into the word *le Sinthôme* in order to mark a difference in the proper use of the term. Foreclosed as a signifier, associated with the domain of the *objet petit a*, woman, you could say, is the symptom of the partition of man. Woman does not exist, but man is a woman who only thinks that he exists. Seminar of 21 January 1975 (manuscript at the Bibliothèque de la Cause Freudienne, Paris).

63. Lacan (1966, 732).

64. See, for instance, the discussion in "Female sexuality" (*Standard Edition,* vol. 21, 228–39).

65. Juliet Flower McCannell has used the notion of an idealized, beautiful feminine Thing to traverse the fantasy of what such a Thing would consist in, and proposed that there is in fact the trace of a feminine subject present in that fantasy: this indicates, McCannell argues, an actual space of feminine *jouissance*, which in itself holds the promise of a love that transcends the phallic constraints of desire. In an interesting reading of Stendhal's *On Love*, she shows how the promise of such a *jouissance* allows for an approach to the other sex, in spite of the fact that there is no common ground between them: "Only an object, raised to the dignity of a Thing, has the possibility of becoming a Subject, subject to suffering from the phallus" (2000, 234).

66. Lacan (1992, 248).

67. Lacan (1992, 282).

68. Patrick Guyomard has developed a critique of Lacan's idea that the cause of Antigone's autonomy should also be the cause of her death; in this perspective, castration, says Guyomard, brings about death as the accomplishment of desire, an idea that can hardly be sustained as the goal of psychoanalysis. Psychoanalysis must be "impure" in its very nature, working with desires and forms of alterity of which death is only one. Guyomard (1992, 44–45, 127–28). Desire is never pure, only corrupted and impure: "Ce 'pur désir' est irrémediablement corrompu par l'impureté de l'alliance et de la filiation" (1992, 75). As Guyomard puts it: "The origin is ambiguous, impure, real and sexuated" (L'Origine est double, impure, réelle et sexuée). Guyomard (1992, 66). Although I agree with his suspicion of the idea of Antigone as pure desire, I disagree with the interpretation that desire is the equivalent of the death drive. In my interpretation, Lacan's analysis of Antigone's pure desire is rather a kind of deduction performed as a critique of the Kleinian theory of the object. This will be explored in greater depth in Chapter 5.

69. As asserted by Kant, beauty does not present any object for us to embrace. Rather, it gives the object its autonomy. In the third critique, Kant shows that beauty is a judgment passed in the subject in reference to an object, but it is neither a property belonging to an object nor anything that could be reduced to a concept. Lacan plays with the Kantian notion of beauty as a symbol of morality, referring to the detachment of the Antigone figure in relation to the viewer. See *Critique of Judgment,* §59, where Kant explains that objects perceived as beautiful are also moral.

70. Lacan (1992, 248).

71. In "Kant avec Sade," Lacan sketches an understanding of *jouissance* as a modern problem. He shows that Sade is a symptom of modernity in the sense that he eradicates Christian moral values while becoming the involuntary victim of an anxiety opening up beyond the death of God; this leaves open the fantasy of an evil God: "Let us interrogate this *jouissance*, precarious in that it hangs, in the Other, on an echo which it only suscitates as it abolishes it, by joining the intolerable to it. Doesn't it at last appear to us to exalt only in itself, in the manner of another, horrible freedom?" (1989, 60).

72. Lacan (1992, 272). Just like in Heidegger's poetics, nothing really happens in tragedy according to Lacan. There is no "true event" because the play takes place under the order of truth: what happens is in fact that things are presented in another way than they were at the beginning, but nothing happens that would change the order that determines the tragedy as such (1992, 265).

73. Philippe Lacoue-Labarthe (1991, 33–34). Lacoue-Labarthe points out that for Lacan, as for Heidegger, the work of art, like the signifier, is itself the creation of the Thing. It creates the empty space, absence, or opening that corresponds to the purification or *catharsis* of the object itself. Philippe van Haute makes a similar argument, linking sublimation to the effect of disappearance, or absence of meaning; beauty, argues van Haute, incarnates the transition point at which the world of meaning loses its self-evidence and appears as vulnerable (1998, 102–20). John Rajchman holds that beautiful objects stand in for our bodies in such a way that they displace the pursuit of a common purpose or good: "Sublimation involves another sort of 'bond' among us" (1991, 73).

74. This means that it cannot be reduced to a conflict between state and family, as Hegel argues in the *Phenomenology*. Lacan (1992, 236).

75. See the discussion of Heidegger's notion of the political in Chapter 3.

76. Yannis Stavrakakis has shown how a political theory could be drawn out of Lacan's concept of the real, and especially how it could be used to enlighten a conception of what he calls an "ambiguous democracy"—a democracy that encircles the real as the impossibility of a totality and of social closure. Such a democracy would then dispense with utopian visions in favor of such an impossibility, and in favor of the antagonisms and failures that all symbolic systems carry in themselves as a result of their necessary alignment with the real: "The importance of the democratic intervention is that, in a double movement, it provides a point of reference, a *point de capiton* for the institution of society, without reducing society to this point of reference. This is achieved because the positive content of democracy is the acceptance of the constitutive lack and antagonism (and consequently hegemony) that splits every total representation of the social field. And the *status* of this lack, as an encounter with the real, is ethical" (1999, 138). This means that an ethics of the real serves as the place of antagonism, of an allowance for the intrinsic conflicts of society to be played out through discussions, elections, conflicts, and renegotiations.

77. Lacan (1992, 275).
78. Lacan (1992, 276).
79. See Chapter 2.
80. Lacan (1992, 262).
81. "Antigone's position represents the radical limit that affirms the unique value of [Polynices'] being without reference to any content, to whatever good or evil Polynices may have done, or to whatever he may be subjected to." Lacan (1992, 279).
82. Doyle (1984, 1–6).
83. Doyle (1984, 106).
84. Lacan (1992, 283).
85. They offer no moral support as a motive for the action. See Eckermann (1986, 542–46).
86. Else (1976, 17).
87. Irigaray (1985a, 219). See also Irigaray (1987, 86, 112).
88. Slavoj Žižek points out that Lacan's analysis of the word *ate* indicates a crucial difference between fantasy space and the real. What lies beyond *ate* is the fantasmatic transformation of the impossible into the prohibited. The absolute demarcation indicated by the limit of *ate* does not move. Incest is such a limit; even if someone was to perform an act of incest, desire would still be structured around the impossibility of having the mother/father as object: other objects are made possible because of this impossibility/castration. Žižek (1993, 115–16).
89. Lacan (1992, 262).
90. Lacan (1992, 284).
91. Lacan (1992, 279).
92. Lacan (1992, 279).
93. Lacan (1992, 282).
94. This is argued by Butler on the grounds that Antigone refuses to become a mother and a wife and welcomes death as her bridal chamber (2000, 76).
95. This has been expanded upon in detail by Zupancic, who relates it to a Kantian aspect in Lacan that makes his subject into something more than an effect of a linguistic structure. Zupancic (1995, 35–44). One may also consider the question to be the focus of discussion in "Subversion of the subject and the dialectics of desire," in *Écrits*. One may of course read this paper as a reflection on the practice of psychoanalysis, but also as if it tells us something significant about the relation between the subject and the symbolic order as such. The position of the Other, Lacan argues, is a position that cannot be represented, strictly speaking: the Other is the locus of the signifier toward which the desire of the subject is directed, but it does not in itself have any meaning beyond occupying such a position. A statement of authority has no guarantee other than its enunciation; it cannot be represented in another signifier, which would appear outside this locus in some way (1977, 310). This is what it means to say there is no Other of the Other, there is no metalanguage (1977, 311).

96. The true formula of atheism is not that God is dead, but rather that he is unconscious, which means that truth is no longer certainty invested in the absolute, but rather certainty invested in the unfortunate accident that is an encounter with the real: *tuche*. Lacan (1998b, 59). In this sense, one may claim that Lacan's notion of man's being is extimate rather than intimate to him, and insert him, as Rudi Visker has done, in a line of contemporary thinkers who have pointed to the truth function as the relation between the singularity of the subject and the invisible domain that is the condition of all subjectivity, rather than as an effect of intersubjectivity or a chain of signifiers (1999, 11). Truth would not then be a function of what one announces, but rather of that which lies beyond the chain of signifiers, in a domain where the signifier does not refer to a signified, a suggestion that would indicate that it is not we who have language, but language that has us (1999, 241).

97. It is tempting to read Antigone's enjoyment of death as a function of the superego. As Alenka Zupancic has pointed out, however, her action shows that the moral law is founded on the real, in the sense of an absolute injunction that cannot be explained or supported through any means other than its own enunciation, and it is not to be confused with the superego. The superego serves the pleasure principle, a pathological and imaginary domain for Lacan (1995, 74, 111–17). The logic of Antigone's ethics as founded in the real has also been explained by Ellie Ragland, who shows that it is not supported by any structure in which her desire would take hold, but rather founded in a real in which desire can no longer be separated from the death drive (1995, 168; cf. also Copjec 1999). This is also the view of Slavoj Žižek, for instance. For Žižek, Antigone's act constitutes a radical break in relation to the symbolic that is typical of the feminine position. A male position corresponds to constructive, edifying *activity* but lacks the radical potential of the feminine. Žižek (1992, 46, 77). For another elucidating discussion on male versus female positions in this regard, see Fink (1995, 115). The notion of the Thing in the *Ethics of Psychoanalysis* precipitates the elaboration of *objet petit a*: the absent cause of desire and therefore of the subject. The aim of psychoanalysis, for Lacan, is to explore the position of the subject in relation to that object, which proves to be different for men and women. Fink puts it this way: "The masculine path might . . . be qualified as that of desire (becoming one's own cause of desire), while the feminine would be that of love. And as we shall see, masculine subjectification might then be to involve the making of one's own otherness qua efficient cause (the signifier), while feminine subjectification would involve the making of one's own otherness qua maternal cause (the letter). They would both, then, require subjectification of the cause or otherness, but of different facets thereof." Fink's discussion is applicable to the example of Antigone, if one translates the letter as another name for what is called the Thing in Seminar VII.

CHAPTER 5

1. Lykke (1989, 148–49, 259–60). Thus Antigone is a much more powerful figure than Electra, who wants to avenge the murder of her father by killing her mother. In her attachment to her father, Electra is a mirror image of Oedipus, as Beauvoir has pointed out (1989, 41).

2. Irigaray (1985a, 219).

3. Irigaray (1993a, 119)

4. Irigaray (1993a, 121).

5. See, for instance, *Sexes and Genealogies*, but also the discussion in *An Ethics of Sexual Difference* and *Speculum of the Other Woman*.

6. Irigaray (1985b, 169).

7. As quoted by Chanter (1995, 180). In her book on Irigaray, Chanter points out that Antigone constitutes a reoccurring frame of reference in the work of Irigaray overall. In an article on Sarah Kofman, she shows the same applies to the French philosopher, who seemed to have taken a melancholic, "Antigonean" relation to the law; neither its subject nor the object through which it can be erected, Kofman shows the impossible place of the female philosopher to be an "Antigonean" position.

8. Irigaray (1985a, 218).

9. Irigaray (1985a, 214–20, 1993a, 107–8, 117–19)

10. Butler (2000, 6).

11. Butler (2000, 35).

12. Butler (2000, 45). Her criticism of the real is emphasized throughout her discussions with Ernesto Laclau and Slavoj Žižek: she is critical of its imposition as a limit that can never be conceptualized or understood outside of Lacanian terminology; in this way, its usefulness for the understanding of the limits of conceptualization of a normative order becomes blurred. Butler, Laclau, and Žižek (2000, 152–53).

13. Butler (2000, 54).

14. Butler (2000, 30).

15. This is also why Butler is critical of feminist psychoanalysts who would argue for the idea that psychoanalysis only sketches positions of desire and do not argue for fixed sexual identities. Butler (2000, 19).

16. Butler's critique echoes that of Beauvoir: paternal power is nothing but a social construction, and psychoanalysis depends on that construction through a collapse between social and symbolic analysis. Beauvoir (1989, 41); Butler (2000, 21).

17. Butler (2000, 71).

18. Butler, Laclau, Žižek (2000, 146).

19. Butler here refers to the work of Orlando Patterson, *Slavery and Social Death* (Cambridge: Cambridge University Press, 1982).

20. Butler (2000, 23).

21. To this extent, the reading of *Antigone* reiterates the critique of psychoanalysis in *Gender Trouble*, where the structural relation psychoanalysis assumes to exist between sex, sexual identity, and desire is taken apart. Butler (1990, 6–7).

22. Žižek's interest in the Real stems from the fact that it is an internal limit to the symbolic system. He has emphasized sexual difference as the epitome of a Lacanian Real for this reason, although the interpretation of sexual difference is also open to hegemonic struggles. Butler, Laclau, Žižek (2000, 110–21).

23. Butler, Laclau, Žižek (2000, 29–30).

24. Butler, Laclau, Žižek (2000, 81).

25. "If we always return to Freud, it is because he started out with an initial, central intuition, which is ethical in kind." Lacan (1992, 38). "We are concerned with the Freudian experience as an ethics, which is to say, at its most essential level, since it directs us toward a therapeutic form of action that, whether we like it or not, is included in the register or in the terms of an ethics. And the more we deny this, the more it is the case. Experience demonstrates this: a form of analysis that boasts of its highly scientific distinctiveness gives rise to normative notions that I characterize by evoking the curse Saint Matthew utters on those who make the bundles heavier when they are to be carried by others" (1992, 133).

26. Lacan (1992, 46).

27. This becomes clear in the last few pages, which discuss the practice of analysis. There it is stated that the analyst cannot give anything but his own desire—something that he does not have rather than something that he has. Lacan (1992, 300–301).

28. The antinomy between law and desire is conditioned by speech, because speech is unequivocal to the function of desire itself. Lacan (1992, 66–67, 82). In "Subversion of the subject . . . ," from *Écrits*, Lacan says that it is precisely because desire is articulated that it is not articulable in an ethical discourse. Lacan (1977, 302). It must be upheld in the form of a foundational prohibition, which, according to Lacan, founds all ethical systems.

29. This cannot be explained in anthropological terms, but only through the function of the symbolic whose function is to designate an impossible object. Lacan (1992, 67).

30. This has been extensively discussed by Thanos Lipowatz, who situates the *Ethics of Psychoanalysis* in a political perspective. Lipowatz reads *Antigone* as a political play that shows that there is a fundamental difference between the symbolic law to which the subject is subjected and the social or societal authorities: this is precisely what the conflicting laws between human and divine are about (1988, 224–26). Yannis Stavrakakis has argued that it is precisely because we are trapped within a field of meaning that is socially constructed that we encounter the failure of representation Lacan calls the real; something is always foreclosed or impossible to represent within the field of social construction, which is also why it is impossible to construct a perfect agreement, a perfect democracy, etc. (1999, 68, 86, 138). Judith Butler has contested the differentiation between the social and the symbolic

in Lacan, aiming to show that they effectively collapse into the same foundational structure of the prohibition of incest, because the paternal law is at the end of both of these orders (2000, 43–55). However, I stick to the proposal that the symbolic law is impossible to represent and that it merely makes up a skeleton of limits that structures the subject. The discussion of the Ten Commandments in the *Ethics of Psychoanalysis* is an example of the fact that the other is in fact impossible to represent because it consists of a prohibition.

31. According to Bernard Baas, Lacan elaborates a transcendental logic of desire in the *Ethics of Psychoanalysis* (1992, 52–53). I would argue, however, that the Thing is different from the function of the Kantian object, not being submitted to any of the categories of epistemological apprehension Kant gives to the object. The Thing is rather related to the needs and drives that color our relation to the other as object. The Thing, according to Baas, defines the origin as lack and the lack as origin (1998, 45–51). But this would, in my interpretation, characterize the *objet petit a* rather than the Thing. What is interesting about the Thing is its double-sidedness: it is not just lack but also matter, which gives it flesh and makes it into a kind of threat that is corporeal and not just fantasmatic.

32. Alenka Zupancic has showed that the subject in Lacan is not simply subjected to the Law, but is the very condition of its enunciation, analogous to Kant's moral law (1995, 35–44).

33. As described in Lacan (1998b, 161–74).

34. See note 25.

35. Lacan's own claim is that ethics begins with the question of desire (1992, 76).

36. Habermas (1987, 7).

37. Lacan (1992, 314).

38. Lacan (1992, 10–11, 22). "The question of ethics is to be articulated from the point of view of the location of man in relation to the Real," says Lacan, thereby promising to elucidate the concept of the Real in the process of discussing the good as a moral value (1992, 11).

39. Lacan explains that it is *not* a genealogy in Nietzsche's sense—thus trying to empty the moral experience of metaphysical content—but rather a genealogy in Freud's sense, thus disassociating the good from rewards such as pleasure and yet showing why the disassociation is so difficult to achieve (1992, 35–36).

40. The formula "there is no Other of the Other" reoccurs throughout Lacan's later writing. He returns to this formula in various forms, most often emphasizing that there is no metalanguage upholding the structure of the symbolic (1966, 812–13). The formula reoccurs in particular in the discussion of feminine *jouissance* in *Encore*, where it makes feminine enjoyment into a function beyond the symbolic, although it is determined by the symbolic at the same time (1998a, 81). In the *Ethics of Psychoanalysis*, it is presented as the domain of the real (1992, 66). See also note 12.

41. Lacan talks about the aim of analysis as an ideal of nondependence, or as "a kind of prophylaxis of dependence." Lacan (1992, 10).

42. Lacan (1998b, 167). Lacan discusses the separation between need, drive, and desire in chapter 4 of Lacan (1998), where he shows that the object of the drive is in fact indifferent because it is never a cause of satisfaction but instead a cause of the drive itself, a cause described as a partial element, such as the mouth, breast, etc. This cause is designated as much in terms of contacts between body parts as with the barriers set up between them: "The impossible is so present in it [the pleasure principle] that it is never recognized in it as such" (1998b, 167). In the *Ethics of Psychoanalysis*, the fragile demarcation line between desire and *jouissance* is negotiated through the relation to the object or fellow being, which has to be "emptied" of any promise of pleasure in order to make the ethical relation function ("There is no law of the good except in evil") because any principle of the good threatens to submit the neighbor to the pleasure principle (1992, 190).

43. Lacan (1992, 306).

44. Lacan (1992, 292).

45. Nancy (1999, 204).

46. Lacan refers to Jeremy Bentham's *Theory of Fictions*, an assemblage of texts published in 1932. Bentham argues that language can be divided into two categories: real entities to which existence can be ascribed—things and persons—and fictitious entities, which cannot exist although we speak about them as if they did—such as values, good and bad. Lacan compares Bentham's theory of functions to his own theory of signifiers: "With relation to institutions in their fictive or, in other words, fundamentally verbal dimension, his [Bentham's] search has involved not attempting to reduce to nothing all the multiple, incoherent, contradictory rights of which English jurisprudence furnishes an example, but, on the contrary observing on the basis of symbolic artifice of these terms, which are themselves also creators of texts, what there is there that may be used to some purpose, that is to say, become, in effect, the object of a division. The long historical development of the problem of the good is in the end centered on the notion of how goods are created, insofar as they are organized not on the basis of so-called natural and predetermined needs, but insofar as they furnish the material of a distribution; and it is in relation to this that the dialectic of the good is articulated to the degree that it takes on effective meaning for man" (1992, 228–29). At this point, Lacan argues for a utilitarian notion of the good that is distributed to sustain a certain system of power. For an elucidating essay on this comparison, see Annexe 1 of the French translation of Bentham, J. Perin, "Réel et symbolique chez Jeremy Bentham," in Bentham (1996). Renata Salecl's essays are helpful in looking at the relation between the subject and the symbolic fictions provided by the big Other: she argues that the corporeal fixation of contemporary culture can be diagnosed as a crisis of belief in the fictions that give the subject his or her identity. Driven by a distrust in even the most basic symbolic entities, such as language, people are now examining the real behind the fiction, an encounter that can be traumatic and potentially threatens social bonds. In the end, a belief in the fiction needs to be sustained for social bonds to exist, whether we talk about Santa Claus, simple polite phrases, or other social codes (1998, 150–51).

47. As Lacan famously puts it, the symbolic order itself is marked by a fundamental lack, the lack in the Other, which causes the dialectics of desire to revolve around the signifier marking the subject as a sexual being (1998a, 204–6).

48. "The Other of the Other only exists as a place. It finds its place even if we cannot find it anywhere in the real, even if all we can find to occupy this place in the real is simply valid insofar as it occupies this place, but cannot give it any other guarantee than that it is in this place. It is in this way that another typology is established [than Freud's second topology for which representations can be repressed], the typology which institutes the relation to the real." Lacan (1992, 66).

49. Such a critique is to be found in, for instance, the essay on natural law. Hegel (1999, 125–28).

50. As Lacan says about the moral law: "The Law puts into balance not just pleasure, but also pain, happiness, or even the pressure of poverty, even love of life, everything pathological, it turns out that desire can not only have the same success, but can obtain it with greater legitimacy." Lacan (1989, 70).

51. Bernard Baas has made a careful and thorough analysis of the distinction between Lacan's *objet petit a* and the Thing. The Thing, for Baas, is above all a point of idealization, while the *objet petit a* is a more primordial cause. The *objet petit a* is that in function of which the Thing gives rise to desire, and what keeps the Thing within the logic of desire. One may therefore speak of the *objet petit a* as the nonempirical, nonobjectifiable cause of desire that keeps us within the logic of desire, while the Thing is the empty representation of the loss itself (1998, 82–83). I will argue, however, with the notion that the Thing could be considered merely as a point of idealization; if it is idealized, it is because it refers to a loss and an irrepresentability that is threatening to the extent that it keeps the subject riveted to a materiality and a kind of embodiment, which make the Thing a function of drives and physical needs as well—this is why Lacan refers to it as the real, even if it is empty of content.

52. Lacan (1992, 230).

53. Lacan believed the mirror-stage was the best description of how things come to mean. The individual is sheltered in a safe state of permanent alienation in the imaginary, where "all the objects of his world are structured around the wandering shadow of his own ego" (1988b, 166). With reference to Klein's "animal intuition," he adds: "The fundamental absurdity of interhuman behavior can only be comprehended in the light of this system—as Melanie Klein so happily called it, not knowing, as usual, what she was saying—called the human ego, namely that set of defences, of denials (négations), of dams, of inhibitions, of fundamental fantasies which orient and direct the subject" (1988a, 17). This means that it is the relation between the imaginary and the symbolic that directs the early Lacan's interests. The imaginary has the function of giving meaning, punching the holes in the symbolic, constructing an overview. It is, however, a necessary supplement to the symbolic rather than a construction in its own right. Meaning dwells in the shadow of that magic name of the father, which saves the subject from dwindling

into psychosis, melancholy, or masochism. Melanie Klein's notion of infantile fantasy, however, is revelatory of the loose status of the primal signifier. For Klein, the child goes through stages that can be described as psychotic before it comes to grip with the distinction between inner and outer reality through symbolization. And symbolization, in Klein as in Lacan, is altogether an affair of castration—separation from the mother. Commenting on Klein's analysis of "Little Dick" from 1930, in "The Importance of Symbol-Formation in the Development of the Ego," Lacan criticized Klein for staying at the level of imaginary fantasies. However, it is Klein's "animal instinct," Lacan says, that has "allowed her to bore through a body of knowledge which was up to then impenetrable" (1988a, 69).

54. In the following, I translate *prochain* by neighbor.

55. It is the superego that is the target of psychoanalysis. Although Freud distinguishes between the superego of "cultural" values and the aggression inherent in the individual superego, he makes clear that analysis must attempt to lower the demands of the superego, regardless of whether they conform with moral norms. (*Standard Edition*, vol. 21, 142).

56. Freud (*Standard Edition*, vol. 21, 111).

57. Lacan (1992, 197).

58. See the discussion in Julien (1995, 125–27). Philippe Julien has written a whole book on the *jouissance* of the other. To love the neighbor as oneself is an impossible principle after Freud; it means releasing the evil and destruction inherent in *jouissance*, submission to a destructive principle (1995, 125–27). The neighbor is himself constituted through a lack or void that threatens to destroy us in our dependence or love: our neighbor wants precisely what we cannot give, which opens an unacceptable rift in him (1995, 147). Paul Moyaert (1996), for his part, has historicized the opening of that rift—for Lacan, there is no turning back to the pre-Freudian or Christian ethical subject. Since Freud revealed the destructiveness of the drives inherent in the modern subject in *Civilization and Its Discontents*, the ambiguity of the neighbor has overturned any notion that might confirm or assess the ethicity of the subject.

59. The myth of the murder of the father, depicted by Freud in *Totem and Taboo*, is announced in a time for which God is dead. But this, in turn, only produces a culture of transgression, where the mythical origin of the Law is produced by and through the desire of the son, who never ceases to waver between submission to the law and transgression (1992, 177).

60. This is argued in several books, most notably *The Sublime Object of Ideology*, where Žižek states that Marxism effectively invented the symptom: "Capitalism is capable of transforming its limit, its very impotence, in the source of its power—the more it 'putrefies,' the more its immanent contradiction is aggravated, the more it must revolutionize itself to survive," and this revolution is produced by the enjoyment that is to be found at its limits: an enjoyment that has to do with overcoming its own constraints in the production of values, where acquisition becomes a value and an enjoyment in itself." Žižek (1989, 52–53). In his essay "Love

Thy Neighbor? No Thanks!" Žižek argues that the impossibility of an ethics of modernity is shown by the presence of surplus value of enjoyment produced by the ideology of the big Other, as represented in capitalism or Nazism: when I submit to the Other, I encounter the real in the form of enjoyment through that very submission (1997, 47). Žižek takes his example from Goldhagen's controversial *Hitler's Willing Executioners*, which argues against Arendt's thesis of evil as banality and lack of reflection. Žižek's claim is that the Holocaust was made possible because the executioners did not only undertake what they were supposed to do; rather they took pleasure in it—a kind of excess produced by serving a totalitarian régime where *jouissance* became a payback for that servitude. Žižek (1997, 56–57).

61. Freud, *Standard Edition*, vol. 1, 297.

62. Freud, *Standard Edition*, vol. 1, 358–59.

63. *Standard Edition*, vol. 1, 318. "Die anfängliche Hilflosigkeit des Menschen ist die *Urquelle* aller *moralischen Motive*."

64. Freud, *Standard Edition*, vol. 1, 383. The Thing is, according to Freud, the constant, nonunderstood part within a perceptual complex. It does little to adapt to reality and does not serve judgment. Although related to the notion of fantasy as introduced later on by the psychoanalytic movement, the Thing is a different concept since it is conceived in a theoretical universe where the Oedipus complex has not yet been introduced. The Thing originates in the gap between psyche and reality, and will sustain that gap no matter how well the psyche learns to adapt.

65. Freud, *Standard Edition*, vol. 1, 317–21.

66. We may, if we like, refer Lacan's notion of the Real to Freud's original conception of matter as a form of psychic impenetrability.

67. As Simon Critchley puts it: "Without a relation to the trauma, or a relation to that which violently disrupts or disturbs the subject (it may be the Good beyond being, God, Kant's moral law, Freud's *das Ding*), there would not be any ethics at all, neither for phenomenology nor psychoanalysis. "Le traumatisme originel: Lévinas avec la psychanalyse," in *Emmanuel Lévinas* (Paris: Collège International de philosophie, 1998), p. 174.

68. As stated in the famous passage from the second of Freud's *Three Essays on Sexuality*: "At a time when the first beginnings of sexual satisfaction are still linked with the taking of nourishment [i.e., in the propping phase], the sexual instinct has a sexual object outside the infant's own body in the shape of his mother's breast. It is only later that he loses it, just at the time, perhaps, when he is able to form a total idea of the person to whom the organ that is giving him satisfaction belongs. As a rule the sexual drive then becomes auto-erotic [*auto-erotism is thus not the initial stage*], and not until the period of latency has been passed through is the original relation restored. There are thus good reasons why a child sucking at his mother's breast has become the prototype of every relation of love. The finding of an object is thus in fact a re-finding of it" (*Standard Edition*, vol. 7, 222).

69. Lacan follows the Freudian logic in making the Thing into an ethical con-

cept; the Thing is an object of *extimacy*, a kind of intimate exteriority or an internal exclusion, inhabiting the subject while remaining inaccessible to it. It is "something strange to me, although it is at the heart of me, something that on the level of the unconscious only a representation can represent" (1992, 71).

70. Lacan (1992, 125).

71. Lacan (1992, 68).

72. Lacan (1966, 835), "La subversion du sujet et la dialectique du désir." See also Chapter 4, note 40. In *Against Adaptation*, Philippe van Haute discusses this formula at length, showing that it is operative not only in the clinical sense of transference, but in the way desire is inscribed in the subject as body. The subject is placed in an interminable displacement between signifiers, which means that it is never identified with one signifier, although it may be represented by one. But the signifier is not an expressible one; we are here concerned with the signifier of desire, which is embodied: "The lack from which desire lives, must always be understood in terms of its concrete bodily form. Without this bodily anchoring desire remains merely virtual. The signifier that inscribes the fundamental indeterminability of the subject concretely in the psychic economy, must, consequently, designate the essential link between the body (life) and language" (2001, 127–30).

73. Lacan (1992, 124).

74. See, for instance, "Peace and Proximity," in Levinas 1996, 161–69.

75. This would also be the task of Lacanian psychoanalysis, as stated by Philippe Julien (1995, 120). In Julien's account, psychoanalysis must be thought within an atheist framework, to which Freud's *Totem and Taboo* gives the key.

76. This is why Lacoue-Labarthe has argued that Lacan's seminar on ethics is in fact an aesthetics, in the same way that Heidegger's readings of tragedy are oriented to aesthetic knowing more than ethical praxis. Just like Heidegger, Lacan argues for a *mimetological* idea of representation: the Thing that guides our eye is always inaccessible, and so images can only be constructed as fictions—in fact, they lack a true origin. In this way, every image is dependant upon the function of signifiers and language rather than being actual mirrors of objects (1991, 31–32).

77. Heidegger (1993, 155–57; *Gesamtausgabe*, 19–20).

78. Heidegger (1993, 159–60; *Gesamtausgabe*, 23).

79. Heidegger argues that traditional concepts of the Thing, such as Aristotle's notion of substance and accidence, are inadequate for the understanding of that which retains the Thing-like quality of the artwork; in fact, the Thing of the artwork is precisely that which withdraws rather than protrudes with graspable qualities. Heidegger (*Gesamtausgabe*, 27).

80. Lacan (1992, 142). See the discussion of the signifier as an empty construction in Chapter 4.

81. The tragic sublime, as Schelling puts it, causes the collapse of intellectual capacities, but it also shows us the tragic hero's overcoming of suffering through his own moral character, which has nothing to do with choice or virtue. The sub-

lime in tragedy is the overcoming of a given condition of suffering through freedom. Schelling (1989, 88–90).

82. Lacan (1992, 112).

83. The formula of raising the object to the dignity of the Thing means also that we move from aesthetics to an ethical register: "Freudian aesthetics is involved [in the seminar on ethics] because it reveals one of the functions of ethics. . . . I am trying to show you how Freudian aesthetics, in the broadest meaning of the term—which means the analysis of the whole economy of signifiers—reveals that the Thing is inaccessible." Lacan (1992, 159). In replacing the object with the Thing, Lacan proposes considerations on aesthetics and sublimation radically different from those of Klein in a text that may well constitute an implicit subject of debate for Lacan: "Infantile Anxiety-Situations Reflected in a Work of Art and in the Creative Impulse" (1929). Klein describes a woman working through her melancholy by becoming an artist. Originally, she is an art collector, but her brother-in-law is an artist and when he removes a painting from her collection, she is greatly disturbed by the empty hole that emerges. She begins to paint herself. The result is successful beyond her expectations and she develops into a real artist, creating among other things an extraordinary portrait of her own aging mother: "The daughter's wish to destroy her mother, to see her old, worn out, marred, is the cause of the need to represent her in full possession of her strength and beauty" (1988, 218). The beauty is a result of a process of repair: "The blank space has been filled," the analysis says (1988, 217).

84. Freud (*Standard Edition*, vol. 14, 215).

85. Freud (*Standard Edition*, vol. 21, 97).

86. See, for instance, the discussion in "Leonardo da Vinci and a Memory of His Childhood," where Freud explains da Vinci as an utterly successful case of sublimation, substituting for an early sexual drive a never-ending thirst for knowledge and a need to express the experience of maternal love through his art. Freud (*Standard Edition*, vol. 11, 119–29).

87. Kristeva (1989, 51–55).

88. Lacan (1992, 281).

89. Lacan (1998b, 85–90).

90. See the discussion in Chapter 4: this is why Lacan makes the beautiful woman into an archetypal Thing, an object of desire that is as unreal as it is untouchable.

91. "The true barrier that holds the subject back in front of the unspeakable field of radical desire that is the field of absolute destruction, of destruction beyond putrefaction is properly speaking the aesthetic phenomenon where it is identified with the radiance of beauty—beauty in all its shining radiance, beauty that has been called the splendor of truth. It is obviously because truth is not pretty to look at that beauty is, if not its splendor, then at least its envelope" (1992, 216–17).

92. Lacan (1992, 244–45, 287).

93. Lacan (1992, 247).

94. Catharsis, for Aristotle, can only follow from fear and pity. The mimesis of tragedy concerns an action that gives rise to fear and pity and produces relief, catharsis, from these emotions (*Poetics* 1449b). By constructing its part as a whole, tragedy depicts the inner necessity that produces the action. The audience experiences relief and balance after having suffered fear and pity. The relief is an effect of the inevitable, a response to the emotions of acute vulnerability that came before. But catharsis is more than relief. Aristotle's argument is more complex. With catharsis, we face a horrifying resolution that came about through fate. It is the sum of these elements that makes tragedy meaningful for us as an art form, the structural components and the emotions they give rise to. Fear and pity are awakened through a reflection on ourselves; in experiencing these emotions we learn to synthesize, which is why tragedy gives us knowledge (cf. 1448b).

95. Amelie Oksenberg Rorty's anthology (1992) gives a good survey of the contemporary discussion. See, for instance, Jonathan Lear (315–37).

96. Nussbaum (1986, 380).

97. "We see . . . a two-way interchange of illumination and cultivation working between emotions and thoughts: we see feelings prepared by memory and deliberation, learning brought about through *pathos*. (At the same time we ourselves, if we are good spectators will find this complex interaction in our own responses.)" Nussbaum (1986, 47).

98. Nussbaum (1986, 4).

99. See, for instance, Friedrich Schelling, in *Philosophy of Art* and in *Philosophical Letters on Dogmatism and Criticism*. The tragic sublime, for Schelling, lies in the acceptance of punishment by the guilty hero who suffers his fate beyond his own doing; by the hero to prove his freedom through losing his freedom "and to perish amid a declaration of free will." Schelling 1989, 259.

100. Lacan (1998b, 54). Repetition just seems to occur; it presents itself as an obstacle, a "hitch" coming back in everyday life over and over again.

101. See, for instance, the comment on Hegel in *The Four Concepts of Psychoanalysis*: there is no choice between freedom or death, as implied in the Master-slave dialectic; the choice of freedom means death, so the only free choice is in fact that of death. Lacan (1998b, 212–23).

102. Lacan (1992, 319, 321). This means, also, that we have to leave the Christian moral framework of suffering, pity, and belief in the good behind us.

103. This is the argument of Lacan, who refers pity and fear to the imaginary (1992, 275).

104. "Desire is nothing other than that which supports an unconscious theme, the very articulation of that which roots us in a particular destiny, and that destiny demands insistently that the debt be paid, and desire keeps coming back, keeps returning, and situates us once again in a given track." Lacan (1992, 319).

105. Lacan (1992, 300).

106. Lacan (1992, 299).

107. This experience is thus related to the double recognition of Oedipus: touching both what he is and what he is not. Lacan (1992, 304).

108. Lacan (1992, 291).

109. This famous injunction is to be found in Lacan (1992, 321).

110. For Jelinek's discussion of her view on Viennese culture and the intentions of her work, see an interview with Adolf-Ernst Meyer in *Sturm und Zwang: Schreiben als Geschlechterkampf* (Hamburg: Klein, 1995), pp. 7–74.

Bibliography

Adorno, Theodor, and Max Horkheimer. 1997. *Dialectic of Enlightenment*. Translated by J. Cumming. London: Verso.

Aeschylus. *The Oresteia*. 1953. Translated by R. Lattimore. In *the Complete Greek Tragedies*, vol. 1. Chicago: University of Chicago Press.

Alford, C. F. 1992. *The Psychoanalytic Theory of Greek Tragedy*. New Haven, Conn.: Yale University Press.

Aristotle. 1927. *Poetics*. Translated by W. H. Fyfe. Oxford: Loeb Classical Library.

Baas, Bernard. 1992. *Le désir pur*. Louvain: Peeters.

———. 1998. *De la chose à l'objet*. Louvain: Peeters.

Beistegui, Miguel de. 1997. *Heidegger and the Political*. London: Routledge.

Benhabib, Seyla. 1992. *Situating the Self*. New York: Routledge.

Bentham, Jeremy. 1996. *Theorie des fictions*. Paris: Editions de l'association freudienne internationale. Annexe 1, J. Parin: *Réel et Symbolique chez Jeremy Bentham*, 3–10.

Blanchot, Maurice. 1963. *Lautréamont et Sade*. Paris: Minuit.

Bouvrie, Synnöve des. 1990. *Women in Greek Tragedy*. Oslo: Norwegian University Press.

Bowra, Cecil Maurice. 1944. *Sophoclean Tragedy*. Oxford: Clarendon Press.

Brennan, Teresa. 1992. *Interpretation of the Flesh*. London: Routledge.

Butler, Judith. 1990. *Gender Trouble*. London: Routledge.

———. 2000. *Antigone's Claim*. New York: Columbia University Press.

Butler, Judith, Ernesto Laclau, and Slavoj Žižek. 2000. *Contingency, Hegemony, Universality*. London: Verso.

Carter, Angela. 1979. *The Sadeian Woman*. London: Virago Press.

Cavarero, Adriana. 1995. *In Spite of Plato*. Oxford: Polity Press.

Chanter, Tina. 1995. *Ethics of Eros*. London: Routledge.

———. 1998. "Tragic Dislocations: Antigone's Modern Theatrics." *Differences* 10, no. 1: 75–98.

Conger, Syndy McMillen. 1994. *Mary Wollstonecraft and the Language of Sensibility*. London: Associated University Press.

Copjec, Joan. 1999. "The Tomb of Perseverance: On *Antigone.*" In *Giving Ground: the Politics of Propinquity,* 233–67. London: Verso.

David-Ménard, Monique. 1994. *Les constructions de l'universel.* Paris: PUF.

de Beauvoir, Simone. 1955. *Faut-il brûler Sade?* Paris: Gallimard.

———. 1989. *The Second Sex.* Translated by H. H. Parshley. New York: Vintage.

———. 1994 [1957]. *The Ethics of Ambiguity.* Translated by Bernard Frechtman. New York: Philosophical Library.

Derrida, Jacques. 1974. *Glas.* Paris: Editions Galilée.

———. 1987. *Psyché.* Paris: Flammarion.

Dettenhofer, Maria H., ed. 1994. *Reine Männersache? Frauen in Männerdomänen der antiken Welt.* Köln: Böhlau.

Doyle, Richard E. 1984. *ATH, Its Use and Meaning.* New York: Fordham University Press.

Düe, Michael. 1986. *Ontologie und Psychoanalyse.* Athenäum: Frankfurt am Main.

Duroux, Françoise. 1993. *Antigone encore—Les femmes et la loi.* Paris: Côté des femmes.

Eckermann, J.P. 1986. *Gespräche mit Goethe.* München: Carl Hanser Verlag.

Eliot, George. 1963 [1865]. "The Antigone and Its Moral." In *Essays of George Eliot,* edited by Thomas Pinney. London: Routledge.

Else, G. 1965. *The Origin and Early Form of Greek Tragedy.* Boston: Harvard University Press.

———. 1976. *The Madness of Antigone.* Abhandlungen der Heidelberger Akademie der Wissenschaften, Heidelberg: Carl Winter Universitätsverlag.

Euben, Peter. 1986. *Greek Tragedy and Political Theory.* Berkeley: University of California Press.

Felman, Shoshana. 1987. *Jacques Lacan and the Adventure of Insight.* Baltimore, Md.: Johns Hopkins University Press.

Felski, Rita. 1995. *The Gender of Modernity.* Cambridge, Mass.: Harvard University Press.

Fink, Bruce. 1995. *The Lacanian Subject.* Chichester, N.J.: Princeton University Press.

Fraisse, Geneviève. 1995. *Muse de la raison*: *Démocratie et exclusion des femmes en France.* Paris: Gallimard.

Fraisse, Simone. 1974. *Le mythe d'Antigone.* Translated by H. M. Parshley. Paris: Armand Colin.

Freud, Sigmund. 1895. *Project for a Scientific Psychology.* In *Standard Edition,* edited by J. Strachey, vol. 1, 295–430. London: Hogarth Press.

———. 1905. *Three Essays on Sexuality.* In *Standard Edition,* edited by J. Strachey, vol. 7. London: Hogarth Press.

———. 1907. "Leonardo da Vinci and a Memory of His Childhood." In *Standard Edition,* edited by J. Strachey, vol. 11; 63–133. London: Hogarth Press.

————. 1925. "Some Psychical Consequences of the Anatomical Distinctions Between the Sexes." In *Standard Edition*, edited by J. Strachey, vol. 19, 248–58. London: Hogarth Press.

————. 1927. "The Question of Lay Analysis." In *Standard Edition*, edited by J. Strachey, vol. 20, 183–253. London: Hogarth Press.

————. 1929. *Civilization and Its Discontents.* In *Standard Edition*, edited by J. Strachey, vol. 19, 59–148. London: Hogarth Press.

————. 1957 [1915]. Instincts and Their Vicissitudes." In *Standard Edition*, vol. 14, 109–40. London: Hogarth Press.

Gallop, Jane. 1982. *The Daughter's Seduction.* London: Routledge.

Gatens, Moira. 1991. *Feminism and Philosophy.* Bloomington: Indiana University Press.

Gauthier, Jeffrey A. 1997. *Hegel and Feminist Social Criticism.* New York: State University of New York Press.

Gearhart, Susanne. 1992. *The Interrupted Dialectic: Philosophy, Psychoanalysis, and Their Tragic Other.* London: Johns Hopkins University Press.

Gellrich, Michelle. 1988. *Tragedy and Theory.* Princeton, N.J.: Princeton University Press.

Green, Andre. 1979. *The Tragic Effect.* Translated by A. Sheridan. Cambridge: Cambridge University Press.

Grosz, Elisabeth. 1990. *Lacan: A Feminist Introduction.* London: Routledge.

Gubar, Susan. 1994. "Feminist Misogyny: Mary Wollstonecraft and the Paradoxes of 'It Takes One to Know One.'" *Feminist Studies*, no 30.

Guyomard, Patrick. 1992. *La jouissance du tragique.* Paris: Aubier.

Habermas, Jürgen. 1987. *The Philosophical Discourse of Modernity.* Cambridge: Polity Press.

Haute, Philippe van. 1998. "Death and Sublimation." In *Levinas and Lacan: The Missed Encounter*, edited by Susan Harasym. New York: SUNY Press, 102–20.

————. 2001. *Against Adaptation: Jacques Lacan's 'Subversion'of the Subject.* Translated by P. Crowe and M. Vankerk. New York: Other Press.

Hegel, G. W. F. 1970. *Vorlesungen über die Ästhetik III.* In *Werke.* Frankfurt: Suhrkamp.

————. 1977. *Phenomenology of Spirit.* Translated by A. V. Miller. Oxford: Oxford University Press. [*Phänomenologie des Geistes*, 1807.]

————. 1996. *Philosophy of Right.* Translated by S. W. Dyde. New York: Prometheus Books. [*Philosophie des Rechts*, 1821.]

————. 1998. *The Hegel Reader.* Edited by S. Houlgate. Oxford: Blackwell.

————. 1999. *On the Scientific Ways of Treating Natural Law*, translated by H. B. Nisbet. In *Hegel: Political Writings*, edited by L. Dickey and H. B. Nisbet.

Cambridge: Cambridge University Press. [*Über die wissenschaftlichen Behandlungsarten des Naturrechts*, 1803.]

Heidegger, Martin. 1954. *Vorträge und Aufsätze*. Pfüllingen: Günter Neske.

———. 1959. *An Introduction to Metaphysics*. Translated by R. Manheim. New Haven, Conn.: Yale University Press. [*Einführung in der Metaphysik, Gesamtausgabe* Bd 40, Vittorio Klostermann: Frankfurt, 1935.]

———. 1982. *On the Way to Language*. Translated by Peter D. Hertz. San Francisco: HarperSanFrancisco. [*Unterwegs zur Sprache, Gesamtausgabe* Bd 12, 1959.]

———. 1992. *The Metaphysical Foundations of Logic. Translated by M. Heim*. Bloomington: Indiana University Press. [*Metaphysische Anfangsgründe der Logik, Gesamtausgabe* Bd 26, 1928.]

———. 1993. "The Origin of a Work of Art." Translated by David Farrell Krell. In *Heidegger: Basic Writings*, edited by David Farrell Krell. London: Routledge. [Der Ursprung des Kuntswerkes, Holzwege, 1950]

———. 1996. *Hölderlin's Hymn "The Ister."* Translated by W. McNeill and J. Davis. Bloomington: Indiana University Press. [*Hölderlins "der Ister,"* Gesamtausgabe 53, 1942.]

———. 2000. *Being and Time*. Translated by J. Macquarrie and E. Robinson. Cambridge: Blackwell. [*Sein und Zeit, Gesamtausgabe* 2, 1977.]

Hölderlin, Friedrich. 1988 [1804]. *Antigonae*. In *Sämtliche Werke*. Frankfurter Ausgabe, Frankfurt: Roter Stern.

Honneth, Axel. 1995. *The Struggle for Recognition*. Translated by J. Anderson. London: Blackwell.

Irigaray, Luce. 1985a. *Speculum of the Other Woman*. Translated by G. Gill. Ithaca, N.Y.: Cornell University Press.

———. 1985b. *This Sex Which Is Not One*. Translated by C. Porter and C. Burke. Ithaca, N.Y.: Cornell University Press.

———. 1987. *Le temps de la différence*. Paris: Librairie Générale Française.

———. 1993a. *An Ethics of Sexual Difference*. Translated by C. Burke and G.C. Gill. London: Athlone.

———. 1993b. *Sexes and Genealogies*. Translated by G.C. Gill. New York : Columbia University Press.

———. 1999. *The Forgetting of Air in Martin Heidegger*. Translated by M.B. Mader. London: Athlone.

Jardine, Alice A. 1985. *Gynesis: Configurations of Woman and Modernity*. Ithaca, N.Y.: Cornell University Press.

Jelinek, Elfriede. 1995. *Sturm und Zwang: Schreiben als Geschlechterkampf.* Hamburg: Klein.

Julien, Philippe. 1995. *L'étrange jouissance du prochain*. Paris: Seuil.

Kant, Immanuel. 1960 [1764]. *Observations on the Feeling of the Beautiful and the*

Sublime. Translated by J.T. Goldthwait. Berkeley: University of California Press.

———. 1993. *Critique of Practical Reason.* Translated by L.W. Beck. 3d ed. New York: Macmillan. [*Kritik der Praktischen Vernunft,* 1788.]

———. 2000. *Critique of the Power of Judgment.* Translated by P. Guyer and E. Matthews. Cambridge: Cambridge University Press. [*Kritik der Urteilskraft,* 1790.]

Kaufmann, Walter. 1957. *Tragedy and Philosophy.* Cambridge: Cambridge University Press.

Kierkegaard, Søren. 1959. *Either/Or.* Translated by D.F. Swenson and L. Marvin Swenson. Princeton, N.J.: Princeton University Press. [*Enten/elder,* 1843.]

Kirkwood, G.M. 1957. *The Poetics of Sophoclean Tragedy.* Oxford: Oxford University Press.

Kitto, Humphrey D.F. 1961. *Greek Tragedy: A Literary Study.* London: Methuen.

Klein, Melanie. 1988. "The Oresteia." In *Envy and Gratitude,* pp. 275–300. London: Virago.

Kristeva, Julia. 1989. *Black Sun.* Translated by Léon S. Roudiez. New York: Columbia University Press.

Krell, David. 1986. *Intimations of Mortality.* University Park: Pennsylvania State University Press.

Lacan, Jacques. 1966. *Écrits.* Paris: Seuil.

———. 1975. *Le Sinthôme.* Unpublished seminar. Available from the Ecole de la Cause Freudienne.

———. 1977. *Écrits: A Selection,* translated by A. Sheridan. London: Tavistock.

———. 1986. *L'Ethique de la Psychanalyse,* edited by J.-A. Miller. Paris: Seuil.

———. 1988a. *Freud's Papers on Technique, 1953–1954, Seminar 1.* Translated by J. Forrester. Cambridge: Cambridge University Press. [*Les Écrits techniques de Freud,* ed. J.-A. Miller, Paris: Seuil, 1975.]

———. 1988b. *The Ego in Freud's Theory and in the Technique of Psychoanalysis, 1954–55.* Translated by John Forrester and Sylvana Tomaselli. Cambridge: Cambridge University Press.

———. 1989. "Kant with Sade." Translated by J. B. Swenson. *October* 41 (winter 1989): 55–104.

———. 1992. *The Ethics of Psychoanalysis.* Translated by D. Potter. London: Routledge.

———. 1998a. *Encore.* Translated by B. Fink. New York: Norton. [*Encore.* Paris: Seuil, 1975.]

———. 1998b. *The Four Concepts of Psychoanalysis.* Edited by J.-A. Miller, translated by A. Sheridan. New York: Norton. [*Les quatre concepts de la psychanalyse.* Paris: Seuil, 1973.]

Laclau, Ernest. 1996. *Emancipation(s)*. London: Verso.

Lacoue-Labarthe, Philippe. 1990. *Heidegger, Art and Politics*. Oxford: Blackwell.

———. 1991. "De l'éthique: A propos d'Antigone." In *Lacan avec les philosophes*, edited by the Collège International de la Philosophie. Paris: Albin Michel, 19–37.

———. 1998. *Métaphrasis*. Paris: PUF.

Levinas, Emmanuel. 1996. *Emmanuel Levinas: Basic Philosophical Writings*, ed. A. Peperzak, S. Critchley, and R. Bernasconi. Bloomington: Indiana University Press.

Lévi-Strauss, Claude. 1969 [1949]. *The Elementary Structures of Kinship*. Translated by J. H. Bell and J. R. von Sturmer. London: Eyre and Spottiswoode.

Lipowatz, Thanos. 1988. *Die Verleugnung des Politischen*. Berlin: Quadriga.

Loraux, Nicole. 1981. *Les enfants d'Athena: Idées athéniennes sur la citoyenneté et la division des sexes*. Paris: PUF.

———. 1991. *Tragic Ways of Killing a Woman*. Translated by A. Forster. Cambridge, Mass.: Harvard University Press.

———. 1995. *The Experiences of Tiresias: The Feminine and the Greek Man*. Princeton, N.J.: Princeton University Press.

Lundgren-Gothlin, Eva. 1991. *Kön och existens*. Göteborg: Daidalos.

Lykke, Nina. 1989. *Rødhaette og Ødipus—brikker til en feministisk psykoanalyse*. Odense: Odense Universitetsförlag.

Macey, David. 1988. *Lacan in Contexts*. London: Verso.

McCannell, Juliet Flower. 2000. *The Hysteric's Guide to the Future Female Subject*. Minneapolis: University of Minnesota Press.

Menke, Christoph. 1996. *Tragödie im Sittlichen: Gerechtigkeit und Freiheit nach Hegel*. Frankfurt am Main: Suhrkamp.

Mitchell, Juliet, and Jacqueline Rose. 1982. *Feminine Sexuality*. London: Macmillan.

Moi, Toril. 1994. *Simone de Beauvoir: The Making of an Intellectual Woman*. Oxford, Blackwell.

Moyaert, Paul. 1996. "Lacan on Neighborly Love: The Relation of the Thing in the Other Who Is My Neighbor." *Epoche* 4, no. 1: 1–33.

Nancy, Jean-Luc. 1991. "Manque de rien." In *Lacan avec les philosophes*, edited by the Collège International de la Philosophie, 200–206. Paris: Albin Michel.

Nussbaum, Martha. 1986. *The Fragility of Goodness*. London: Cambridge University Press.

Oliver, Kelly. 1996. "Antigone's Ghost: Undoing Hegel's *Phenomenology of Spirit*." *Hypatia* 11, no. 1 (winter 1996): 67–90.

Ott, Hugo. 1988. *Martin Heidegger*. Frankfurt: Campus.

Pippin, Robert B. 1989. *Hegel's Idealism: The Satisfactions of Self-Consciousness*. Cambridge: Cambridge University Press.

Pöggeler, Otto. 1990 [1963]. *Der Denkweg Martin Heideggers.* Pfullingen: Verlag Günther Neske.

Poovey, Mary. 1984. *The Proper Lady and the Woman Writer: Ideology As Style in the Works of Mary Wollstonecraft, Mary Shelley and Jane Austen.* Chicago: University of Chicago Press.

Rajchman, John. 1991. *Truth and Eros.* London: Routledge.

Reeder, Jörgen. 1990. *Begär och etik.* Lund: Symposion.

Ragland, Ellie. 1995. *Essays on the Pleasures of Death.* London: Routledge.

Rabinowitz, Nancy Sorkin, and Amy Richlin, eds. 1993. *Feminist Theory and the Classics.* London: Routledge.

Richardson, William. 1991. "La vérité dans la psychanalyse." In *Lacan avec les philosophes,* edited by the Collège International de la Philosophie, 191–200. Paris: Albin Michel.

Rilke, Rainer Maria. 1986. *Selected Poems.* Translated by A. E. Flemming. New York: Methuen.

Rorty, Amélie Oksenberg, ed. 1992. *Essays on Aristotle's Poetics.* Princeton, N.J.: Princeton University Press.

Roudinesco, Elisabeth. 1997. *Jacques Lacan.* Cambridge: Polity Press.

Rousseau, Jean-Jacques. 1933 [1762]. *Émile.* London: J. M. Den and Sons.

Sade, D.A.F. 1987a. *La nouvelle Justine.* In *Oeuvres complètes,* vol. 6. Paris: Pauvert.

———. 1987b. *Historie de Juliette ou les prospérités du vice.* Paris: Pauvert.

Salecl, Renata. 1998. *(Per)versions of Love and Hate.* London: Verso.

———., ed. 2000. *Sexuation.* Durham: Duke University Press.

Sapiro, Virginia. 1992. *A Vindication of Political Virtue: The Political Theory of Mary Wollstonecraft.* Chicago: Chicago University Press.

Schelling, F. W. 1856. *Werke.* Stuttgart: Joseph Cotta.

———. 1989. *The Philosophy of Art.* Translated by D.W. Scott. Minneapolis: University of Minnesota Press.

Schlegel, A.W. 1966 [1908]. *Vorlesungen über dramatische Kunst und Literatur.* In *Kritische Schriften und Briefe.* Stuttgart: Kohlhammer Verlag.

Seaford, Richard. 1994. *Reciprocity and Ritual.* Oxford: Clarendon Press.

Segal, Charles. 1986. *Interpreting Greek Tragedy: Myth, Poetry, Text.* Ithaca, N.Y.: Cornell University Press.

———. 1995. *Sophocles' Tragic World.* Cambridge, Mass.: Harvard University Press.

Sophocles. 1986. *Antigone.* Edited and translated by A. Brown. Warminster: Aris and Phillips.

Stavrakakis, Yannis. 1999. *Lacan and the Political.* London: Routledge.

Szondi, Peter. 1978. *Versuch über das Tragische, Schriften 1.* Frankfurt am Main: Suhrkamp.

Steiner, George. 1984. *Antigones.* Oxford: Clarendon Press.

Taminiaux, Jacques. 1995. *Le théâtre des philosophes.* Paris: Minuit.

Vernant, Jean-Pierre, and Pierre Vidal-Naquet. 1990. *Myth and Tragedy in Ancient Greece.* Translated by Janet Lloyd. New York: Zone Books.

Visker, Rudi. 1999. *Truth and Singularity.* London: Kluwer Academic Publishers.

Whitford, Margaret. 1990. *Luce Irigaray.* London: Routledge.

Wohl, Victoria. 1998. *Intimate Commerce: Exchange, Gender and Subjectivity in Greek Tragedy.* Austin: University of Texas Press.

Wollstonecraft, Mary. 1985 [1792]. *Vindication of the Rights of Woman.* London: Norton.

————. 1989. *Works of Mary Wollstonecraft.* Edited by Nora Crook. London: William Pickering.

————. 1994 [1798]. *Maria or the Wrongs of Woman.* London: Norton.

Zak, William F. 1995. *The Polis and the Divine Order.* Lewisburg, Penn.: Bucknell University Press.

Zeitlin, Froma. 1996. *Playing the Other.* Chicago: Chicago University Press.

Žižek, Slavoj. 1989. *The Sublime Object of Ideology.* London: Verso.

————. 1992. *Enjoy Your Symptom.* London: Routledge.

————. 1993. *Tarrying with the Negative.* London: Routledge.

————. 1994. *The Metastases of Enjoyment.* London: Verso.

————. 1997. *The Plague of Fantasies.* London: Verso.

Zupancic, Alenka. 1995. *Die Ethik des Realen.* Wien: Kant und Turin.

Index

Cultural Memory | *in the Present*